Julie Vullnetari is Research Fellow in the School of Global Studies, University of Sussex. She holds a DPhil in Migration Studies from the University of Sussex, and has published widely in peer-reviewed international journals such as *International Migration* and *Global Networks*.

Russell King is Professor of Geography at the University of Sussex and Director of the Sussex Centre for Migration Research. He is the co-author of *Out of Albania: From Crisis Migration to Social Inclusion in Italy* (2008), and editor of the *Journal of Ethnic and Migration Studies*.

REMITTANCES, GENDER AND DEVELOPMENT

Albania's Society and Economy in Transition

JULIE VULLNETARI AND RUSSELL KING

I.B. TAURIS
LONDON · NEW YORK

Published in 2011 by I.B.Tauris & Co Ltd
6 Salem Road, London W2 4BU
175 Fifth Avenue, New York NY 10010
www.ibtauris.com

Distributed in the United States and Canada
Exclusively by Palgrave Macmillan
175 Fifth Avenue, New York NY 10010

Library of Development Studies 4

ISBN 978 1 84885 487 1

A full CIP record for this book is available from the British Library
A full CIP record for this book is available from the Library of Congress

Library of Congress catalog card: available

Printed and bound in Great Britain by CPI Antony Rowe, Chippenham
Camera-ready copy edited and supplied by the authors

CONTENTS

LIST OF MAPS & ILLUSTRATIONS

Maps

Illustrations

LIST OF TABLES

ABBREVIATIONS

ABA	American Bank of Albania
AENEAS	EU Programme for Financial and Technical Assistance to Third Countries in the Area of Migration and Asylum
ALSMS	Albanian Living Standards Measurement Survey
BoA	Central Bank of Albania
CADSES	Central European, Adriatic, Danubian, South Eastern European Space
CARDS	Community Assistance for Reconstruction, Development and Stabilisation
CESS	Centre for Economic and Social Studies
DFID	UK Department for International Development
EA	Economic Aid
EBRD	European Bank for Reconstruction and Development
EC	European Commission
ERRC	European Roma Rights Centre
EU	European Union
FAO	Food and Agriculture Organisation
FDI	Foreign Direct Investments
GDP	Gross Domestic Product
GoA	Government of Albania
GP	General Practitioner
HDI	Human Development Index
IKA	Greek Institute of Social Insurance for Industry and Services
ILO	International Labour Organisation
IMF	International Monetary Fund
INSTAT	Albanian Institute of Statistics (*Instituti i Statistikës*)
INSTRAW	United Nations International Research and Training Institute for the Advancement of Women
INTERREG	EC initiative aimed at interregional cooperation in the EU

IO	International Organisation
IOM	International Organization for Migration
LFS	Labour Force Survey
METE	Ministry of Economy, Trade and Energy
MFI	Micro Finance Institution
MG	MoneyGram
MOLSAEO	Ministry of Labour, Social Affairs and Equal Opportunities
MTO	Money Transfer Operators
NAP	National Action Plan
NATO	North Atlantic Treaty Organisation
NBG	National Bank of Greece
NELM	New Economics of Labour Migration
NGO	Non-Governmental Organisation
NSDI	National Strategy for Development and Integration
NSGE-DV	National Strategy on Gender Equality and Domestic Violence
NSM	National Strategy on Migration
ODA	Official Development Aid
OECD	Organisation for Economic Co-operation and Development
PBI	Profile Business Intelligence
RA	Readmission Agreement
RDA	Regional Development Agency
RDS	Regional Development Strategy
SAA	Stabilisation and Association Agreement
SCMR	Sussex Centre for Migration Research
TCN	Third Country National
UNDP	United Nations Development Programme
VARP	Voluntary Assisted Return Programmes
VARRP	Voluntary Assisted Return and Reintegration Programmes
WTO	World Trade Organisation
WU	Western Union

PREFACE AND ACKNOWLEDGMENTS

This book has its origins in a funded research project, for the successful completion of which a number of individuals and institutions were of crucial importance. Here, we would like to express our gratitude to them. First, we thank the United Nations International Research and Training Institute for the Advancement of Women (INSTRAW) for their invitation to tender for, and then for commissioning us to carry out, the project 'Gender and Remittances: Building Gender-Responsive Local Development' 2007–09; and to the United Nations Development Programme (UNDP) for their co-funding of the project. We are particularly grateful to Ms Diana Lopez who was the overall project coordinator at INSTRAW, for her tremendous support and encouragement throughout the project. The study was part of a six-country comparative research: Albania, the Dominican Republic, Lesotho, Morocco, the Philippines, and Senegal. Our Albania-Greece team was based at the Sussex Centre for Migration Research (SCMR) of the University of Sussex. Russell King was Principal Investigator and Julie Vullnetari was the main researcher. The latter carried out all the field research and hence took the lead in writing the empirical chapters which are the heart of this book. Russell King's main contribution was to Chapters 1, 2 and 8.

Fieldwork for this research took us to three study villages in the commune of Pojan, part of the Korçë district in south-east Albania, to Korçë town itself, and to Albania's capital Tirana. Our data collection in these various locations was successful thanks to the hard work of a number of individuals who assisted us with information, by administering questionnaires in the villages, or providing accommodation and support during our stay there: Ms Vasilika Vasili, Ms Arjana Kolami, Mrs Ylvere Lëngu, Mrs Mynefe Xhuti, Mr Ylmi Lumalasi, Mrs Moza Rrushiti, Mr Erjon Xhuti, Mrs Alie Spaillari, Mr Besim Vullnetari, Mr Mergim Xhuti,

Ms Juliana Kelo and Mr Feridon Kelo. Their dedication as well as the insights they provided during our long discussions were crucial to the success of the fieldwork. We thank Ms Entela Hasku in Tirana for transcribing most of the in–depth interviews carried out in both Albania and Greece. In the villages and in Korçë we would like to thank the key stakeholders – local authority representatives, civil society leaders and academics – who provided us with information through discussions, e-mails, and in-depth interviews.

Our fieldwork also took us to Greece where we would like to acknowledge the support of many Albanian migrants and key community leaders: above all Ervin, Edi, Jani, Mrs Mimoza Dako, Mrs Irma Loli, Mrs Anila Tërshana, Edlira and Lilionfi. A special thank you goes to Ms Eda Gemi who carried out the in-depth interviews with key stakeholders in Athens. We are also very grateful to the key stakeholders themselves who agreed to participate in these in-depth interviews, as well as in the focus-group discussions held in Thessaloniki. Representatives from the Greek Ministry of Interior and of Foreign Affairs, from the Greek Ombudsman, local authorities, the Albanian Consul General in Thessaloniki, the private sector, researchers, academics, and leaders of migrant organisations took time away from their busy schedules to inform our research with their views and suggestions.

We take here the opportunity to extend our appreciation to Prof Lois Labrianidis and the Department of Economics at the University of Macedonia in Thessaloniki, for providing the facilities in which our focus-group discussions with the key stakeholders in this city were organised. These discussions benefited greatly also from the support and technical assistance of Ms Zana Vathi, Ms Anjeza Dielli and Mr Agron Elezi.

At the SCMR in Sussex, we are very grateful to Dr Adriana Castaldo for her valuable assistance with some of the statistical analysis of our survey data for Albania.

We would also like to thank the I.B.Tauris team who worked closely with us during the preparation of the manuscript for publication, as well as two independent referees for their valuable comments and feedback.

A special thank you goes to Mr Nigel Eastwood for preparing the camera-ready format of the book.

Last, but by no means least, our deepest gratitude goes to the migrants, returnees and their families interviewed in Albania and in Greece, all of whom remain anonymous for ethical reasons but who were essential to the success of the research. For the wonderful hospitality they provided us in their homes, for allowing us to intrude into their lives, and for sharing with us their joys and worries, we are enormously grateful.

Julie Vullnetari and Russell King, Sussex, UK

1

INTRODUCTION

Given the mainstreaming of gender into social science in recent decades, including major advances in gendering both migration and development, it comes as something of a surprise to find that remittances – the main functional link between international migration and development – have hardly ever been examined from a gender perspective. This is the gap – a significant one, we believe – which this book seeks to fill. This monograph is the first detailed, book-length study of gender and remittances. Our research is set both within a general economic and social development framework, and also within a particular context of post-communist transition in Albania, a small country in south-east Europe.

Albania may be small but in other senses it is an iconic country for this research topic. Ruled for forty years by the notorious dictator Enver Hoxha, Albania was Eastern Europe's harshest and most isolated communist state. Part of this isolation was the practical and ideological banning of migration, seen as an act of treason, and the virtual imprisonment of the country's population behind an impregnable, electrified, fortified border. Small wonder that, when the communist regime fell in the early 1990s, Albanians were so keen to see the outside world, which they had been denied access to, even knowledge of, for so long.

A second reason why Albania is such an apposite setting for this research is the severity of its poverty and the scale of the emigration which took place after 1990. Albania was the poorest of the Eastern bloc's communist countries and remains, on many indicators, the least developed European country today.[1] Not unrelated to this, emigration since 1990 has been on a scale unmatched by any European country in recent decades – indeed probably no other country in the world has seen such a dramatic loss of its population as took place in Albania during the 1990s.

Remittances, in turn, are the logical response to this dual situation of widespread poverty and mass emigration. They are the linking mechanism through which migrants seek to survive and even prosper, supporting their family members who remain in Albania and trying to build a future for all concerned. Since the early 1990s, Albania has constantly come near the top of the world list of remitting countries, not for the total amount of remittances (because Albania is a small country compared to the likes of 'big' emigration countries like India, Mexico or Morocco), but for the relative importance of remittances when measured in per capita terms or as a percentage of Gross Domestic Product (GDP).[2]

In this opening chapter we 'set the scene' for the rest of the book. We justify the importance of the research topic of 'gendering remittances' and we reinforce further the relevance and uniqueness of the Albanian case for such an investigation. We also set out the research questions: these guide the empirical analysis which constitutes the heart of the book. Then we describe the methods used to collect our research material. Finally, a chapter-by-chapter outline is given, in order to demonstrate to the reader how the component parts of the book are sequenced and fit together.

Why Gender Remittances?

In recent years, migration has played an increasingly prominent role in the international debate on development. Rather than being 'condemned' as a symptom or result of underdevelopment, migration nowadays is seen as a route towards development and as a major strategy for alleviating poverty.[3] A key role in this new debate on migration and development (or 'the migration–development nexus') is played by remittances. International agencies such as the World Bank, the UN and the International Organization for Migration (IOM), as well as the governments of countries which have experienced mass emigration, such as Albania, are increasingly focusing on maximising both the quantity and effectiveness of remittances as a strategic development tool. Their aims are to bring much-needed foreign exchange to balance national accounts and to channel towards development-inducing investment, and to sustain and improve the livelihoods of households and families with migrants abroad.

But remittances are overwhelmingly seen in economic and financial terms. The dominant questions always seem to be: How much is remitted? What are remittances needed for? How can they be more effectively invested for development purposes? Yet, in strongly patriarchal societies such as Albania, important questions need to be asked about the micro-dynamics of remittances – who sends, who receives, who makes decisions on how remittances are spent? Gender plays a fundamental role in the mechanics of remitting. Certainly, within Albania, the 'traditional' picture would suggest that these mechanisms and decisions on remittances are taken overwhelmingly by men. But remittances are almost never analysed through a gendered perspective.

At the same time, within the field of migration studies, there has been an important move in recent years to study mobility processes within a gendered analysis. But this gendering of migration has not been extended to remittances. What currently exists within the fast-developing field of 'migration and development' is a strong emphasis on remittances as a potentially powerful mechanism for the development of migration-origin societies on the one hand, and on the other, a strong discourse on 'gendering migration' in the migration studies literature. Yet these two dominating narratives – 'remittances and development' and 'gendering migration' – have hardly ever been brought together. Our book does exactly this, both at a conceptual–theoretical level, and with reference to our extensive new research on Albanian migration to, and associated remittance flows from, Greece, the main destination for Albanian migration since 1990.

About the Book

This book examines the role of gender in the relationship between migration – especially international migration – and development, with specific relevance to remittances. It responds to the clarion call for research into gendering remittances put forward in a landmark paper by Ramírez *et al.* (2005) issued as part of the INSTRAW (United Nations International Research and Training Institute for the Advancement of Women) initiative to stimulate work in this field. Our analysis is situated in the context of a small post-communist country in south-east Europe – Albania – and the migration of its citizens to neighbouring Greece, a member country of the European Union (EU) and an important trade partner for Albania. The post-communist years in Albania have been dominated by large-scale migration, both abroad and internally. By 2010, nearly 1.5 million Albanians, equivalent to almost half of the country's resident population, were estimated to be living abroad, principally in Greece and Italy (World Bank 2011: 54). The highly dynamic character of post-1990 Albanian migration, placed against almost half a century of zero emigration during the communist era, makes Albania a veritable laboratory for the study of migration and development (King 2005).

The early 1990s movements abroad – especially to Greece – were strongly male-led, i.e. men migrated first and their wives followed through family reunification later, and the latter were fewer in numbers. Over the years the male to female ratio has become more balanced, and there is now a settling-down of migrants throughout Greece, with migrant couples having more secure jobs, while their children are enrolled in Greek schools.

Although Albanians live throughout Greece, there is a relative concentration in the northwestern regions which border Albania and an absolute concentration in the two most important Greek metropoles – the capital, Athens, and the second biggest city, Thessaloniki. The latter was the site for our part of the research in Greece.

Our fieldwork started in three villages in the district of Korçë, south-east Albania, where we surveyed a large sample of remittance-recipient households, plus some returnees from Greece. From here, we 'followed the migrants' (cf. Marcus 1995) to their main destination city in Greece, Thessaloniki. The transnational household was thus the unit of our analysis, although the perspectives and experiences analysed are those of individual women and men. As such, our empirical material was collected through two main research instruments. First, we administered 350 socio-economic questionnaires with remittance-receiving households in rural Albania; these questionnaires took the form of short, structured interviews in a face-to-face setting. Second, the research team carried out 45 semi-structured in-depth interviews and group discussions with remittance-sending Albanian migrants in Greece, and with residual families and returnees in rural Albania. In addition, our research was informed by the views and perspectives of several key informants at local, regional and national level in both countries. These included government representatives and policy-makers, academics, remittance transfer companies, representatives of migrants' associations and local non-governmental organisations (NGOs). These data are set against a background of analysis of existing statistical datasets provided by institutions such as the Albanian Institute of Statistics (INSTAT), the Central Bank of Albania (BoA) and the World Bank.

Our research aimed to identify the ways in which remittances are sent, received and used within the context of gendered transnational households. We sought to address the following key research questions:

- How do men and women within transnational households send and receive remittances?
- How do these transnationally-linked men and women utilise remittances? Are they used purely for survival, for consumption purposes, or do they invest in their future livelihoods and in 'social capital'?[4]
- What opportunities do household members have to link the utilisation of remittances and their ongoing investments within local development plans (to the extent that such plans exist)?
- How can public policies better provide options for building sustainable livelihoods and social capital?

Related to the final question in the above list, our research had a strong policy-oriented component, reflected in the roundtable discussions and in the interviews with key informants, who were mostly local and national stakeholders. Expanding the policy dimension of our research, the project also aimed to:

- further increase awareness and improve access by women-headed remittance-recipient households to productive resources while augmenting their assets and strengthening their capacities;
- provide relevant information and support to local and national governments in order that they can more clearly identify and formulate policies to optimise the utilisation of remittances for sustaining local livelihoods and building social capital; and,
- enhance the capacity of key stakeholders to integrate gender into their policies, programmes and projects, especially those which link remittances to local development and building social capital.

Finally, overarching all the above, is the fundamental and recursive relationship which our research addresses between gender and remittances. In other words:

- How do prevailing gender relations in Albania and amongst Albanian migrant households shape the sending, receiving and utilisation of remittances?
- And how do the earning, transmission and decision-taking over remittances shape gender relations in transnational migration households?

Methods and Sites of Data Collection

Migration is a complex phenomenon that can best be researched and understood through an equally complex approach of mixing different disciplines, methods and sites. This is what we do in this book. First, the multidisciplinary approach is reflected in the use of mixed perspectives primarily from human geography, sociology and anthropology, but also drawing to a certain extent on economics, history and politics. This essential interdisciplinarity of the research field of migration studies has been powerfully advanced in recent years by, *inter alia*, Castles and Miller (2003: 21–2), Cohen (1995: 7–8) and King (2002).

Second, our methodology is a combination of quantitative and qualitative instruments of primary data collection and analysis, which offers significant benefits through the synergies created by their complementarity. For example, questionnaires are useful in providing the numerical significance of various aspects such as remittance sums and incomes, thus allowing researchers to understand the scale and distribution of certain phenomena under study. The limitations of this technique are that its codification with specific meaning in order to gather certain information forces responses to pass through previously determined categories; and there are often unrecognised assumptions by (ethnocentric and powerful) researchers which are built into the questions and not easily undone (INSTRAW 2006). These limitations can be counterbalanced by using in-depth data collection techniques such as interviews and participant observation. These 'softer' approaches allow interviewees to build their own context and make their views and opinions heard. In addition, they potentially enable researchers to place 'non-dominant, neglected knowledges at the heart of the research agenda' and to present reality through the eyes of the research participants and not of the researchers themselves (Smith 2001: 25). One of the most well-known examples of such quantitative–qualitative synergies is Massey's (1987) ethnosurvey, which he designed to study undocumented migrants and the processes of migration between Mexico and USA. Closer to our own research area, the mixed-method approach has been successfully used by Anderson *et al.* (2006) to study migrants from the eight Eastern European countries joining the EU on May 2004, who lived and worked in the UK prior to and after this date. Hatziprokopiou (2006) also used such a strategy in his doctoral research where he examined the integration of Albanian and Bulgarian migrants in Thessaloniki.

In our own research we employed a socio-economic household questionnaire, combined with in-depth interviews and group discussions involving migrants, their families, returnees, as well as key community figures and other stakeholders such as academics, policy-makers and representatives of NGOs. We explain these in more detail when we discuss our fieldwork sites later on. Besides primary data collection we pay due attention to existing large statistical datasets published and analysed by relevant institutions such as INSTAT and the World Bank. In addition, we critically survey (in Chapters 2 and 3) the extant literature on the links between migration, remittances and development from a gender perspective – worldwide and in the context of Albania.

The third element of our approach is multi-sited ethnography. Inspired by Marcus' (1995) theorisation, we 'followed the people' (migrants) and 'the thing' (remittances) from origin to destination areas and back again. Starting from the village, we follow the 'village outward' approach (Baily 1992), tracing the migrants to their destinations and, for those who return, back to the village. Furthermore, we are guided by the transnational literature in migration studies, which argues that migrants retain and nurture ties across both the country of origin and that of destination, thus requiring the inclusion of both these locations in research (Glick Schiller *et al.* 1995; Levitt and Jaworsky 2007; Vertovec 1999). We see remittances as part of the 'economics of transnational living' (Guarnizo 2003) and more specifically as a transnational gendered social practice. We take the transnational household as the unit of analysis, where most migration decision-making takes places, while at the same time acknowledging the role of individual women and men and complex gendered dynamics within such households. Needless to say, the perspectives and experiences presented in this book are those of individuals, whose gendered identities and behaviours are played out both within the micro-dynamics of families and households, and within the broader hegemonic patriarchal structures of Albanian (and also Greek) society.

Field Sites in Albania

Our fieldwork in Albania was carried out in a cluster of three villages in the district of Korçë, south-east Albania, and in the town of Korçë itself.[5] Korçë is the most important regional centre of the south and south-east, located along one of the principal transport and trading routes that link Albania with the Balkans and the EU through Macedonia and Greece. Map 1 provides details on this regional and administrative setting. Situated at a generally high elevation above sea level, almost 60 per cent of Korçë's prefectural terrain is dominated by mountains. But it also has two of the most fertile plains in the country, making it a major area of agricultural production (Korça Regional Council 2005). During the communist years the district developed an industrial base which included food-processing factories, ore extraction mines, brewing and a glass plant, as well as one of the biggest textile combines in the country. Whilst the latter two became obsolete as the regime collapsed, food-processing has been revived and is a major employment sector for the district's labour force, especially women. Trade and commerce have also grown considerably, but rapid growth is particularly observed in the garment industry, which is characterised by small (semi-) foreign-owned (especially Greek) businesses (Korça Regional Council 2005). In fact, more than a quarter of all foreign enterprises in the Korçë region are Greek, making it one of the most important poles of Greek investment in Albania (Belba 2005: 88). The labour-intensive garment factories are important employers of women, whereas men work mostly in construction.

The Korçë region is also known for its large-scale emigration. A large share of these movements are directed from its hinterland – especially mountain villages, which have lost as much as 30 per cent of their population in the last 15 or so years – towards the urban areas of the region itself (Korçë Municipality 2005: 15). But many have also moved to more distant places internally and abroad; in fact, Korçë district scores highly as a top sender of both internal and, especially, international migrants (Carletto *et al.* 2004: 27). Internally, almost 60 per cent of migrants have moved to Tirana, but Durrës and Vlorë are also important destinations (Korça Regional Council 2005: 24). The majority of international migrants have moved to neighbouring Greece, but other destinations include Italy, the USA, Australia and Macedonia.[6] The overall balance of these movements is an inter-censal population loss due to both types of migration of almost 60,000 individuals at the district level (Carletto *et al.* 2004: 24). The 2001 census enumerated a population of 142,909 for the district, around 55,000 of whom lived in the town of Korçë (INSTAT 2004a). By January 2008, the population registers counted almost 200,000 people living in the district.[7]

The villages of Pojan, Zvezdë and Kreshpanj in Pojan commune were our three study villages. The selection of this locale was based on the criteria that: a) it is a sending area with a significant proportion of migrants in the population; b) a substantial proportion of households receive remittances from abroad; c) it is sufficiently typical of migrant-sending communities in (that part of) the country. In December 2007, population registers held by local and regional authorities recorded around 7,000 residents in all three villages, with Pojan being by far the largest and Kreshpanj the smallest in the commune.[8] In terms of population, the villages are interesting for three reasons. First, the population is quite mixed along religious – Muslim and Orthodox Christian – and ethnic lines – ethnic Albanians, Evgjit or 'Egyptians' and Roma.[9] Considering that the latter two are probably the most marginalised communities in Albania, the area lends itself very favourably to the study of the effects of migration on such groups. Second, some of the Orthodox Christian population here lays claim to forms of Greek citizenship, a process which is intensified because of the advantages of such belonging in terms of easier access to entry visas and work permits in Greece (de Rapper 2005; Kretsi 2005). And finally, Pojan has experienced a certain degree of in-migration from more remote mountainous villages in the district. This last point is relevant because it illustrates that migration is rarely a simple one-way process; even areas of out-migration can attract in-migrants from less-favoured places, as well as returnees from earlier out-migration.

The main economic activity in the Pojan area is farming, most of it at subsistence levels. There are also some non-farm businesses, the majority of which are in the retail trade and hospitality sector, especially small grocery shops and bars. The services sector is dominated by transport. Many day labourers commute to Korçë for work – men in construction, women in garment factories; others are hired in the local farms.

Map 1 Albania – location map of administrative districts. Korçë is a large district in south-east Albania

Data Collection in Albania

For the selection of the households to be surveyed in the villages, two criteria were followed: a) that they had at least one member of their family living and working in Greece; and b) that they received remittances from this migrant member in Greece. The remittance recipient – who was not always the head of the household – was selected as the respondent for the quantitative survey. In a follow-up phase, a number of them were re-visited for in-depth interviews. In total, we carried out 350 household questionnaires, where the majority of respondents were women. These were combined with 25 semi-structured in-depth interviews held with a selection of the questionnaire respondents and returnees; the female to male ratio was almost 2:1. In addition, we organised two group discussions: one with remittance-recipient men and the other with Roma and Evgjit women, some of whom migrated seasonally to Greece. Finally, we also employed ethnographic observation throughout the course of our engagement with the interviewees, as well as by participating in various community activities.

We included key informants in the research through in-depth interviews. Eight such interviews were carried out with the heads of villages, the head of the commune, leaders of local NGOs, the business community, regional government representatives and academia; some of these were based in the town of Korçë.

The survey and interviews were all in the Albanian language. The questions in the household survey focused on four themes:

- The *demographic situation* of the household: biographical data on the respondent and the principal remitter such as age, gender, education, marital status, occupation and migration duration (the latter for the remitter only); as well as on household composition.
- The *housing situation*: information about ownership of the dwelling, location, access to water, electricity, telephones and the Internet.
- Information about *financial remittances* sent by the principal remitter such as sums, frequency, remitting channels, their proportion of overall household income, their uses, decision-making on their use, actual investment of remittances in local businesses and future plans in that regard; as well as *in-kind remittances* and their type.
- Data on various *other financial aspects* of the household, such as local household income *excluding* remittances, and use of financial products such as loans and bank accounts.

Given that in-depth interviews were conducted as follow-ups to the survey, the information gathered through them broadly covered these same themes, but went deeper into details of gendered roles, decision-making, expectations, arrangements and outcomes that took place within households. Although there was some structure around these themes, ample encouragement was provided for the interviewees to contribute their opinions and experiences on other issues they considered important.

Sites in Greece

Greece was selected as a pairing destination country because it met the criteria in terms of: a) the concentration there of a significant proportion of Albanian migrants; b) the age or duration of the migratory process – much of the very first post-communist migration was directed to Greece and the flow continues to this day. The second criterion is important since well-settled migrant communities will have developed well-established remittance patterns. In addition, the degree of organisation of the diaspora – hence the opportunity for an analysis of collective remittances – is also expected to be higher for such communities.

The focus of our fieldwork in Greece was Thessaloniki, where we built on networks and knowledge from previous research we had carried out on Albanian migration there (Vullnetari 2008; Vullnetari and King 2008). Our fieldwork covered the Thessaloniki conurbation, the built-up urban surface consisting of the municipality of Thessaloniki, i.e. the inner city in the centre, and the various neighbourhoods (also known as administrative districts) adjoining it.[10]

Thessaloniki is an important destination for migrants from the study villages. This reflects the general trend for the Albanian immigrant population in Greece as confirmed by other research, according to which Thessaloniki is second only to Athens in terms of the size of the Albanian migrant community (Rovolis and Tragaki 2006). In addition, whilst most of the research on Albanian migration has focused on migrants in Athens in particular, Thessaloniki had, until recently, attracted limited academic attention.[11] Furthermore, since this city is rather close to the origin villages, yet is a large metropolitan area, we were interested in the cross-border dynamics of migration and the resulting transnational practices between our study villages in Albania and this Greek city (see Map 2).

Thessaloniki is the most important economic centre in the north of Greece. The 2001 census recorded a population of 1.1 million in the Prefecture of Thessaloniki, 70 per cent of whom lived in the conurbation (Hatziprokopiou 2006: 82). More than 7 per cent of all Albanian migrants in Greece live in this Prefecture. As generally in Greece, here too Albanians constitute more than half of the migrant population (Hatziprokopiou 2006: 311). They are employed primarily in services (31 per cent), construction (28 per cent) and agriculture (13 per cent). Around

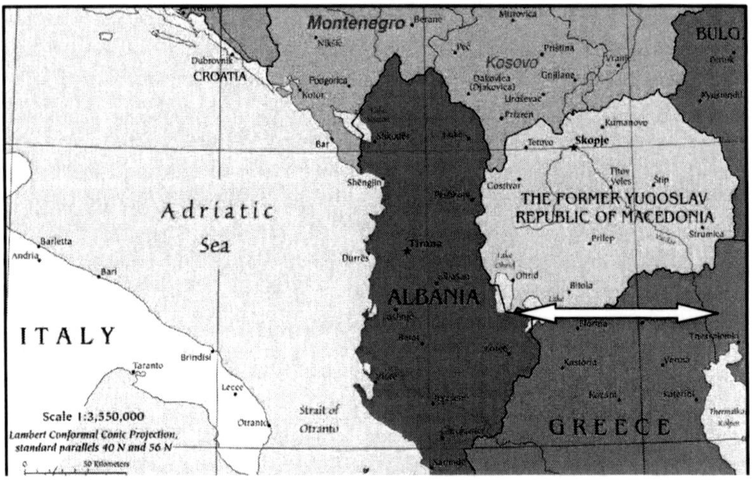

Map 2 Transnational fieldwork sites, Albania–Greece.
Source: Adjusted from Central Balkan Region map 2003, courtesy of the University Libraries, The University of Texas at Austin, available online at: <http://www.lib.utexas.edu/maps/europe/central_balkan_pol_2003.jpg> [last accessed: December 2010]

half of Albanian women work in the domestic and care sectors. The character of the Thessaloniki economy has affected female employment particularly with regard to its share in manufacturing, recording higher employment shares in this sector than country-wide – 25 per cent compared to 9 per cent (Baldwin-Edwards 2004a; Hatziprokopiou 2006: 83). This is related to the dominance of the industrial, especially manufacturing, sector, a significant part of which consists of family-run and labour-intensive small businesses. These are typical places of employment for Albanian women (Hatziprokopiou 2003: 1043–4).

Finally, Thessaloniki's long history of multiculturalism, hosting various populations from all over the Balkans and the Mediterranean, is regenerated with the recent immigration and settlement in the city of populations with diverse ethnic, social, religious and cultural backgrounds. In some cases these historical relations have been revived and reshaped into vital transnational links facilitated by geographical proximity. At the heart of this stand the cross-border social networks which channel not only migrants' mobility, but also trade, transport and investment (Hatziprokopiou 2006: 85, 106–8).

Data Collection in Greece

For the selection of respondents in Thessaloniki the relevant criteria were that they: a) originated from the Korçë area in Albania; and b) sent remittances to Albania. We conducted 20 semi-structured in-depth interviews with remittance-sending migrants, the majority of whom were men, reflecting thus the remittance-sending pattern in Albanian migration. As in Albania, we engaged with a number of stakeholders and key informants such as representatives of the Greek Ministry of Interior and that of Foreign Affairs, of the Greek Ombudsman, of local authorities in Thessaloniki, of financial institutions involved in remittance transfers between Greece and Albania, leaders of migrant organisations, researchers, academics and key migrants with businesses in Greece and Albania. Their views and suggestions were collected through in-depth interviews and two group discussions. The languages used were Greek and Albanian.

Some Ethical Issues

Respondents and interviewees in both countries included men and women in order to enable us to understand how each group – and particularly women – are involved in the remitting process. The survey and the interviews were conducted only when full consent was given by respondents, and were administered in a relaxed and transparent manner. However, we want to highlight some ethical issues that are often overlooked when discussing research on remittances.

First, it is important to note the personal and private nature of matters such as income and wealth, whether locally generated or remitted. This affects the degree to which respondents are willing to be forthcoming about such issues, something which has also been experienced by other researchers (see for instance Wong 2006). Second, there is a social dimension to remittances linked to the perceived 'success' of the migrant abroad, as well as to the degree s/he performs his/her duties towards parents, spouse and children. For these reasons, self-reported income and remittance sums should be considered with a degree of caution. In some instances they may be inflated in order to 'upgrade' the social status that comes with higher remittances (especially, in the Albanian family context, when they are sent/expected from 'dutiful' sons or husbands). In other cases local incomes and remittances may be downplayed when there is a perception on the part of the respondent that the information will somehow end up at the local tax or welfare assistance office. Furthermore, when answers are solicited from family members in origin areas about their migrant sons, daughters or spouses (as the main groups of remitters), the researcher needs to bear in mind that these may be reluctantly provided (if at all) when migrants are undocumented. Aware of these concerns, we tried to show sensitivity about them and conducted our research with respect for privacy, confidentiality and respondents' agency.

Outline of the Book

We round off this opening scene-setting chapter with an overview of the chapters which follow.

Chapter 2 maps the conceptual and theoretical terrain on which the empirical research is subsequently built. It surveys the four key domains in the chapter's title – gender, remittances, migration and development – and the connections (or lack thereof) between them. It reviews the now-voluminous literature on migration and development (the migration–development nexus); the strategic role of remittances in the nexus; the burgeoning literatures on gender and migration, and gender and development; and thereby highlights the lack of attention paid to gendering remittances. In reviewing the literatures on these various domains, reference is made to certain 'classic' migration settings where the migration–development–remittance experience has been particularly well documented (e.g. Mexico, Morocco, the Philippines), although not from a gendered perspective. Regarding the gender–remittance nexus, the main question that seems to have been asked in the very small number of studies that have approached this interaction is: are women 'better' remitters than men? That is to say, do they remit more, and are they more reliable remitters? Conventional wisdom has it that they are, but sound empirical evidence on this is scarce and contradictory. Moreover, we contend that this question is too simplistic; what we need to 'unpack' are the patriarchal gender structures which surround the remittance process and which condition the ability of women to send and spend such income flows.[12]

Chapter 3 reviews the scale and impact of Albanian migration since 1990: by 2010 there were more nearly 1.5 million post-1990 migrants living abroad, 600,000 of them in Greece where they constitute around 60 per cent of the immigrants in that country. Italy is the second most important destination, with around 400,000 Albanians. Regional patterns show a greater intensity of outmigration from southern Albania, where the fieldwork was carried out. Since the early 1990s, remittances have been a major plank supporting the Albanian economy – accounting for around 15–20 per cent of GDP – and sustaining a large share of Albanian households, especially in rural areas. Remittances have topped $1 billion per year since 2004. In terms of the contribution of remittances to the overall economy, Albania comes close to the top of the ranking of countries worldwide. The chapter reviews the studies made of Albanian remittances, noting that none of them have adopted a gender perspective. The final section of the chapter reviews the evolution of gender dynamics in Albania. Despite a measure of gender equality achieved under communism, Albania remains (and in some respects has become more so since 1990) a deeply patriarchal society. Several potential relationships between patriarchy, gender, migration and remittances are mapped out as hypotheses to be examined in subsequent chapters on the basis of the field research we carried out.

The focus of *Chapter 4* is the main unit of analysis in our research, the transnational household spanning both Albania and Greece. We start by briefly discussing the profiles of our respondents and their families in terms of their gender, age, education level, marital status, occupation, and for those family members living in Greece, duration of migration, and where possible, spatial distribution. This sets the scene for an in-depth analysis of the typology of transnational households within which remittances are transferred. The three main types are: the extended family residing in the village, whose adult son works in Greece and sends remittances to his parents; the nuclear family (wife and children) residing in the village, whose husband/father works in Greece and sends remittances to his wife; older parents of migrants, residing in the village on their own, whose adult children and their families live and work in Greece – remittances are usually sent by sons and received by fathers. Other, less common patterns and typologies are also mapped out. In the last section of this chapter we discuss the various ways in which these transnational households maintain their family cohesion across borders.

In *Chapter 5* we turn to the core of our research, namely the analysis of remittances and the way that gender shapes, and is shaped by, them. Our focus is on financial remittances sent by individuals within transnational households. Our gendered analysis of the remitting process considers sums, channels and frequencies of transmission. We also pay due attention to the gendered patterns of sending and receiving remittances. The types of transnational household where males remit as opposed to those where females do so, are discussed in turn.

In *Chapter 6* we continue with this analysis, but extend it to include development. Here we consider how remittances are used generally, and by men and women, by paying attention to some less-researched, but equally important aspects. Thus, social development, and the social dimension of remittances are at the centre of our analysis in this chapter. In addition, we also discuss the gendered complexity of non-monetary transfers, namely socio-political, technological and in-kind remittances. We interpret all these in the light of the post-communist transformation over these last two decades, which also helps us to untangle some of the ways in which remittances and gender shape each other.

After the discussion at a micro-level in the previous three chapters, in *Chapter 7* we scale up our analysis and examine the relationships between migration, development, remittances and gender from a local, regional and national perspective. The main axes of our analysis remain remittances and gender, structured around two threads. First, we discuss the relevant policies and programmes which have been proposed or implemented thus far in Albania, and specifically in our research area. Secondly, we draw substantially on expert opinion based on in-depth interviews, informal conversations and group discussions with key stakeholders both in Albania and Greece. We pay particular attention to the potential for development in the rural areas of origin, where remittances could be used to efficiently generate sustainable livelihoods. In this discussion we include some of the key factors that would ensure the optimisation of such remittance use for investment, as well as the ways in which gender shapes such entrepreneurial activities.

In the *final chapter* the main theoretical arguments and empirical results of the book are reviewed, and the extent to which our research has contributed 'new knowledge' is evaluated. We assert that our findings are significant and original, and contribute, through the specific focus on gender and remittances, to moving forward the debate on migration and development. We draw out the implications of the research for policy-makers, both in Albania and more generally.

2

MIGRATION, GENDER, REMITTANCES AND DEVELOPMENT: A THEORETICAL PERSPECTIVE

The purpose of this chapter is to lay the theoretical foundations of the book, setting out a series of conceptual issues which will help to scaffold the empirical analysis presented in subsequent chapters. We review each of the four keyword domains in the chapter's title and the connections – or lack thereof – between them. Hence we survey migration and development, remittances and development, gender and migration, gender and development, and gender and remittances. Alongside our analysis of these linked conceptual domains, we also review a selection of empirical literature, paying particular attention to some 'classic' migration settings, such as Mexico and the Philippines, where the migration–remittance–development experience has been thoroughly researched, albeit often without paying much attention to gender as an analytical category. In introducing a gendered analysis we note, on the one hand, the expanding literatures on gender and migration and on gender and development, but also, crucially, the lack of attention paid to gender and remittances. This *lacuna* is the *raison d'être* of this book.

In focusing on what we call the gender–remittance nexus, we discover that a number of simplistic stereotypes have started to emerge, without much supporting evidence. The dominant stereotype is the widely quoted statement, or assumption, that women are 'better' remitters, and users of remittances, than men. We review the limited findings in the literature to back up this assertion, and find the evidence contradictory. A second analytical stereotype that we need to question is the assumption that it is valid to compare males and females as remitters and remittance receivers as if they were competing in the remittance game on a level playing field. In other words, we argue that asking whether men or women are better remitters is not the right question (King and Vullnetari 2010). We need to look behind the simple binary comparison and delve into the gender structures and dynamics of the migrant-sending society, including the transnational component of that society which has developed through migration abroad. Only then can we understand the gendered questions of who sends, receives, utilises and decides about remittances.

Migration and Development

Recent years have seen a growing interest from academic researchers in a range of disciplines such as economics, sociology, anthropology and geography, as well as from development planners and policy-makers, into the linkages between migration and development – or what has come to be known as 'the migration–development nexus' (Van Hear and Nyberg Sørensen 2003). The nature of these linkages remains complex and multifaceted, and hence much debated.[1] The complexity derives from a number of factors including: origin and destination country perspectives; macro or micro analyses; distinguishing causes from impacts; differences between short-term versus long-term effects; various types of migration (internal vs. international, temporary vs. permanent, low-skilled vs. highly-skilled etc.); and variations from one geographical and historical context to another. Challenges of measurement often frustrate proper documentation of the effects of migration on development and vice-versa. It is well-known that good statistics on migration, especially in poor countries, are elusive; and measuring development throws up its own conceptual and ideological challenges, beyond the quality of the data. Moreover, in an era of increasing global interdependencies, isolating the specific migration–development dynamics from broader trends of global social transformation and inequality becomes ever more difficult (Glick Schiller and Faist 2009). Indeed, many would argue that detaching migration–development dynamics from these wider processes is a mistaken approach, since they can only be fully understood *within* the framework of globalisation, societal transformation and international and regional inequality (Castles 2010). Yet, the temptation to make sweeping generalisations must be tempered with the necessity to take specific geographical and historical circumstances and contexts into account.

We suggest that, fundamentally, the debate on the linkages and causalities within the migration–development nexus revolves around four main questions:

- Does underdevelopment cause migration?
- Does migration lead to underdevelopment?

- Does migration lead to development?
- Does development lead to further migration?

At the end of the book we will come back to these questions and see which of them are most relevant to the Albanian experience.

The four questions can also be seen as pointers into different theoretical and ideological interpretations of the migration–development debate. Three main positions structure this debate: one optimistic, one pessimistic, and the third one more contextual and nuanced. The optimistic view stresses 'development'; the pessimistic one 'underdevelopment'; whilst the 'middle way' reflects a more pluralist reading of the various theoretical debates. As de Haas (2010) points out in his lucid review of the migration–development theoretical field, the debate has swung back and forth like a pendulum: from developmentalist optimism during the 1950s and 1960s, to neo-Marxist pessimism during the 1970s and 1980s, and then back towards more optimistic scenarios in the 1990s and 2000s. These discursive shifts have reflected wider paradigm shifts in development theory across economics and the social sciences since the mid-twentieth century. Let us now take each of these interpretations in turn.

Pessimism

The pessimistic view derives from structuralist, neo-Marxist, cumulative-causation and dependency theories by which migration is not so much a simple response to underdevelopment but, rather, one of its fundamental expressions. Migration therefore hinders development in migrant-origin countries (but aids it in destination countries), thereby exacerbating underdevelopment and inequality. Underdevelopment causes migration, which in turn drains resources and leads to underdevelopment, more migration, and so on in a vicious circle. This is the classic model of cumulative causation (Myrdal 1957), a self-reproducing downward spiral, leading to the 'development of underdevelopment' (Frank 1969) in parts of the world such as Latin America and Asia.

According to this line of thinking, emigration is caused by the penetration of foreign capital from core to peripheral zones within the world economic system (Castles and Miller 2003; Sassen 1988; Wallerstein 1979). The consequent dislocation of labour from rural to urban areas, and from periphery to core, only serves to fuel the process of capital accumulation in core areas. Origin countries and particularly their rural areas are impoverished by the loss of their young, active and creative population cohorts, especially when they are highly educated. This leads to brain drain, often made worse when those going abroad experience de-skilling. Back home, mass outmigration disrupts labour markets leading to shortages of workers in key sectors like agriculture and rural industry; in a study of migration from Yemen, for instance, children had to replace the adult male labour lost to emigration (Fergany 1982: 762).

We deal with remittances in more detail in the next part of this chapter, but it is worth noting here that the pessimists view the developmental impact of remittances negatively. Because it is often the better-off who migrate from rural areas, inequality increases through the backflow of remittances and the poor get relatively, if not absolutely, poorer. Furthermore, it is argued, remittances are not development-inducive because they are often spent on what are considered 'unproductive' purchases, thus hindering any structural change to ease dependency on them (Lewis 1986; Lipton 1980). Instead, sending areas become structurally dependent on remittances, which can only be sustained by yet more migration. Remittances may also inhibit long-term gender development through their role in maintaining traditional rural structures and systems, which are often very biased in favour of men – as landowners, village chiefs, family patriarchs etc. (Rempel and Lobdell 1978).

Finally, return migration brings only disillusionment, according to the pessimistic interpretation. When migrants return, not only do they not bring new skills with them (because they have been de-skilled abroad or have done jobs which are irrelevant to their home settings), but they represent a negative selection. They come back because they are failures or are retiring. The successful ones, the best and the brightest, are the least likely to return. Not only do they stay in the destination countries, they become integrated there and gradually sever their links to the home country, thereby cutting any hope for any positive development contribution (Cerase 1974).

Optimism

One of the unifying features of the pessimistic scenario reviewed above is that the agency of migrants is denied: they are seen as pawns of the system, dragged hither and thither by the demands of capitalism, and then routinely discarded when they are exhausted or no longer needed. Migrants' agency is restored by the 'optimistic' interpretation of the migration–development relationship. In this scenario, migration is seen as an individual or household response to underdevelopment, and a personal solution to the condition of poverty. Remittances and return migration can turn a condition of underdevelopment into a pathway towards development. Depending on which variety of the optimistic theory is followed, migration either cancels itself out once the economic gap between sending and receiving areas narrows (the neoclassic equilibrium approach), or stimulates further migration through the 'demonstration effect' that successful migration generates. In short, the optimistic view turns the assumptions, arguments and mechanisms of the pessimistic interpretation on their head. A 'virtuous circle' replaces the 'vicious' one.

Another way of characterising the positive interpretation of migration's contribution to development is that it is a win-win-win situation: the country of origin, that of destination, and the migrants themselves, all gain; the country of origin because it can 'export' its unemployment and benefit from remittances, the country of destination because it receives a 'free' supply of ready-made labour willing to work for lower wages and in tougher jobs than its own workers will accept, and the migrants themselves because they escape poverty and improve their lives and the life-chances of their families. This of course is a somewhat sanitised view of the reality of migration, but it it useful as a theoretical blueprint (see also King and Vullnetari 2009a).

The optimistic or 'developmentalist' scenario has two different theoretical interpretations: the neoclassical equilibrium model which dominated economic thinking in the 1950s and 1960s, and the 'new economics of migration' model, reliant especially on the developmental potential of remittances, which has held sway for the past two decades (de Haas 2010: 230–2). The neoclassical view sees migration as a factor-equalising mechanism by which workers are transferred from labour-surplus (low-wage, high-unemployment) countries or areas to labour-deficit regions (with high wages and zero unemployment). The very transfer of labour equalises factor prices (wages in the case of labour) and hence the spatial disequilibrium which drove migration in the first place is narrowed, and there is no further need for migration (Massey *et al.* 1993). In the purest form of the neoclassical model, which assumes perfect information and no barriers to movement, return does not take place; returnees would thus represent only those who failed or miscalculated (Cassarino 2004). However, later versions of the model saw returning migrants, and their savings and training accumulated whilst abroad, as major potential stimulants of investment and home-country development (Griffin 1976; Kindleberger 1965; Miracle and Berry 1970).

The neoclassical theory viewed migrants as atomistic individuals motivated only by utility maximisation, and disregarded their membership of households, families, and communities. Neither return nor remittances were part of this theory. These unrealistic assumptions were relaxed in – indeed they were the essence of – the new economics of labour migration (NELM) which took root in the 1990s following a landmark paper by Stark and Bloom (1985; see also the excellent review of the field by Taylor 1999). The distinctive contribution of the NELM was twofold: first, it saw the family and household as the fundamental decision-making unit for migration (and other livelihood decisions); and second it blended income maximisation with risk aversion. In this way migration (of one or more members of a family) was part of a portfolio of economic strategies, each of which could be a potential income earner but also a hedge against failure in another branch of the family portfolio. So, migration to wage-work could be an insurance against crop failure or market-price collapse, while agricultural production could also cushion against the failure of the migration project. Remittances and return were thus key components of the NELM household model (de Haas 2010: 242–6).

Remittances (less so return) have been the dominant element in the recent and still-current positive interpretation of the migration–development nexus espoused by a number of key players in the international development area, such as the World Bank, the EU, the Organisation for Economic Co-operation and Development (OECD), various UN organisations and the IOM (Glick Schiller and Faist 2009; Kunz 2008). Whilst stopping well short of explicitly encouraging migration by removing all barriers to international movement, these bodies see migration both as a route out of poverty and as a key stimulus to home-country development. The latter aim is attained, so the narrative goes, largely through 'managing' migration and maximising the positive economic effects of remittances. Typical of this genre is the following statement from UNDP (2009: 2–3, 5):

> Most migrants, internal and international, reap gains in the form of higher incomes, better access to education and health, and improved prospects for their children. Surveys of migrants report that most are happy in their destination [...] Migrants boost economic output, at little or no cost to locals [...] In migrants' countries of origin, the impacts of movement are felt in higher incomes and consumption, better education and improved health, as well as a broader social and cultural level. Moving generally brings benefits, most directly in the form of remittances sent to immediate family members. However, the benefits are also spread more broadly as remittances are spent – thereby generating jobs for local workers – and as behaviour changes in response to ideas from abroad. Women, in particular, maybe liberated from traditional roles. [...] While not a substitute for broader development efforts, migration can be a vital strategy for households and families seeking to diversify and improve their livelihoods [...] Large gains to human development can therefore be achieved by lowering the barriers to movement.

Strong echoes of the 'optimistic' articulation can be read in this statement. It is a clear vindication (without much solid evidence, however) of the triple-win scenario for sending countries, receiving countries, and the migrants themselves. The NELM is represented by reference to the role of migration in diversifying migrant livelihoods, remittances are given a key role in stimulating home-country development, 'social remittances' are alluded to by the phrase 'behaviour changes in response to ideas from abroad' (more on social remittances presently), and the gender empowerment effect is also acknowledged – although there is no mention as to how this comes about.[2]

Return migration is seen as less relevant to the development stimulus that migration can bring to migrants' areas of origin. This is partly because return migration stops remittances. But this is also partly because of the lessons of the past, in particular the disappointing developmental results of the return migrations during the 1970s and 1980s of the labour migrants who had departed in the early postwar decades. There is, however, renewed attention to getting the more highly-skilled emigrants to return, or at least to re-engage with their homelands, through various 'return of talent' and 'brain regain' policies operated by individual governments and by bodies such as the IOM. It has also become increasingly apparent that many migrants, including those established abroad for a long time, behave transnationally, involving themselves simultaneously in their ethnic communities abroad and their origin countries, without a definitive return taking place (Guarnizo 2003; Vertovec 1999). A final perspective on return is the way in which circular migration has been promoted recently as an efficacious solution to the migration–development dynamic. Allowing labour to move temporarily where it is in demand allows the international labour market to function efficiently without uprooting migrants from their home communities permanently; moreover such a strategy avoids the social, cultural and economic costs of long-term-settled migrants with their families and different ways of living.

A Pluralist, Contextualist, Critical View

The optimistic interpretation of the positive synergy between migration and development is essentially a 'Northern' or 'First World' optic, promulgated by developed states and international organs like the World Bank which are the main regulators of the global economy. This 'view from the North', which is also reflected in some of the work of the Global Commission on International Migration and the UN's High-Level Dialogue on Migration and Development, both operative during the 2000s, continues to drive academic and policy debates (Glick Schiller and Faist 2009: 5). The 'Southern perspective', advocated for instance by Castles and

Delgado Wise (2008), is a minority voice in these asymmetric international debates where the migration interests of the rich, often former colonial countries seem to hold sway,[3] even if cloaked in the rhetoric of helping the less developed countries, usually by pushing the benefits of financial remittances in an uncritical way.

As Faist (2008) and Glick Schiller and Faist (2009) argue, we need to retain a critical stance towards most narratives and interpretations of migration and development, and the too-simple progression from the idea of migration as a problem resulting from, and endemic to, underdevelopment (the pessimistic view) to migration as a solution to the development challenge (the optimistic view). This 'middle way' or third position is more sensitive to the complexities and interdependencies of the age of globalisation. It is not an 'either/or' situation, but rather a complex set of interactions between migration and development where the positive and negative impacts of migration on source countries are intertwined. Part of this complexity is the recognition, following Giddens (1984), that both structure and agency play crucial roles in understanding the heterogeneity of migration–development interactions, enabling us to move beyond the rigidly deterministic formulations of the structuralist school, or the false aggregation of atomised individual decision-makers in the neoclassical model.[4]

If there is a criticism of this third perspective, it is that it is *too* ambivalent. It sees the migration–development relationship as 'unsettled' (Papademetriou 1991), 'unresolved' (Appleyard 1992), and as 'complicated, uncertain, ambivalent, and unexplored' (Hermele 1997: 134). To fall back on the escape clause 'it depends on the circumstances' (Hermele 1997: 135) may seem an indecisive stance but it does open up to the great variety of migratory contexts around the world, both now and in the past.

Three Questions for Albania

We round off this discussion by posing three 'middle-range' theoretical questions which have both general bearing on the migration–development nexus and more specific relevance to the Albanian case which is the empirical focus of the book. The first concerns the balance of positives and negatives over the short versus the long term. Fischer *et al.* (1997) argue that, on the whole, empirical evidence reveals that migration has positive effects for the destination countries and (less convincingly so) origin countries in the short run; but it is much more difficult to pin down 'migration-induced long-term development effects' (1997: 122). In the long run, they note, migration rarely brings far-reaching socio-economic changes that advance development in origin countries. But part of the difficulty here is that, over the longer term, the specific effects traceable to migration become more difficult to identify and disentangle from other processes – for example globalisation, structural reform, or tourism. This is certainly a relevant issue for Albania where, because of the suddenness of the onset of large-scale migration in the early 1990s, the short-term effects (relief of unemployment, remittances etc.) are rather easy to see, whereas the long-term effects on the Albanian economy and society are not yet clear.

The second question interrogates the logic of the so-called 'root causes' approach to solving the migration–development problem. If we accept that underdevelopment – poverty, unemployment, economic stagnation, social inequality, deficient infrastructure, poor life prospects etc. – leads to migration (a starting-point that most analysts, of whatever 'school', seem to accept), then can the migration be stemmed by addressing these root causes of migration? (Lipton 1980). Interest in root causes comes from two sources: destination-country governments wishing to control the migration pressure they feel their country is under, particularly if it is geographically adjacent to migration-source countries (such as Greece and Italy with Albania, Spain with Morocco, the US with Mexico etc.); and origin-country governments wanting to offer better life-chances to their populations so that the latter are not placed in a position where they feel they have to migrate to survive and improve their lot. Politically, too, a government which cannot organise its economy such that many people do not have to migrate is in an ignominious position. We believe that this question, too, is relevant to the Albanian case. Put simply: what measures need to be put in place to convince Albanians not to migrate in such large numbers, without of course denying them their human right to migrate should they so wish? We return to this question in Chapter 7.

The third question grows out of a re-evaluation of the 'root causes' approach. The root-causes philosophy is based on the proposition that the best migration (control) policy is development: i.e., once a country or region becomes 'developed', the need to migrate will be removed. The empirical evidence, on the whole, does not sustain this hypothesis. Actually, economic growth and development tend to coincide with increases in migration rates, because socio-economic development enables, and inspires, more people to migrate. This mechanism leads to the notion of the 'migration hump' – alluding to the inverted U-shaped curve on the graph of the relationship between migration (vertical axis) and development (horizontal axis). Initially development and migration proceed in tandem (because very poor people are too poor to migrate) until a certain level of development is reached (the top of the 'hump') when migration decreases because people (on an aggregate level) no longer feel the necessity to migrate to improve their lives (Martin 2004; Martin and

Taylor 1996). Our question here is: when will Albania reach the top of the hump?

Remittances and Development

International remittances are money that migrants earn abroad and send to members of their families who remain in origin areas. Considered by many as the most visible, beneficial and largest-scale direct impact of migration, these capital transfers are often vital to migrant-origin economies; as well as contributing valuable foreign currency to national income and the balance of payments, they are 'safety nets for poor regions' and a powerful tool to reduce poverty, as many studies have shown (see, *inter alia*, Jones 1998: 18; Kapur 2004: 18; Taylor 1999: 67). Policy makers, development economists and social researchers alike have been concerned for some time to find ways to best harness them, and the literature generated is overwhelming.[5]

The 'Remittances Mantra'

In terms of both absolute amounts and expressed as a proportion of a country's gross domestic product (GDP), the magnitude of international remittances is impressive. The global total was estimated at $336 billion in 2008; the onset of the global economic crisis provoked a fall of 6 per cent to $316 billion in 2009 (Ratha *et al.* 2010). Of course, questions must be asked about the accuracy of these figures (see Gammeltoft 2002; Ghosh 2006). Moreover, remittances sent through formal channels such as banks or money transfer operators like Western Union are thought to be 'only the tip of the iceberg' (Puri and Ritzema 1999: 3). Unrecorded flows, i.e. financial transfers through friends, family, self-carrying cash during return visits etc., as well as in-kind remittances such as furniture, clothes etc., have been estimated to constitute between 35 and 75 per cent of the official flows (Ghosh 2006; Puri and Ritzema 1999; Spatafora and Freund 2004). In spite of these figures, it must be remembered that often the poorest countries do not participate so much in international migration, because very poor people do not have the financial and human resources to move abroad. Consequently, they are more dependent on Official Development Aid (ODA) as an income source (Ghosh 2006). This has to be reflected in policy considerations whereby international remittances, although an important source of external development finance, need to be considered as complementary, rather than as a substitute for ODA (Nyberg Sørenson *et al.* 2002; Ratha 2003).

For a decade or so now, remittances have been 'talked up' as the major contribution migration can make to development in the poorer countries of the world, even if the very poorest – countries and people – are excluded. If we look at the world rankings of total remittances and, more pertinently, as a share of GDP (UNDP 2009: 159–62) we see three groups of countries in the upper ranks:

- for total remittances, large countries with big migrant and diaspora populations as a result of extensive emigration over many decades (China, India, Pakistan, Bangladesh, the Philippines, Mexico, Morocco);
- on the GDP share criterion, many small, often island countries (Haiti, Jamaica, Honduras, El Salvador, Lesotho), alongside non-oil Middle Eastern countries (Lebanon, Jordan, Yemen);
- also on the GDP share measure, those former Eastern bloc countries which have experienced mass emigration in the last two decades as a result of poverty and an often chaotic post-communist transition (Albania, Moldova, Armenia, Kyrgyzstan, Tajikistan).

For most of these countries listed above, remittances constitute 10–40 per cent of GDP, lower for some of the larger countries because of the sheer size of their economies; and in most cases too remittances outweigh ODA and Foreign Direct Investment (FDI).

Given that remittances are a kind of 'bottom-up' development initiative, generated by individual migrants rather than by governments, international development agencies or NGOs, they are often promoted as a more effective, and 'cheaper', form of development. Unlike FDI and ODA, they cost nothing (discounting, that is, the human cost of migration). Moreover, their distribution is usually dispersed, like a sprinkler system, feeding cash directly into mainly rural households in areas of high outmigration; unlike FDI and ODA which are often concentrated in expensive and high-prestige projects at discrete, often urban, locations. Hence, to quote a senior World Bank official, 'remittances are beautiful'.[6]

But, this 'remittances mantra' is also now being questioned by more critical voices. One of the first sceptical notes was introduced by Kapur (2004); others have followed (*inter alia*, Carling 2008a; de Haas 2005; 2007b; Kunz 2008). Within developing countries there are concerns that the bulk of these transfers go to the better-off, since they constitute the majority of international migrants. Thus, the inequalities that existed before migration took place are reinforced (Lipton 1980). In their extended survey of the role of migration for the development of several countries in Eastern Europe and Central Asia, Black *et al.* (2007: 41) also concluded that remittances had increased income inequalities for countries such as Albania and Serbia.[7] Nonetheless, poor people may benefit from international remittances through the trickle-down or multiplier effect, for instance related to increased demand for local goods and services (de Haas 2007a; Taylor 1999). This effect is said to be wider and to affect poverty reduction more significantly in rural areas, particularly from remittances transferred by lower-skilled migrants, since they come mostly from rural areas. Research points out that the low-skilled remit more than their highly educated counterparts, particularly as a proportion of their total earnings (Lowell 2002: 20). The multiplier effect for poverty reduction was also clear in the multi-country study by Adams and Page (2003). They found that a 10 per cent rise in the share of international migrants for a country resulted in a 2 per cent decline in the share of people living on $1 a day. A figure of 2 per cent might not seem impressive at first sight, but at an individual level the difference it makes can be significant.

Most of the debate over remittances and their developmental impact takes it for granted that only the financial flows resulting from international migration are involved. But the role of internal migrants should not be overlooked, even if the data on internal remittances are scarce, and the amounts sent or received per capita are generally much lower. Nevertheless, in some countries they affect a wider base of people and are important for food security and poverty reduction (Rempel and Lobdell 1978: 329; World Bank 2006a: 65). Overwhelmingly in African, but also in some Asian and Latin American countries, studies have found that internal remittances are an important part of the income portfolio for rural residual families (Deshingkar 2006).[8] In China they have been estimated to contribute 10–30 per cent of the per capita income for rural households (Murphy 2005: 235); they were shown to provide an important safety-net for poor households in Bangladesh (Afsar 2003); and they were found to reduce 'the level, depth, and severity of poverty' in rural Ghana (Adams 2006).

Why Remit?

Any discussion on motivations to remit is drawn back to the seminal paper on this topic by Lucas and Stark (1985) which, as Carling points out (2008b: 583), has been cited three times more than any other paper on remittances. An early excursion into the 'new economics' of migration, Lucas and Stark (1985) looked at remittances at the household level, with empirical evidence from Botswana. Their typology of reasons to remit was made up of three categories: 'pure altruism', 'pure self-interest', and an intermediate category they called 'tempered altruism or enlightened self-interest'.

Remittances have an *altruistic* function if migrants derive utility from their family's utility. The migrant thus cares about his/her family's poverty, health and well-being and responds accordingly. This implies several things regarding the theory and operationalisation of remittances (Hagen-Zanker and Siegel 2007). There is a positive relationship between adverse conditions in the receiving households and the amount of remittances sent. Second, remittances should increase with migrant income (since the migrant has more income from which to remit), and decrease with the income of the recipient household (whose 'needs' are thus reduced). Third, remittances will increase at times of crisis, such as crop failure, environmental disaster, or the health costs of a sick family member. Remittances thus have an important responsive or counter-cyclical pattern. Finally, remittances may decrease if there are other remitters in the family, since the migrant feels less accountable if he/she knows that the residual family has other support.

At the other extreme, migrants send remittances out of *self-interest*, which breaks down, in the Lucas and Stark typology, into three specific motivations. The first is the aspiration to inherit: this is the 'purest' form of self-interest, although the promise of inheritance may be used as a blackmailing device by the household head (e.g. the migrant's father) to secure remittances. According to the inheritance motive, remittances increase with the recipient household's assets and income, the probability of inheriting (dependent on the age and health of the parents, the number of siblings, the inheritance system – primogeniture, partible inheritance amongst all siblings or only males etc.), and the migrant's own wealth and income (Hagen-Zanker and Siegel 2007). Note that the relationship between remittances and the receiving household's wealth is reversed here (i.e. it is positive) compared to the altruism motive (where it is negative).

Second, in the self-interest category, remittances may be sent to demonstrate laudable behaviour and thereby enhance social prestige. Whilst such a 'good' reputation is usually aimed at the eyes of the home community as a whole, there may also be a 'demonstration effect' within the family. For instance, in a three-generation setting, remittances sent to the migrant's parents may put moral pressure on the migrant's own children to take care of him/her in old age. It is also the case that the social prestige of 'good remitting' from migrant children reflects on the recipient family, who lose respect and accumulate shame if their migrant children are not seen to be faithful remitters – the implication being that the parents did not bring up their children to be loyal to their families.

Third, the migrant sends remittances self-interestedly to be invested in assets such as land, housing, livestock or a business in preparation for a return home. Usually this involves relying on another family member such as a parent or sibling to manage the assets during the migrant's continued absence. Such an 'agent' must be on good terms with the migrant and be trustworthy, otherwise tensions may result, as they sometimes do. To the extent that these assets or the business might be shared between family members when the migrant returns, self-interest blends with altruism here.

This last circumstance brings in the final category of the Lucas and Stark typology, *tempered altruism* or *enlightened self-interest.* This involves a variety of situations in which the migrant and the family at home mutually benefit from migration through some form of implicit contractual arrangement. Loan repayment is one obvious example, whereby remittances reimburse the family for financing the costs of migration, and also, over the longer term, repay parents for their human capital investment in the migrant's upbringing and education. Another example is where the migrant leaves his/her children behind in the care of family members and the remittances are, at least partly, for the costs of childcare. A third variant of this hybrid motivation set is an arrangement of co-insurance, which is the perfect illustration of the NELM situation. Here the migrant 'trades' remittances to support the recipient household at times of 'shocks' (market failure, health costs etc.) in return for 'reverse remittances' at times of crisis for the migrant, such as during the initial job search and subsequent periods of unemployment abroad. As Hagen-Zanker and Siegel (2007) point out, risks at home and risks in the destination country have to be non-correlated for such a co-insurance scheme to work well. In their empirical work in Botswana, Lucas and Stark (1985) found evidence of mutually beneficial contractual arrangements of co-insurance and loan repayment.

According to Carling (2008b), the many studies on remittances carried out since Lucas and Stark's foundational article have done little more than confirm that altruism is important in explaining remittance-sending, but it does not fully explain remittance behaviour; yet the balance between altruism and self-interest is often difficult to probe and disentangle. Carling's conclusion (2008b: 585–6), that the *context* and *type* of migration are vitally important, is fully consistent with the approach that we develop in our own empirical investigation in this book. Hence we distinguish, for instance, between seasonal and long-term migration; between situations where the single migrant leaves his/her family behind as opposed to nuclear-family migration; between remittances sent to spouse and those sent to parents; and so on.

A final point concerns the normative setting by which remittance-sending is subject to *moral values* of *expectations* and *entitlements* on the part of the recipient (Carling 2008b: 586). Emigrants feel 'socially obliged to remit' (Carling 2008a: 55) or are conditioned to do so by their upbringing and the nature of their surrounding community, which may have established a 'remittance culture' based on its transformation into a remittance economy. A family with a 'deviant' migrant who fails to remit is pitied or socially marginalised by the surrounding community, so that further pressure is brought on the errant migrant to reform his/her ways in order that family reputation can be restored (Stark 2009: 152).

Uses of Remittances

The most powerful economic argument for remittances' development potential is the simple yet surprisingly under-emphasised one that they derive from returns to labour in high-income countries and are transferred and used in low-income countries where their 'real' value is proportionately greater, depending on the cost-of-living differential between the two. However, quite apart from this 'enhanced value' argument, it is the *use* of remittances in the migrant's country of origin that is the crux of the long-standing debate over migration's contribution to development.

A common division – surely too simple – is often made between so-called 'productive' uses of remittances (investments in farming, industry, services and other enterprises) and 'unproductive' spending (food, clothing, housing, consumer goods, family rituals etc.). Two problems arise from this dichotomisation. First, such definitions are based on a narrow economic perspective, which does not reflect socio-economic realities in less-developed countries and ignores the essentially private nature of remittance transfers, which are not specifically designed to stimulate national development (cf. Koc and Onan 2004; Nikas and King 2005; Orozco 2007). Second, there are disagreements over exactly what should be classified as 'productive' and 'non-productive'. As Oberai and Singh (1980: 236–7) suggest, consumption-oriented expenditure 'should not be interpreted as mainly unproductive; in an economy in which levels of living are low, consumption expenditure may often be functional and may induce significant improvements in labour productivity'. Remittances affect the well-being of families by enabling them to improve their diets, their accommodation, dress better and thus constitute a healthier and more productive workforce and population. Furthermore, through remittances there is increased access to better education and health, as well as improved continuation of family rituals and obligations, which beneficially affects families' social status and psychological well-being.

Nevertheless, many economists and others have expressed concern over the viability of remittances as a development stimulus. Their main worry is the channelling of most remittances into consumption, however defined, or even worse, into 'conspicuous consumption' (lavish and over-large housing, expensive consumer goods, and excessive spending on family and community rituals such as weddings and funerals). In his classic review paper, Lipton (1980: 12) claimed that at least 90 per cent of remittances were used on everyday consumption, although the variety of migration–development contexts that have evolved over the decades surely make this a figure that is hard to justify nowadays. In Lipton's ranking, productive investments came only fourth. Even then, he characterised them as 'consumptive investments' – eg. purchase of land to enjoy landowner status, hiring workers to achieve employer status, or small and economically marginal businesses such as grocery stores or cafés. De Haas (2010: 237) goes on to list other negative aspects of remittance use which vindicate the 'pessimistic' framework: purchase of land drives land-price inflation, to the cost of local farmers who cannot expand their holdings; consumer goods are generally imported, causing a 'leakage' of remittance income back out of the country and falling demand for locally-produced goods (eg. furniture); households supported by remittances disinvest in farming and withdraw their labour from the rural economy.

Whilst most researchers agree that the primary use of remittances is consumption in order to ensure the survival of the family at a reasonable and hopefully improved level of well-being (including in refugee situations; Jazayery 2002), other analysts argue that migrants and their families use remittances in ways that are completely rational given their personal and family circumstances as well as the structural economic, socio-cultural and political contexts in which these decisions are made (Guarnizo 2003: 674). Investments in children's healthcare and education, 'unproductive' in the short term, can yield vital long-term economic and human development benefits. Even where consumer goods are imported (which they may have to be because they are not produced locally), employment is generated by the need to transport, maintain and service them. Likewise, the construction of new housing, which has so often been vilified by commentators, can generate considerable multiplier effects through employment, demand for construction materials, and subsequent house maintenance and decoration. In emigration countries as far apart as Mexico, Morocco, Albania and Bangladesh, research has shown that remittances have provided a considerable number of jobs for residents within the country (de Haas 2010; Guarnizo 2003).

Finally, from a macro-economic perspective too, remittances can make a big contribution to foreign exchange earnings and capital formation, although the latter may often be for small and medium enterprises. In their study of 11 transition countries in Central and Eastern Europe, Léon-Ledesma and Piracha (2004) found that remittances contributed significantly to increasing investment levels. They were also considered as vital for economic growth in many Latin American countries (Orozco 2007). However, more conservative conclusions suggest that this might be exaggerated and that, beyond development in small-scale initiatives, remittances have not in fact proved to be the prime mover for economic take-off or sustained growth (Ghosh 2006). It is also important to observe that they may increase inflation and impede structural adjustments (Ammassari and Black 2001; Russell 1986). In the absence of overarching and well-planned strategies, the sustainability of such 'remittance economies' cannot last long. This difficulty is increased in volatile political situations, as Black *et al.* (2007) found in the Balkans and Central Asian countries.

Gender, Migration and Development

Having comprehensively surveyed the main arguments and supporting literature on the interactions between migration, remittances and development, we now introduce gender into the discussion. Our key point is that while gender perspectives have made major impacts on the literature and thinking about migration and development, a gendered analysis of remittances, the main linking mechanism between migration and development, is still missing.

Gendering Migration

Despite the fact that gender is one of the fundamental structuring parameters of human life, it was not brought into migration studies until the landmark writings of Phizacklea (1983) and Morokvasic (1984). Prior to that, migration was somehow silently assumed to be a 'male thing', with women following, if at all, only as dependents, meaning wives and homemakers. Increased awareness of women's role in migration has revealed a feminisation of migration, both quantitatively and qualitatively. Nowadays, women constitute half of all international migrants and for some countries, such as the Philippines, they are in the clear majority (King *et al.* 2010: 78–9). Qualitatively, women are increasingly participating in migration as 'autonomous agents' (Deshingkar and Grimm 2005); they have moved from being 'marginal subjects' in the migration process to 'social actors' (Campani 1995). This feminisation trend is particularly strong in Latin America and South-East Asia, but less so in South Asia and Africa; it is strong in some Eastern European countries, such as Poland and Ukraine, but not so evident (yet) in others, such as Albania. The differential gendering of migration streams demonstrates that such regional variations are affected by local cultural norms, as well as by demand in certain gender-specific labour sectors of the economy. Even where migration remains largely male-dominated, female migration has been on the increase, partly through family reunion migration but also in order to access employment in labour-market niches perceived as 'female' such as domestic service, care work, and garment factories (IOM 2005a; Piper 2005).[9]

For the past two or so decades, then, migration has been appreciated as a fundamentally gendered phenomenon that requires sophisticated analytical tools and theories that move beyond sex as a dichotomous variable. A gendered analysis involves much more than counting the numbers of male and female migrants or even comparing and contrasting the migration behaviours and experiences of men and women. Rather, as Hondagneu-Sotelo has argued in her work on Mexican migration to the United States, 'gender *organizes* migration… gender relations facilitate or constrain both women *and* men's immigration and settlement' (1994: 3; her emphases). Theoretical formulations of gender and migration see gender as *relational* – the migration behaviour of one sex cannot be understood without reference to the behaviour of the other sex – and also *situational* and *contextual*, dependent on specific space-time circumstances (Bjerén 1997: 226; Piper 2005: 1).

Space does not allow a detailed review of the various contextual and situational outcomes, since the literature on gender and migration has grown very rapidly in the last two decades. What we can do is direct attention to a few contrasting examples drawn from the context of work and family migration from underdeveloped countries, helped by useful overview papers by Ghosh (2009), Piper (2005) and others.[10] The key questions become: how do culturally-embedded and socially-constructed gender relations in poor countries constrain the migration behaviour of women (especially) and men? And to what extent is migration an empowering transition for women, in that through the migration experience, gender relations get modified in their favour?

Research in Bangladesh has shown highly differentiated migration patterns by gender, and hence contrasting gendered effects. Like other South Asian countries (but not Sri Lanka), it is overwhelmingly male migrants who go abroad; female migration is subject to serious restrictions and, where it takes place, it is mainly internal and localised. Male migration abroad is seen as more rewarding, leading to upward social mobility, even though the quality and conditions of the work performed overseas are harsh and demeaning. However, for the women left behind, male migration can be disadvantageous and disempowering. Men's control over women increases as a result of migration: women are discouraged from going to work outside the home, and motherhood and care are becoming more central to women's identity. Where remittances are not sent, women may find themselves with insufficient food or reduced access to healthcare, forcing some, against the prevailing cultural norms for women's behaviour, to resort to low-paid seasonal agricultural work (Black 2009: 31–4).

Other research in Bangladesh has documented how female migrants from rural areas to Dhaka moved from having no income of their own prior to migration, to 80 per cent of them having earned enough through migration to put them above the poverty threshold. In turn these migrant women played a significant role in social change in origin communities, especially through encouraging and financing the education of their siblings and other relatives, including other women and girls (Afsar 2005: 6). Other effects are cross-generational: still in Bangladesh, migration was found to lead young Bangladeshi migrant men to challenge their father's power and authority within the family (Piper 2005: 25).

Kabeer's (2000) comparative study of Bangladeshi women in London and Dhaka shows how gendered cultural norms combine with locational influences to determine women's lives and labour market choices. She finds that, paradoxically, women living in Bangladesh had greater labour market choice than their migrant counterparts in London; this was unexpected given the overall socio-economic status of women in the two countries. Women in Dhaka could renegotiate the practice of *purdah* (including restrictions on their attire and public appearance) with their husbands and the local community in order to legitimise their work in garment factories, whereas in London women were forced by this cultural practice to restrict their employment to home-based work. This paradoxical outcome also reflects the 'time-warp' that many established migrant communities are caught in, whereby the cultural and social practices that dominate are those that prevailed in the country of origin at the time of migration, rather than those which are contemporary to the home society: this condition, too, is found in many immigrant communities (Ghosh 2009: 33).

Morocco and the Philippines – two other major emigration countries with widespread and differentiated migration patterns – provide further evidence of contrasting gender dynamics. De Haas (2007a) has shown that Moroccan (international) migration does not play a significant role in gender relations in Morocco. Where emancipation and empowerment do take place, the effects may last only during the migration episode; gender relations revert back to their previous state after return occurs. This pattern is replicated by many other studies, which generally show that women are less willing to return-migrate than men, since the former anticipate losing the greater agency they gained in the host-country context (also through access to paid work), whereas men, who often feel emasculated by their work and social position as migrants doing menial work in the destination country, are keener to return in order to restore their patriarchal power within the family (King 2000a).

However, contrary to the image of Moroccan women migrating only as part of male-led family migration to Europe, Salih (2001) has shown how increasing numbers of Moroccan women have migrated individually. Partly, it seems, their story has been submerged beneath the hegemonic male model of Moroccan migration. Increasingly, more educated Moroccan women are taking an independent route to migration, often within established networks of kinship links abroad, whilst others migrate to escape difficult situations at home, such as a husband-initiated divorce or spousal or paternal abuse. Yet the price paid for such independent migratory action is often extreme. One of Salih's research participants had migrated to Italy independently, married an Italian and started a family. Her father then excluded her from his life, threatening that, if she returned to Morocco, he would take away her passport. When she eventually returned to Morocco for her father's funeral, she found the family had lied to others, saying she had married a Tunisian (i.e. a fellow-Muslim Arab) in Italy (Salih 2001: 662).

The Filipino case is instructive because it is a country where there are rather separate and independent migrations of men and women, reflecting the more liberal nature of society and the legal system, which recognises the right of women to migrate independently.[11] Males have a long tradition of seafaring migration and of migration to manual and service jobs in the Gulf, whereas women migrate mainly as domestic workers to a variety of destinations – Europe (especially Italy and Spain), the Middle East, Singapore etc. Once again, any empowerment that Filipina migrant women achieve comes at a price. They are able to access reasonably well-paid jobs as domestic helpers, carers and nurses,[12] yet they have to sacrifice their personal freedom (especially if the nature of their work requires them to 'live-in' with their employers) and their right to family life by leaving their children behind, either in the care of relatives or by hiring a local, lower-paid child-carer. This 'diverted mothering', whereby a migrant woman devotes her time to caring for the children of her employer, whilst simultaneously hiring someone else to help bring up her own children in the home country, is one of the gendered ironies of 'global care chains' (Anderson 2000; Ehrenreich and Hochschild 2003; Kofman 2004). Of course, married male migrants who migrate on their own are also detached from their families and children, so that the challenges of 'transnational fathering' should also be recognised (Parreñas 2008).

The effects of these gender-differentiated migration patterns from the Philippines are mixed but some generalisations can be made on the basis of the existing literature. For instance, Filipino left-behind husbands may take on the child-rearing and household roles whilst their wives worked abroad, but gender roles revert back to their pre-migration pattern upon the wife's return. Similarly, when men were the migrants and women the stay-at-homes in the Philippines, the extra agency that the women enjoyed as temporary family heads and remittance managers tended to disappear when husbands/fathers returned and tried to reassert their patriarchal position. It also appears to be the case that transnational 'single' parenting – either on the part of the migrating parent or the one left behind – is more effectively carried out by women than by men, the latter experiencing greater difficulty in adapting to the new arrangements demanded by distant or lone parenting (Ghosh 2009: 26–8; McKay 2007; Parreñas 2000; 2003; 2005; 2008).

These few examples, drawn from some of the major theatres of gendered global migrations, barely scratch the surface of the rich material that is available in the literature on gender and migration. We conclude that, indeed, migration can be both a cause and consequence of women's empowerment; or, if you prefer, empowerment can be both a cause and consequence of migration. *Potential* effects are likely to be most wide-ranging in less-developed countries where women often have minimal control over resources and a limited voice in household decision-making, due to age-old patriarchal structures combined with restricted exposure to new ways of thinking (Piper 2005: 25). Hugo sums up: migration can be 'an empowering experience for women … [if it is favourably] … influenced by the context in which the migration occurs, the type of movement, and the characteristics of the women involved' (2000: 288). According to him, empowerment is most likely to take place when the migration draws women from rural to urban areas (either internally or internationally), separates them from their wider family group, engages them in employment outside the home and in the formal economy, takes place over an extended period, and gives them legal and humanitarian protection. Later, we will see how the Albanian case responds to these ideal conditions.

Gendering Development and Globalisation

Just as there is now an established literature on gender and migration, so there is one on gender and development, which has developed more or less in parallel to that on gendering migration.[13]

Following Sassen (2000), we can identify three phases in the development of literature on gender and development. The first phase focused on the rural, agricultural setting and was particularly concerned with the effects of the installation of cash crops and wage labour – often by foreign firms actualising the modern version of the colonial plantation system – and the way this new capitalist farming economy was dependent upon household subsistence production. A gendered division of labour was created between males working in commercial agriculture for wages, and women who took care of subsistence agriculture, thereby subsidising the wage labour of men. Starting in the 1970s, a rich and critical literature developed on this gendered dual system, whereby the 'invisible' labour of women in subsistence agriculture, producing food and other necessities, supported modern capitalist farming and, moreover, contributed to the extremely low wages paid on commercial plantations and mines, whose products were geared to lucrative export markets (see Boserup 1970 for the classic study; also Deere 1976 and other literature cited in Sassen 2000). Far from being the 'drag' on development that modernist readings of development regarded subsistence farming as, feminist analyses revealed the true dynamics of this mutually interlocking process of 'modernisation' and 'development' (Smith and Wallerstein 1992).

The second stage focused on the internationalisation of industrial production and the feminisation of the new industrial proletariat that was created in the new industrial zones spawned by global capital in less-developed countries. This, in essence, is the well-known 'Sassen thesis' (1988), whereby predatory foreign capital exploits the 'new international division of labour' (Froebel *et al.* 1980) by implanting low-grade manufacturing jobs in offshore locations where labour, especially female labour, is cheap, malleable, and expendable. The effect has been to mobilise a disproportionately female workforce, which had hitherto been outside the industrial or wage economy (often engaged in subsistence production), and was ripe for bringing in to labour-intensive industrial complexes, typically those manufacturing garments or assembling electronics products. The dislodging of women from their rural, subsistence hinterlands in poor countries often was the first stage which then led to their subsequent migration once the factory closed, downsized or shifted, or the women were laid off because of illness, age, or pregnancy. Again, there is an abundant literature on this aspect of the feminisation of the development process (see, *inter alia*, Chant 1992; Enloe 1988; Nash and Fernandez Kelly 1983; Safa 1995; Sassen 1988).

The third phase of scholarship looks at how men and especially women are impacted by the new global economy of the late twentieth and early twenty-first centuries. We stress here the various facets of globalisation which incorporate women, poverty and mobility in different ways. A useful starting-point is Sassen's notion of women as protagonists of 'counter-geographies of globalisation' (2000). Sassen sees women as both 'victims' but also 'heroes' of hegemonic globalisation forces which place household survival in the global South increasingly in the hands of women, including migrant women. These new conditions of economic globalisation's impact on poor and transition countries include increases in unemployment, the closure of small and medium enterprises which can no longer compete with cheap manufactured imports, the shutting-down of large nationally-operated industries under neoliberal regimes of market capitalism, the collapse of farming as a viable livelihood, and the general rise in uncertainty about how livelihoods can be sustained.

According to Sassen, a key component of the new 'counter-geography' is the way that, 'through their migration, work and remittances, women enhance the revenue of deeply indebted countries and offer new profit-making possibilities to "entrepreneurs" who have seen other opportunities vanish as a consequence of global firms and markets entering their countries or to long-time criminals who can now operate their illegal trade globally' (2000: 503). This leads, in the words of Sassen, to 'growing numbers of traffickers and smugglers making money on the backs of women'. This is a scenario which many think rings true for Albania where much NGO and inter-governmental attention has been given to issues of smuggling and trafficking of young women into sex work in Europe. As a result, this has become the dominant framing narrative of female migration from Albania, and has undoubtedly ended up by creating a falsely exaggerated picture of its scale and effects. For this very reason, we do not draw further attention to this stereotyping discourse in this book.[14]

Gender and Remittances

Sassen's excessive attention to women's incorporation into mobilities of smuggling and trafficking – in which she specifically mentions Albanian and Kosovan prostitutes in London – is re-balanced by Kofman (2004) who offers a broader if less ideologically-powerful interpretation of women migrants in the new global economy. Both Sassen and Kofman refer to the vital role of remittances generated by these various categories of migrant women, and Kofman helps to widen the picture by paying particular attention to the under-researched role of highly-skilled migrant women in global circuits of migration (Kofman 2000; 2004; also Raghuram 2004). All these authors, however, stop short of *gendering remittances*. It is also revealing that Carling (2008a), in his 'interrogation' of remittances, does not include the 'gender question' in his 'eight fundamental questions' about remittances and remittance-related policy.

The preceeding sections of this chapter have shown that 'gender and remittances' has lagged far behind the other analytical dyads we have surveyed – migration and development, remittances and development, gender and migration, and gender and development. This is surprising given the sharply-increasing policy interest in remittances as a developmental strategy for poor countries, seen in recent years. Conventional wisdom seems to suggest that women are more frequent remitters than men, even though they often do not earn as much as the latter (Nyberg Sørensen 2005). Empirical evidence on the topic, however, has so far been inconclusive and results vary by indicators (total sums remitted, shares of income remitted, remitting frequency, consistency of remitting over time, sender–receiver relationship), country of origin, research methodology and even within the same migrant group.

Most of what exists on gender and remittances is scattered in general studies on remittances, which usually refer to the sex of remitters rather than to the important gender dynamics that shape individual and household decision-making about remittances. In order to understand these gendered social realities we need to know more than just the sex of the remitter or recipient. Below, we undertake a critical survey of the existing literature organised around the central themes which are most frequently discussed in this respect: who are better remitters, what motivates remitters, the effect of gendered remittances on expenditure and work patterns in origin communities, and the impact of remittances on gender roles.

Are Women 'Better' Remitters than Men?

This seems to be the central question in most discussions, often fuelled by a presumption that women remit more, and are more reliable remitters over time, because it is their 'nature' to be altruistic rather than motivated by pure self-interest. However, the issue is much more complex.

At least in some countries, the evidence does show consistency. For instance, in the Thai context researchers agree that women – especially migrant daughters – remit more than men (see Curran and Saguy 2001; Osaki 1999; Vanwey 2004). Piotrowski (2009) showed that not only did daughters send more remittances than sons to their parents living in rural Thailand, but migrant sisters provided more assistance than migrant brothers to siblings. According to Osaki (1999), Thai women's stronger commitment to providing economic support to their households left behind can be explained by the gender roles prevalent in Thai society. Thus, men are expected to devote themselves to monastic life or engage in politics and administration, whereas women have a responsibility to ensure the well-being of the family.

For other migrant groups, however, findings are less clear-cut. The best example of this is Mexico, one of the most researched migrant nations worldwide. In her in-depth qualitative study of Mexican families who lived in the US, de la Cruz (1995) argued that women remitted more frequently and were more reliable remitters than men, but this was based on a very small sample. Using a different methodology – a split household model – Taylor (1987) came to contrary conclusions in his analysis of Mexico–US migration. Both expected remittances and non-migration cash income contributions were found to be significantly lower for females than for males. He argued that lower remittances by women may have been due to their lower earnings or their lesser willingness to remit. Indeed, as Grassmuck and Pessar (1991) observed, Mexican migrant men lived austere lives in the US, and saved and remitted more as they considered their migration to the US as temporary. In contrast, Mexican women did not remit but spent their income abroad on expensive durable goods serving to root the family in the US, thus hoping to avoid return which might mean giving up new-found freedoms enjoyed abroad.

In a recent study of Oaxacan internal and international migrants Cohen (2010) also finds that migrant women living within Mexico remit less than their male counterparts – an average of 500 and 650 pesos [roughly $37 and $48] per month respectively. The difference was even greater for those working in the US; migrant women living there sent back half of men's remitted amounts, $130 versus $250.

Research findings are also inconclusive in the case of Filipino migrants who, like Mexicans, have received much scholarly attention in migration studies. Tacoli (1999), researching Filipino migrants in Rome, concluded that women's commitments and obligations toward their households back in the Philippines were generally stronger than those of their male counterparts. Young single women sent twice as much in remittances as did their male counterparts and this support was more consistent and reliable than that of the latter. Married women also sent more money to their children than their male counterparts. In contrast, drawing on a representative sample of 1,128 Filipino households with overseas workers, Semyonov and Gorodzeisky (2005) found that men remit more than women, even after controlling for variations in occupation, destination countries, and socio-demographic variables. Their analysis also demonstrated that the average income of households with men working overseas was significantly higher than of those with women overseas migrants; this difference was fully attributed to the earnings disparities and to differences in the amount of remittances sent home by overseas workers.[15]

In contrast to Thailand and the Philippines where, according to prevailing gender relations, women are expected to be the backbone of the family, in other societies financial responsibility for the family is firmly placed upon men. According to Cai (2003) Chinese sons remit more than daughters to their elderly parents in line with the stronger filial responsibility the sons carry towards their households of origin. In the Albanian context, migrant men generally remit more than women to their respective parents. Here, the highly patriarchal relations which frame traditional Albanian society do not allow married migrant women to remit to their own kin, and a wife's income is generally destined for her husband's parents and siblings, not her own (King *et al.* 2006); more on this later. Other research which has found men to remit more than women includes that of Agarwal and Horowitz (2002) on Guyana and Markova and Reilly (2006) on Bulgarians living in Spain.

A recent survey of migrants from 18 countries originating in Latin America, the Caribbean and Ghana and living in the USA, the UK and Germany is one of the few which investigates the relationship between gender and remittances among a large respondent sample (Orozco *et al.* 2006). The results are mixed along the lines discussed above, and show variations for different countries of origin. The study found that men sent more remittances than women overall, suggesting a positive relationship with income. The exceptions were migrants from Mexico and the Caribbean, where the opposite was the case. On the other hand, women in all migrant groups remitted more than men did to non-spouse relatives – children, parents, siblings and more distant relatives – suggesting more altruistic motives. This particular result was especially significant in the case of Ghanaian migrants. Finally, women overall were also more reliable remitters over time (Orozco *et al.* 2006: 12–13).

What Motivates Women and Men to Remit?

A second strand of literature relates to the motivations and micro-determinants of remittances, and is structured around the two propositions reviewed earlier: individuals remit either because of altruistic motives or because of self-interest. Generally, the assumption is that altruistic motives lie behind females remitting, in contrast to self-interest motivating male remitters. Some of the literature reviewed in the previous sub-section lends weight to this argument. However, as Lucas and Stark (1985) argue in their seminal work on Botswana, both motives, caring for others and for one's own future interests, can co-exist. Lucas and Stark found that sons remitted more than daughters, and especially to households with large cattle herds; sons are the most likely to inherit and cattle are the dominant form of inheritable wealth in Botswana. But, the motives overlapped as it was not clear-cut if these herds were of the household as separate from the remitting sons, or whether the household looked after the cattle of the remitter as well as their own. Similarly, Hoddinott (1994) demonstrated that there was a strong link between internal migrant sons remitting to their parents in rural Kenya and future inheritance of land – land being the inheritable wealth in Kenya. The co-existence of altruism and self-interest was also considered to be behind the motivation to remit by Ghanaian migrant women living in Toronto (Wong 2006). They sent money to their female kin in order to fulfill their obligations according to the matrilineal cultural norms, but also as a 'reward' for the provision of childcare in Ghana.

In their Dominican study de la Brière *et al.* (2002) showed how gender combined with destination as determinants for remitting behavior. Migrant women in the US sent home more money and did this as part of an insurance contract with their parents. For example, they remitted more when their parents were ill, while their male counterparts in the US did not do so unless they were the sole migrant in their family. However, sending remittances in anticipation of a future bequest from parents was pursued by both men and women, although this was significant only for international migrants to the US as opposed to internal migrants.

The Gendered Impact of Remittances in Origin Communities

Beyond the motivation for remittances, male and female remitters may have different preferences about the ways in which their remittances should be spent. De la Cruz (1995) found that Mexican migrant men directed their remittances to personal investments such as housing, land, cattle and agricultural production, as their intention was to return to Mexico for good. Migrant women also used their remittances in investment, but theirs were more often targeted at the family, notably education and business opportunities. An IOM (2005b) study in Moldova similarly uncovered markedly gendered remittance expenditure patterns: female migrants tended to spend their remittances on current expenses such as food, clothes and household equipment, as well as on what were coined as 'special' expenses, i.e. on education and health; whereas Moldovan male migrants had a preference for consumer durables such as cars and housing.

Spending patterns may also be influenced by the gender of remittance recipients. This has been included in some of the literature on intra-household expenditure patterns which suggests that the distribution of resources depends on individuals' bargaining power within the household – often favouring men. For instance, using female headship as proxy for bargaining power in their study on Sri Lanka, De and Ratha (2005) demonstrated that when the household head was female, remittances had a positive impact on the health and education of the children; when the man was the household head the positive impact of remittances was limited to asset accumulation. McKay (2005), who researched the use of remittances in farming in the northern Philippines, found that Filipina migrants had different ideas and preferences about the use of their remittances from their husbands who remained in the villages. Migrant women wished to buy land and plant staple crops such as rice, reflecting both their importance in a sustainable subsistence against future shocks, and traditional notions of social mobility. Their husbands, on the other hand, envisaged social mobility through modernity, which they could achieve by using their wives' remittances to plant cash crops such as beans, or purchase chainsaws for logging.

In addition to expenditure, the impact of gender and remittances in origin areas can be reflected in the working patterns of men and women recipients. Amuedo-Dorantes and Pozo (2006) argued that an increase in international remittances for Mexican male recipients was associated with a decline in formal employment and an increase of informal jobs. In contrast, rural female recipients showed higher levels of withdrawal from labour overall, suggesting that this was a way of escaping low-paid employment in the informal economy. In a similar study using panel data from El Salvador, Acosta (2007) concluded that upon receiving remittances women withdrew from the labour market much more than men – by 42 per cent and 9 per cent respectively. In addition, both men and women in remittance-recipient households worked fewer hours per week. Increased levels of remittances coming into residual households are thought to be one of the major factors behind the withdrawal of women from the labour market in Albania during the 1990s (Konica and Filer 2005).

Impact of Remittances on Gender Roles

A number of researchers have discussed how remittances have impacted on gender roles of senders and recipients, although the nature of such impacts varies. For instance, Abdi (2006), in her research on Somali migrants in the US, clearly demonstrated how, even for a highly patriarchal society, gender relations and expectations had changed significantly with women increasingly assuming the role of 'breadwinner' in the household. Similarly, Lindley's (2009) study of the Somali diaspora in London showed how migrant women had come to occupy an important economic role as income-earners, which had resulted in a feminisation of remittance sending. Meanwhile, Wong (2006) found that remittances sent by Ghanaian migrant women in Toronto served to strengthen women's position of power within the matrilineage – as senders and as recipients – although contestations by male relatives were common. Other scholars have asserted that long-term absences of male remitters from home restructure the intra-family negotiating context, resulting in remittance-recipient wives gaining more decision-making power over the use of remittances. At times they are supported in this by matrilineal networks, as Conway and Cohen (1998) found in their study in Oaxaca in Mexico. As regards the limited prior work on Albanian migration, King *et al.* (2006) found that remittances had, if anything, reinforced the patriarchal power relations amongst the community living in London. However, this was based on fieldwork carried out in the early 2000s, soon after their arrival in the late 1990s, and nearly all of those interviewed originated from the conservative rural highlands of northern Albania.

Conclusion

This chapter has ranged widely over the literatures and concepts associated with and connecting migration, development, remittances and gender. We have shown that, whilst migration and development have been increasingly subject to, and enriched by, gendered analyses, the field of remittances – one of the main connecting forces between migration and development – has not. The following chapters will empirically rectify this oversight by looking at the highly instructive case of Albania. In order to theoretically frame our ensuing analysis we round off this chapter by deploying a conceptual model which we think is particularly useful for analysing the gender–remittance nexus. The framework is called *gendered geographies of power* and has been advanced by Mahler and Pessar (2001).

The model was put forward to better study how gender operates across transnational space; given the obvious transnational nature of remittances, this framework is highly suited to our purpose. The driving-force of the model – its kinetic energy, if you will – is power. Mahler and Pessar turn to the concept of power geometry elaborated by Doreen Massey (1994). According to Massey, the particular conditions of modernity – and, we would add, post-modernity – have produced various combinations of space–time compression and interconnections (but also blockages and barriers) between places and spaces. As she points out (1994: 149), different people and institutions exert power over how flows (of people, trade, images, money etc.) take place: 'some individuals imitate flows and movement, others don't; some are more on the receiving end of it [power]; some are effectively imprisoned by it…'.

Two other components of the model are *geographic scale* and *social location*. The first captures the variable spatial and social scales at which gendered power can be expressed and exerted across transnational terrains – such as the remittance corridor between Greece and Albania. Gender relations and ideologies can be reaffirmed or reconfigured between states (by way of gendered migration policies, such as recruitment agreements for particular categories of workers or restrictions on family reunion), or at the level of individuals and families, via the way that migration and development reshape (or reinforce) gender dynamics. In the case of *purdah* mentioned earlier, the socio-spatial scale is the female body.

Finally, by social location, Mahler and Pessar (2001: 445–6) refer to individuals' and families' 'positions within power hierarchies created through historical, political, economic, geographic, kinship-based, and other socially stratifying factors'. For the most part, Mahler and Pessar assert, people are born into a social and geographical location that confers on them certain entitlements and advantages, but also disadvantages and barriers to their actions (such as access to migration or to a decent livelihood). Migration, if it can be achieved, enables people to move from one geographical location to another (obviously) but also to achieve social and economic mobility as a result. On the other hand, multiple hierarchies of nationality, class, race, gender and sexuality operate at various levels to affect both an individual's social location and his/her potential to change it.

We find this an intuitively attractive model because it enables us to organise and operationalise our Albanian material in the following way. Geographical and social location are 'given' by our choice of empirical field: rural, poor, south-east Albania on the one side, and the better economic environment of Greece, especially Thessaloniki, on the other. But Albanian migrants have distinct and to some extent socially disadvantageous positions in the latter place too, where they are 'offered' only low-status work, a marginal position in society, and an uncertain legal status. Yet, as our results will show, these conditions can change for the better. Geographic scale ranges, as hinted above, across a number of levels: from the macro or state-level institutional dynamics of Greek migration policy and border control; to the effects of migration and remittances at the still-macro regional dynamics of the 'migration and remittance corridor' that leads between the villages and northern Greece, spanning the border territory; to the effects of migration and remittances on the meso-level communities (villages) and neighbourhoods (in Greece) that the migrants and their families inhabit; and finally down to the micro-level intra-family, inter-personal relations that develop through the migration process of individuals along with, or separated from, their kinship members. Between these geographical locations and social positions, and along the channels and pathways beaten out by migrants going one way and remittances the other, flow the gendered power dynamics of decision-making, authority and influence in which individuals' social agency is expressed, denied or enhanced.

3

ALBANIAN MIGRATION, REMITTANCES AND GENDER DYNAMICS

This chapter, as its title implies, is in three parts. First, we review the scale and impact of Albanian migration since 1990. We contextualise this massive exodus within key features of Albanian society, the country's exit from communism as well as the post-communist events which more specifically shaped these migratory moves. We pay particular attention to the typology of Albanian emigration and its dynamic evolution over the last two decades, including a brief note on migrants' processes of integration in the major destination countries of Greece and Italy. We then continue with a discussion of the impact that this migration has had on Albania. Here, we focus above all on remittances – financial and in-kind – which are probably the most significant economic aspect of Albanian migration. We discuss their impact at macro-level, especially in terms of volumes and relation to macro-economic indicators, and continue with an assessment of their role in the lives of individuals and families. We then look at gender and the way this has shaped and been shaped by migration and remittances. The final section of the chapter reviews the evolution of gender dynamics in Albania.

The main function of this chapter in the overall scheme of this book is to provide detail on the Albanian context. Its purpose, however, is not merely descriptive and factual; throughout we present a number of potential relationships between patriarchy, gender, migration and remittances, mapped out as hypotheses to be examined in subsequent chapters on the basis of our field research.

Migration in Albania

Albania emerged as one of the last countries in Europe from behind the 'Iron Curtain' in the early 1990s. Throughout most of the half century under communist rule, emigration was regarded as an act of treason; those who dared to cross the border illegally were punished severely. For those few who managed to 'escape', retribution was meted out on their families, condemned as 'unpatriotic' and sent to suffer in isolated and harshly-run labour camps. Internal movements too were highly regulated. Symbolic of the paranoia of the Enver Hoxha regime was the construction of hundreds of thousands of defensive concrete bunkers, whose remains still litter the Albanian landscape – see Illustration 1.[1] When the 'regime' collapsed in 1990–91, it was as if a dam had burst open. Twenty years later 1.44 million Albanians – equivalent to 45 per cent of the 3.2 million people currently living in Albania (World Bank 2011: 54) – were estimated to have emigrated and be living abroad, primarily in Greece and Italy. Table 1 is compiled from more detailed estimates provided by the Government of Albania (GoA) for 1999 and 2005. These figures combine documented and an estimate of undocumented migrants. Most data from the major host countries are broadly compatible with these,[2] except that the Italian sources indicate a total of at least 400,000 rather than 250,000 Albanians by the late 2000s (Caritas/Migrantes 2009: 86, 90).

Illustration 1 Communist-time concrete bunkers, south-east Albania, 2006

Table 1 Estimates of Albanians living abroad, 1999 and 2005

Country	1999 (Barjaba 2000)	%	2005 (GoA 2005a)	%
Greece	500,000	67.3	600,000	54.9
Italy	200,000	27.0	250,000	22.9
USA	12,000	1.6	150,000	13.7
UK	5,000	0.7	50,000	4.6
Germany	12,000	1.6	15,000	1.4
Canada	5,000	0.7	11,500	1.0
Belgium	2,500	0.3	5,000	0.5
Turkey	1,000	0.1	5,000	0.5
France	2,000	0.3	2,000	0.2
Austria	2,000	0.3	2,000	0.2
Switzerland	1,000	0.1	1,500	<0.1
Netherlands	?	?	1,000	<0.1
TOTAL	742,500	100	1,093,000	100

Source: Barjaba (2000) and GoA (2005a: 36).

It is clear from the table that around half of Albanian emigrants – 600,000 – live and work in neighbouring Greece, where they constitute about two-thirds of the total non-EU, 'non-ethnic Greek' immigrant population. The second-largest immigrant group in Greece is the Bulgarians, with a share of only 5 per cent. Considering that the total Greek population is less than 11 million, the Albanian community has a considerable presence there, accounting for around one in twenty of the *de facto* population. Initially, up to the time of the first Greek regularisation of undocumented immigrants, the vast majority of Albanians in Greece were men, mostly young working-age individuals. After the 1998 regularisation many women were able to join their husbands, and their share in the total Albanian immigrant population in Greece rose quickly to 41 per cent in 2001 (Baldwin-Edwards 2004a: 5; Cavounidis 2004: 41–3).

Italy is the second most important destination for Albanian emigrants, with around 400,000 Albanians living there. According to the well-regarded Ismu Institute (quoted in Bonifazi 2007: 130), their presence in mid-2005 was 13.7 per cent of total immigrants, just ahead of Romanians, 13.0 per cent, and Moroccans, 12.2 per cent. As in Greece, the share of women in the total number of Albanian immigrants in Italy has grown sharply, reaching 40 per cent in 2001 (Bonifazi and Sabatino 2003; King 2005). Regarding other countries to which Albanians have emigrated, it appears that the UK and the USA are gaining ground, although data on these two countries are scarce, partly due to the non-significance of the Albanian community as a share of total immigrant population there. Furthermore, it is unclear whether the figure for the USA includes 'historical migrants' who settled before the start of the communist era in Albania.

Indeed, the post-1990 mass emigration was not without historical precedent, as Albanians have traditionally emigrated far and wide in search of labour and due to wars and regional feuds. Perhaps the most significant historical exodus was the emigration of around 200,000 individuals after the lands of Albanian lords fell under the Ottoman conquest during the fifteenth century (Tirta 1999). Later, many Albanians migrated within the frontierless Ottoman Empire; their mobility, known as *kurbet*, literally 'exile' or 'living away from home', reflected the poverty of their mountainous agro-pastoral homeland and the lack of alternative employment options. During the late-nineteenth and early-twentieth centuries Albanians migrated in significant numbers to the United States; most of this overseas migration was from the south of the country.

Contemporary Albanian migration is taking place under very different circumstances from these early moves. In particular, its massive concentration over a short period of time as the country moved almost overnight from total closure to large-scale out-migration marks it as a significant and unique case. Van Hear (1998: 119) has described it as 'a new migration order', whilst Carletto *et al.* (2006) talk about a 'country on the move'. As we shall see in the following sections and chapters, Albania represents a unique laboratory for the study of migration and development (King 2005: 133). This has potential particularly for comparative conclusions with other countries mentioned in the previous chapter, which have a longer and more continuous tradition of emigration.

Chronology

As regards the Albanian post-communist mass emigration, three distinct phases can be identified. The first, during 1990–93, was triggered by the violent and chaotic exit of the country from 45 years of communist oppression, poverty and almost hermetical closure to the outside world. The first sign of this exodus was the 'embassy occupation' in July 1990 when around 5,000 people climbed the walls of Western embassies in Tirana and requested protection. Illustration 2 reproduces scenes from the embassy of the Federal Republic of Germany, where around 3,200 refugees, gathered in the garden and residence, listen to the news that Germany won the Football World Cup and that the refugees are allowed to be transferred to Germany. Refugees sheltered in other embassies were also eventually allowed to leave for the West (Vickers and Pettifer 1997: 27). In the three years that followed, thousands more commandeered ship flotillas to Italy, while others trekked from all over the country towards and over the harsh mountains along the southern frontier, to reach Greece. As

Illustration 2 Albanian refugees inside the embassy of the Federal Republic of Germany, Tirana, 8 July 1990. Original photo by Peter Gebert

it was impossible to keep records, especially for the movements to Greece, numbers are unknown, but some estimates suggest that around 200,000 left the country during 1991 and 1992.

The second episode followed the collapse of the infamous pyramid investment schemes in 1997. During 1993–96 there was rapid economic growth, primarily due to migrants' remittances from abroad. An unknown but clearly considerable share of them was invested in high-interest private 'saving' schemes, which flourished due to the underdeveloped financial sector in the country (Jarvis 2000). Many non-migrants also put money into these schemes, sometimes selling their houses and other assets to do so. At their height in 1996, the pyramids had attracted deposits equivalent to half of the country's GDP (Korovilas 1999: 409). Their collapse in early 1997 brought down the government and led to a period of political and economic turmoil verging on civil war in some parts of the country. This situation produced another boat exodus to Italy and larger but unquantifiable crossings of the Greek border.

The third moment refers to the migration influenced by the Kosovo crisis of 1999–2000. The Albanian economy recovered rapidly after the fall of the pyramid schemes, principally due to yet more remittances sent by more emigrants. However, in 1999, around half a million ethnic Albanian refugees from Kosovo entered the country, fleeing the ethnic cleansing of Milosevic's regime. The Kosovan refugee crisis destabilised the already fragile economic and demographic situation, especially in northern Albania, geographically the most remote and poorest region of the country. As Kosovar Albanians moved onwards to European asylum destinations, many citizens of Albania mixed themselves in with them.

During this first post-communist decade Albanians spread themselves beyond Greece and Italy – their initial destinations – to other EU countries such as France, Germany, Belgium and the UK, and to North America, principally the USA to join the historical diaspora there. The 'diasporisation' of the emigration process is thus picking up pace (Mai 2005).

In the intervening years of these episodes and since 2000, emigration has continued, but at a steadier rate. Meanwhile, large numbers of Albanian migrants have benefited from the regularisation programmes, especially in Greece and Italy. These have taken place in 1995, 1998 and 2002 in Italy, and in 1998 and 2001 in Greece, leading to family reunification and the subsequent stabilisation of migrant communities there. The last decade has been a period of relative stability and economic growth in Albania. However, politics remains highly conflictual and democratisation processes continue to suffer from allegations of corruption and disregard for the rule of law, while the country's infrastructure is in a dire state. Under these circumstances, the typology of Albanian emigration has undergone profound changes.

Typology

Based on research and observations carried out during the first post-communist decade, Barjaba (2000) first suggested an 'Albanian model' of emigration, refined in later papers by Barjaba and King (2005) and King (2005). This model has the following distinguishing features: migration is *intense* (a rate of emigration much higher than any other Eastern bloc country); it is largely *economically driven* – a form of '*survival migration*'; it has *a high degree of irregularity*, with many undocumented migrants; it displays lots of *to-and-fro movement*, especially with Greece; and it is *dynamic and rapidly evolving*, especially as regards new destinations and routes of migration. In the decade since 2000 these features have changed significantly, as migratory flows have become steadier. Also, large numbers of migrants in both Greece and Italy, where the degree of irregularity was highest, have – as noted above – benefited from regularisation programmes and many are now settled and focused on life in their 'new' home. This has affected the back-and-forth movement which has considerably diminished, although it is still carried out by young men from poorer households, and also by some couples from the Roma and Evgjit minorities in southern Albania. Finally, although emigration continues to be considered by Albanians as the most effective way of coping with the country's poor economic conditions (King 2005: 141), many Albanians have also migrated to study, or to unite with their spouses abroad. Migration has thus evolved in terms of reasons, patterns, typologies, routes and not least destinations. Let us look at some of these in a bit more detail.

First, there is an increase in emigration of the 'elite' – students, academics, scientists and intellectuals – which has raised concerns over a 'brain drain'. Financed by affluent parents as students, or making use of special entry programmes such as that run by the Canadian government, many of them do not return. According to a study by the Centre for Economic and Social Studies (CESS) in Albania, 50 per cent of Albania's lecturers, researchers and academics emigrated between 1990 and 2005 (Gedeshi and Black 2006). Second, the male-led feature of Albanian migration, whereby men migrated first and then women followed, is less applicable to migration beyond Greece and Italy. Although some women took the tough and dangerous routes to Greece, Italy, and beyond, travelling on steep mountain paths, in rubber dinghies and in the back of lorries, most of the first-decade emigration was dominated by male migrants. However, participation of Albanian women as a share of Albanian migrant communities abroad has increased in recent years, as noted above. More independent female migration has occurred among the highly skilled, especially to destinations such as the USA and Canada (see Orgocka 2005). Finally, there is also a trend of 'migrating grannies' – grandmothers who migrate to join their children's (often sons') families abroad (King and Vullnetari 2006). The principal aim of this particular migration is to provide childcare, thus freeing the migrant wife to participate in paid employment. Transnational grandparenting is one of a number of strategies Albanians have adopted in order to maintain family cohesion across borders. However, these are often frustrated and interrupted by immigration regulations, which impact heavily on how intergenerational relations and reciprocal care within households are performed.

Albanian migrants' integration in the two major host societies has been a very difficult process. Initially received as 'Adriatic brethren' who had survived brutal communist oppression, they were soon vilified and stigmatised as 'primitive', 'untrustworthy' and 'dangerous' (Lazaridis and Wickens 1999: 648; Zinn 1996). Gendered stereotyping in Greece and Italy has fixed Albanian men as 'criminals' and Albanian women as 'prostitutes', thereby helping to justify their marginalisation and treatment. The two key shaping factors for such a heavy stigmatisation have been the irregular status of Albanians throughout most of the 1990s, and the construction of negative images by the local media, exploited in turn by politicians for their own political ends (Baldwin-Edwards and Kolios 2008; Barjaba and King 2005; King and Mai 2002). However, in spite of these enormous challenges, Albanian migrants in both countries have managed to attain a high degree of socio-economic integration, reflected in their good command of the host language; high employment rates; moves to more stable and better-paid jobs; improved living conditions; wide geographical spread throughout Greece and Italy; and high rates of school enrollment for their children (see for Greece Gogonas 2007; Hatziprokopiou 2003; 2006; Kokkali 2010; Labrianidis and Hatziprokopiou 2005; Labrianidis *et al.* 2004; Pratsinakis 2005; and for Italy King and Mai 2004; 2008). They have achieved this progress through individual and family efforts rather than through formal diaspora action or lobbying on the part of 'ethnic' organisations. Although some return has taken place, by and large Albanian migrants are there to stay.

This massive population mobility abroad has been combined with large-scale population relocations internally. The primary direction of these moves has been from rural to urban areas and from the northern and southern mountainous hinterlands towards the more socio-economically advanced coastal districts in the west of the country. Particularly the south and south-east, where our research took place, have been heavily affected. This combination of internal and international migration has sharply redrawn the population map of Albania, and has affected economic and social life and opportunities in unequal ways. Undoubtedly, one of the most significant factors in this process has been the flow of remittances, a more detailed analysis of which follows.

Migration and Remittances in Albania

The migration of such a significant share of Albania's population abroad (and internally) has had a considerable impact on the country's development in terms of demography, spatial redistribution of the population, social changes and economic trends. Remittances have been key to all this.

Remittances: the Macro-Perspective

According to estimates from the Bank of Albania (BoA), which is the central financial regulatory authority in the country, there has been a substantial inflow of remittances into the country since the first emigrants moved to work abroad. In order to appreciate their volume and related significance in macro-economic terms, let us examine Table 2.[3]

Table 2 Flow of migrants' remittances to Albania and their macro-economic significance, 1993–2009

Year	Total remittances sent (US$ million)	% of GDP	% of exports	% of trade deficit	Remittances per capita (US$)
1993	275	22.3	224.5	92.1	86.7
1994	378	19.4	267.4	92.8	118.0
1995	385	15.5	190.7	85.8	118.3
1996	500	18.6	237.3	71.5	152.1
1997	267	11.6	188.8	55.7	80.2
1998	452	14.8	219.0	76.8	134.8
1999	368	10.0	133.6	58.9	109.1
2000	530	14.3	205.4	60.0	170.0
2001	615	15.2	203.2	53.0	167.7
2002	632	13.9	191.2	55.0	172.3
2003	778	12.8	172.5	57.7	212.2
2004	1028	13.7	170.4	61.0	280.4
2005	1169	14.0	177.1	64.0	266.1
2006	1171	12.8	148.0	55.4	272.8
2007	1295	12.0	120.4	44.0	276.9
2008	1171	9.2	127.8	33.0	269.4
2009	1111	9.0	110.0	33.0	247.8

Source: Bank of Albania in Uruçi (2008: 4); updated

We observe that remittances increased during 1992–96, fell by nearly half in 1997, and increased again thereafter (with a slight decrease in 1999), exceeding $1 billion in 2004. Although the billion threshhold has been retained, the year-on-year growth was very slow up to 2007. The two years that followed marked a slight decline, also confirmed by BoA's household surveys. Thus, according to the 2008 survey, the total volume of remittances amongst respondents fell by 16 per cent compared with the previous year, whereas average remittances per household were down by 20 per cent (Rëmbeci 2009: 108). The survey was repeated in 2009 with a slightly different sample, and the results suggested a continued decline – average remittances per household were down by 7 per cent, while those per immigrant by 25 per cent (BoA 2010a: 27).

We suggest two main factors have influenced this downward trend. First, there is the migration cycle. Albanian migration is maturing with increased levels of regularisation, followed by increased reunification with spouses and children; hence less incentives to remit. Second, there is the socio-economic situation in both Albania and host countries. Greece and Italy, which together host around 80 per cent of Albanian migrants, have been heavily affected by the recent global economic crisis. As we write, Greece is undergoing painful fiscal measures threatening jobs, lowering purchasing power and contracting the economy as a whole. Consequently, the crisis has impacted on migrants' jobs and living standards, thus lessening remittance flows towards Albania (King and Vullnetari 2009a). Despite declared GDP growth, Albanian socio-economic conditions do not show significant improvement. Especially those conditions which would attract migrant remittances for economic investments such as the physical and administrative infrastructures, continue to be inadequate and plagued by a myriad of problems.

Over the last two decades the Albanian economy has come to rely heavily on these migrant remittances, especially as it now lacks a substantial production and manufacturing base (de Zwager *et al.* 2005; Nikas and King 2005). Representing between 9 and 22 per cent of the country's GDP over the years, remittances have surpassed by several times the amount of Foreign Direct Investment (FDI), as well as the amount of foreign aid received from international institutions (King 2005: 149; Konica and Filer 2005; Piperno 2005; Uruçi and Gedeshi 2003). Throughout much of the period covered by Table 2, remittances amounted to twice the revenues from exports, confirming that labour is effectively Albania's most important export (de Zwager *et al.* 2005). These financial transfers have been conducive to macro-economic stability by enabling management of the huge trade deficit of more than 20 per cent of GDP per year through the foreign exchange they provide; they consistently cover more than 50 per cent of it on average (de Zwager *et al.* 2005; Lundström and Ronnås 2006: 50). Furthermore, through their use as business capital, they have addressed the deficiency of the country's financial sector to supply such capital (Kilic *et al.* 2007; Kule *et al.* 2002; Léon-Ledesma and Piracha 2004). However, there has also been ongoing concern that remittances appreciated the Albanian Lek against foreign currencies, affecting thus the competitiveness of Albanian (especially farm) producers (de Zwager *et al.* 2005).

In spite of calls for caution on this over-reliance on remittances, it seems that little has been done to plan for a post-remittance era in Albania (Nikas and King 2005). True, the effects of the global economic crisis for the Albanian economy have, so far, been less devastating than anticipated. Germenji (2010) suggests that the main reasons for this include a low level of integration of Albania's economy into the global markets and an underdeveloped stock exchange. That Albania's is a largely cash-based economy also helps, especially when considering home-ownership which is usually through cash and less through bank-drawn mortgages. Nonetheless, on the longer-term effects the jury is still out.

Utilisation and Impact on Households and Individuals

While the impact of remittances may be unclear at a macro-level, there is overall consensus amongst researchers and other stakeholders that remittances in the Albanian context have been crucial for the economic survival and poverty alleviation of many individuals and households (De Soto *et al.* 2002; Gedeshi *et al.* 2003a; IMF 2006; King 2005; World Bank 2007). According to various surveys, they constitute a significant share of recipient households' annual income – between 41 and 45 per cent; even higher in rural areas (de Zwager *et al.* 2005: 39–40; Frashëri 2007: 66, 68; Lerch and Warner 2006). However, less agreement is reached when it comes to their impact on inequality. Do remittances meaningfully differentiate non-poor from poor households? Do they decrease or increase inequality?[4]

When we consider the use of remittances by households in Albania, their significance as a tool for survival and poverty alleviation becomes apparent. This is confirmed by a number of quantitative and qualitative studies (Arrehag *et al.* 2005; Carletto *et al.* 2004: 35; De Soto *et al.* 2002; de Zwager *et al.* 2005: 51; Frashëri 2007; Gedeshi 2000: 62; Gedeshi *et al.* 2003a; Kring 2007: 25, 33; Konica and Filer 2005; Kule *et al.* 2002: 235; Piperno 2005: 132). Drawing on these, we can suggest that remittances are used as follows, in approximate order of importance:

- for basic survival needs such as food, clothing and utilities;
- to improve the quality of dwellings through repairs, replacement of roofs, windows and doors; bringing piped water inside the house; moving the toilet indoors; generally enlarging and refurbishing dwellings; as well as purchasing furniture, domestic appliances and small generators to substitute the failing electricity supply;
- to maintain life-stage traditions such as weddings, funerals, births etc., thus securing the social respectability of the family;
- to purchase urban land and/or construct new houses;
- to finance the education of young family members;
- for health-related expenses;
- as savings, although not always in the bank.

Scanning the Albanian landscape, it is clear that very significant sums have been invested in construction, whether on repairs and refurbishment of dwellings, or to build or purchase new houses. This is partly a result of the deplorable housing situation of most Albanians as they emerged from the communist era (Misja 1998). But dwellings are also considered as a safe investment option in situations where other avenues are limited or not easily accessible, as has been the case here. The wider literature on migrant remittances and savings has also shown that building or improving the house in the home country is a near-universal objective of migrants (see de Haas 2007b; also King 1986). In Greece, for instance, most emigrants who were remitting from Germany in the 1960s and 1970s also invested in construction and housing for similar reasons (Nikas and King 2005). Finally, as Smith and Mazzucato (2009) show in their research among Ghanaian transnational networks spanning the Netherlands and Ghana, investment of remittances in houses should not be seen exclusively in economic terms; they are simultaneously couched in social and cultural dimensions which are often just as important.

In the Albanian context, the new houses are often built once other more immediate needs of the family have been met. Initially considered as homes for the migrant and his/her immediate family, the purpose of houses soon changes along with the migratory project. When the reality of returning becomes more unlikely, these houses become signifiers of belonging and proof of achievement, to be enjoyed only during visits or holidays (Dalakoglou 2009). The majority of them, however, are built in urban or most often peri-urban areas, rather than in the villages of origin. Remittances from abroad thus enable an internal move away from villages or small towns of origin (Vullnetari 2008). The migrant (usually a man) may continue to live abroad and send remittances, whilst part of his family may move from the village to the city, where he can then join them upon his return (King *et al.* 2003). At least this is the plan, often postponed and, perhaps, never to be achieved.

Some remittances have been invested in business enterprises, often in the retail and hospitality sector, as well as in transport- and construction-related activities (see Castaldo and Reilly 2007; de Zwager *et al.* 2005; King *et al.* 2003; Papapanagos and Sanfey 2001; Nicholson 2004a). They are often small concerns, usually employing only immediate members of the family, sometimes more extended kin (Nicholson 2001). Investments in the production and manufacturing sector have so far been negligible (de Zwager *et al.* 2005; Piperno 2005), although there are some signs that this is changing (Kilic *et al.* 2007: 10). In rural areas remittances are also invested in farming (Gedeshi *et al.* 2003b; Germenji and Swinnen 2004), often resulting in the farm activity being reoriented towards less labour-intensive production, such as the livestock sector (McCarthy *et al.* 2006). Whilst agriculture may be an income development strategy for older farmers, it hardly holds any prospects for youth who are keen to leave for the cities at the first opportunity (Fuga and Dervishi 2002). International migration, and the remittances gained from it, are thus used to pull rural youth – and many households – out of agriculture and take them to the city (see also Miluka *et al.* 2007).

Important for improving living conditions are also in-kind remittances. However, recent research suggests that their share of total remittances has somewhat decreased – 13.5 per cent in 2005, compared to 17 per cent in the mid-1990s (de Zwager *et al.* 2005: 21; Misja 1998). Nowadays there are more goods available locally, most often through imports, which ironically are fuelled by financial remittances. Often, women send in-kind remittances to their own kin, to substitute for not being able (because they are not 'allowed') to send cash (Smith 2009). We now turn our attention to this gender dimension of the flows.

Gendered Remittance Processes

Although remittances in Albania have been intensively investigated, a gendered perspective on the analysis is largely lacking, with some exceptions (see King *et al.* 2006; King and Vullnetari 2009b; Smith 2009). While substantial evidence exists on their use, as we outlined in the previous section, almost no information is provided as to how this decision-making process is gendered. Nor is there much information about who sends and who receives remittances and the power (im)balances and shifts that may consequently arise within households. The limited evidence points to a sharply gendered process, reflecting dominant gender relations in Albania, which are highly patriarchal. Below we outline some of the key questions at the heart of this debate, and which we explore in more depth throughout this book.

First, who receives these remittances? The surveys which have included this variable in their analysis as well as the qualitative studies we referred to above (above all King *et al.* 2006; Smith 2009), point to parents as the group targeted by most migrants – 55 per cent according to figures from the Albanian Living Standards Measurement Survey (Carletto *et al.* 2004: 35) and up to 94 per cent in recent BoA surveys (Frashëri 2007: 71–2). Next come the spouse (wife) and children of the migrant (men), followed by siblings and less often other relatives. None of the quantitative surveys, however, asks further if it is the mother or the father among parents who most often receives these remittances. King *et al.* (2006) found that it was overwhelmingly the father, but their study was based on a rather small sample originating from northern Albania, known for its enduring patriarchal relations.

Second, who sends remittances? In the few surveys where these are mentioned, migrating offspring are the primary remitters, followed by husbands, siblings and other relatives, approximately in that order. Once again no gender distinction is made for the first group, with few exceptions, which point to sons as primary remitters in the vast majority of cases. Thus, they comprised 60 per cent of all remitters in one of the

IOM/ILO surveys, and 72 per cent and 80 per cent of all remitters in the much larger 2006 and 2008 BoA surveys respectively (Balliu 2007: 23; Frashëri 2007: 72; Rëmbeci 2009: 122). In these studies daughters comprised 8 per cent, 19 per cent and 15 per cent of remitters respectively. Analysing the 2002, 2003 and 2004 ALSMS data in a longitudinal approach, Duval and Wolff (2010: 80, 84) also conclude that daughters are much less likely to remit compared to sons.

Third, what types of remittances are sent by men and by women, and what conditions this choice? The ethnographic research of King *et al.* (2006) and Smith (2009) offers some insights into these issues. Their evidence suggests that while men overwhelmingly remit money, women send more in-kind, especially to their own kin. When they send money this is often labelled as a 'present' or a 'gift' both by senders and receivers, even when amounts are significant. For married women the permission of their husbands to send money to their own kin is important, leading to what Smith calls 'official' and 'unofficial' monetary remittances, i.e. money sent with the husband's knowledge – and approval – and that sent 'in secret'. It is often easier for women to send money if they are themselves employed in the host country; even then, the husband's permission needs to be obtained before proceeding.

Finally, how are decisions made around sums, the frequency of remitting, and their utilisation in Albania? How do gender relations shape, and get shaped, in the process? We will delve into the general issue of gender relations in Albania in the next section, but for now we briefly tease out the context into which these remitting patterns can be placed, drawing primarily on our own previous ethnographic work around some of these themes (King *et al.* 2006; King and Mai 2008; King and Vullnetari 2009b). As we showed earlier in this chapter, there are two key features of Albanian migration which are immediately relevant to our discussion, both of which are shaped by the highly patriarchal gender relations that typify the Albanian society.

On the one hand, there is the largely economic character of Albanian migration; after all, most migrants emigrated in order to improve their and their families' living conditions. Therefore, single migrant men will send remittances to their parents. Upon marriage, Albanian patrilocal traditions require the wife to move into the husband's home, where they will live with his parents and unmarried siblings. Often, the parents continue to make the most important decisions, especially financial ones. Some things change with the migration context, but not much. Upon family reunification with his wife and children in the host country, the migrant son continues to send remittances to his parents, although their volume decreases. Once married, a woman becomes part of the husband's household; hence, her (financial) responsibilities are to *his* parents and not hers. Her income is thus part of *his* family's income, and is generally pooled under the husband's management, to be sent to *his* family. However, some cash remittances may be sent to the wife's own parents; these are largely regarded as 'presents'. Furthermore, the focus of the young family is now on life in the 'new' home.

On the other hand, patriarchal gender relations limit women's mobility – they seldom emigrate on their own, unless they are highly skilled, of professional background and from urban areas. University students constitute one such group, moving to pursue undergraduate or postgraduate courses abroad. As we have shown earlier in this chapter, the majority of Albanian women have emigrated either with their husband, or to join him abroad. This type of migration also conditions the process of remitting and decision-making. Thus generally, migration abroad and remittances do not seem to significantly improve women's autonomy; rather as King *et al.* (2006) argue, the '*gendered geography of power*' (cf. Mahler and Pessar 2001) is enhanced during migration through the economic impact of remittances.

Based on these analyses, we conclude this section by drawing a number of broad generalisations. First, most remittances are sent and received by male members of the family, typically from a young single male emigrant to his father. When the father has died, it is the migrant's mother who becomes the head of the household and consequently the remittance recipient. Even when the migrant man is married and his wife lives in Albania with his parents, the pattern often remains the same.

Second, the largest amounts are sent by young single migrant men who support parents and siblings in Albania, and by married men who support their wife and children there. When the wife and children join their spouse/father in the host country, the focus turns towards life in the new destination; hence flows to migrants' parents are reduced drastically.

Third, married female migrants generally do not send remittances to support their own kin. If the married woman is in paid employment abroad, her income is often pooled together with that of her husband under his control. Some of this income may be remitted to Albania, but often to *his* parents, according to traditional gendered family roles. Remittances to support *her* parents are expected from *her* brothers (if they exist) and not her. Daughters-only families are thus quite disadvantaged, although alternative strategies are designed in many such cases, as we shall see later.

Fourth, remittances are higher in the first years of migration as it is then that the needs of the family are most urgent. Once these have been met, and especially when the migrant marries and is joined by his immediate family in the host country, remittances often decrease.

Fifth, in the majority of the cases, remittances are not sent at regular intervals or in constant sums, but they fluctuate according to the needs of the family in Albania, and the availability of work in host countries.

Sixth, remittances are higher from those living and working in Italy than those in Greece, and higher still from migrants settled in the UK. These differences reflect prevailing wage rates.

Finally, the vast majority of remittances are sent informally – often the migrants bring their cash with them when they visit, or they may give this to other relatives and friends who visit Albania. The banking system is used rather little, even though a large share of migrants have bank accounts in their host countries.

Gender Relations in Albania: Focus on Women

Albanian society has been traditionally based on two tenets: the central role of the family unit and strong patriarchal social relations. Historians and anthropologists classify it as fitting the typology of 'Balkan patriarchy' (Kaser 1996: 383). This typology is distinguished by patrilineality (membership in the family follows the male line), patrilocality (wives move into the house of the husband's father), strong blood ties, blood-feuds and bride-price. According to Halpern *et al.* (1996), both gender and age play a critical defining role in the social system which forms the basis for this complex of hierarchical values. As such, positions within the family and society are ascribed according to gender, whereby males have supremacy, and women are subordinated within the context of a 'protective' family. In terms of age, the eldest males have authority over younger ones, and likewise with females, with the result that the youngest wife in the family has the least power.[5]

Pre-Communist Times and the Kanun

Various ethnographers have documented the features mentioned above, especially in the north of the country (for key readings see Backer 1983; Durham 2000; Young 2000). Particular attention in this context has been paid to the *Kanun* of Lekë Dukagjini, an unwritten body of customary laws which served as a 'complete moral and legal framework' (de Waal 2005: 72) in regulating all aspects of life amongst some communities in the north from around the fifteenth century (see for instance Carver 1999; Shryock 1988; Tarifa 2007; Whitaker 1981). The *Kanun* reflected and shaped these patriarchal relations and was observed by Catholics and Muslims alike. Although other codes of customary laws were in use – such as the *Kanun* of Skënderbeg in some northern regions or the *Kanun* of Labëria in the south-west (de Waal 2005: 254) – they do not feature prominently in most analyses of gender relations.[6] Perhaps the reason is the strong importance and centrality of the customary behaviour and practices (as enshrined in the *Kanun* of Lekë Dukagjini) in the daily life of its adherents up to 1945, and even into the 1990s, as de Waal observed in the Mirditë region (2005: 68–72).[7] In contrast, in those areas which had experienced early migration – mainly the south and the south-east – the local customary canons had lost their importance by the mid-twentieth century. The geographical position of these southern communities in broad river valleys, and in particular their experience of large-scale migration, had opened up avenues for outside influences and changes in the societal system, including gender relations.

Zog's interwar government (1925–39) tried to tackle women's position in society by introducing legislation aiming to bring more gender equality, but implementation largely failed (Musaj 2002; Whitaker 1981: 153). On the eve of World War II, female illiteracy stood at around 90 per cent and was especially high in rural and north-eastern areas; there were only 21 female teachers countrywide, and girls constituted less than 3 per cent of secondary school students (Hall 1994: 83; Logoreci 1977: 157–8).

Gender Relations under Communism and during the Post-Communist Transformation

Inspired by Marxist ideology for equality as well as for practical reasons, women were soon recruited into the partisan units fighting Italian and Nazi occupation during World War II (Logoreci 1977: 158). The 1946 post-war constitution, as well as other legislative acts in the years that followed, gave Albanian women unprecedented rights for a traditional society (Gjonça *et al.* 2008). These policies and the general socio-economic changes throughout the country significantly improved their position, especially with regard to their education and participation in public life. By 1989 female illiteracy had been brought down to just 8 per cent and rates of participation at various levels of education had greatly increased (Brunnbauer 2000: 152; Gjonça *et al.* 2008). Equally, between 1970 and 1990, around 30 per cent of the People's Assembly representatives were women, in contrast to a participation rate of zero prior to 1945 (Lamani 2003: 25). Finally, around 80 per cent of working-age women were employed by 1989 (Bezhani 2001: 2). Other improvements have been noted in the more private sphere such as narrowing the age gap between marriage partners, marrying for love and not through family betrothals, and increased opportunities for women to file for divorce (Uçi 2003).

Nonetheless, the roots of patriarchy in the private sphere were not fundamentally shaken by communism. First, there was little if any redistribution of household chores and care tasks within the family: women continued to look after the house and care for the children and the elderly *in addition to* working in their paid jobs; men continued to enjoy more free time – to rest, watch television or go out with friends. Second, men were disproportionally represented in the top managerial and executive positions, whether in public administration or other professions. Third, men took up the majority of non-agricultural work – where this existed – leaving women to do the most difficult jobs in primitive agriculture (Sjöberg 1991). However, a rigorous and systematic evaluation of the achievements and failures during the communist period in general, and in the field of gender relations in particular, is yet to be made.

The collapse of hardline communism in 1990 and the power vacuum that resulted from the dissolution of the omnipresent state brought about a re-invention of tradition and a regeneration of patriarchy (Schwandner-Sievers 2006: 224). However, these too had undergone transformations during the communist years (Nixon 2009). Women were affected quite adversely in the process. As Nixon (2006) suggests, this post-communist transformation was accompanied by 'highly oppositional gender roles', which were reflected in the widening of the gap between the public and domestic spheres. The first became overwhelmingly the domain of men wherein masculinity was 'idealised as strong, decisive and profit-making', while femininity was increasingly associated with 'values of domesticity, caring and childrearing…'. As the concept of women's emancipation was stigmatised by association with the communist past – which was seen as having sought to destroy the family – it became widely rejected (Brunnbauer 2000; Nixon 2006).

Sporadic studies carried out during the early- and mid-1990s provide some rare insights and confirm that, while customary practices and norms had not been eradicated completely as proclaimed by the communist propaganda, a number of important changes had taken place. In her study of property relations and rights in three rural areas of Albania – Pukë in the north-east, Vlorë in the south and Lushnjë in the west – Wheeler (1998) found that by 1995 rural families had generally retained their patriarchal character. Property rights continued to be collective (family) rather than individual, sons were preferred over daughters for inheritance, and a woman's relationship to property within the family was through her father or husband. These features were particularly strong among households in the north. However, changes had occurred in that the position of divorced and widowed women had improved, and particularly the family structure had become more nuclear and flexible. These findings could reflect the legacy of the communist period, as well as post-1990 socio-economic changes, especially large-scale internal and international migration. In another study Senturia (1997) examined Albanian women's work and its effect on reproductive health by following a cohort of nearly 1,200 pregnant women during 1993–94. She documented the harsh reality of their everyday life and the gendered distribution of tasks at home. Here is an illustrative quote from one of her interviewees: 'I go to work during the day. I come home and cook and clean. On Sundays, my husband rests while I prepare the big meal. Even on the day of rest I work. I am tired' (Senturia 1997: 384).

Women's Employment and Political Participation

The transition from a centrally-planned to a market economy was accompanied by large-scale job losses for women, more so than for men (Saltmarshe 2001); the latter emigrated in large numbers abroad. This inequality in the labour market continues and is noted in pay, types of job, opportunities for employment and sexual harassment. For instance, whilst three quarters of working-age women (15–54) were in the labour force in 1991, by 2002 less than half of women in this age group were formally economically employed. For working-age men this indicator was reduced from 85 per cent to slightly less than 75 per cent over the same period of time (Moreno-Fontes Chammartin and Cantú-Bazaldúa 2003).[8] Women also earn significantly less than men – on average 68 per cent of male wages – both because they work fewer hours and because they earn less per hour (World Bank 2006b). Even at the end of the second post-communist decade men own 92 per cent of all property in the country, and receive approximately 84 per cent of GDP (UNDP-Albania 2008: 13).

Employment of highly skilled women in the public sector is nevertheless significant. However, here too they work in lower-paid jobs such as in welfare, education and health, whilst within the same sector they hold substantially fewer decision-making positions than their male counterparts (ISB 2008). Professional women participate particularly in NGOs, including in executive and advisory structures (UNDP-Albania 1999). Although most NGOs have worked on issues concerning women such as their emancipation, domestic violence, and participation in political life, the overall enhancement of women's political and socio-economic position in society has not been significant. This is particularly the case for rural women. Some authors have questioned these effects of 'implanted' civil society from outside (Sampson 1996; UNDP-Albania 2005: 115, 120). Particularly concerning is the disjuncture between urban professional women, a number of whom are actively involved in these NGOs as well as many public administration departments on the one hand, and rural women on the other. By the late 1990s the women's movement in Albania was still practically non-existent in rural areas (UNDP-Albania 1999: 39);

and by 2005, of the 100 registered women's NGOs, only six focused on rural women (UNDP-Albania 2005: 84).

Rural women are among the most disadvantaged and have few off-farm employment options. In national statistics they are considered as fully employed by reason of *the family* having a plot of land. However, agriculture is based primarily on the (often unpaid) labour of family members and continues to be dominated by low-productivity subsistence farming. Unemployment is simply not an option for most of these individuals (World Bank 2006b). Following Sassen's (2000) thesis, these women's 'invisible' labour in subsistence agriculture thus supports capitalist structures which have penetrated Albania in the last 20 years. The women are the victims as well as the heroines of the new global economy, since much of the survival of their family depends on their (often unpaid) labour, as we shall see in the following chapters (see also Vullnetari 2009).

Owning and running a business is even more difficult due to limited time to devote to business, lack of confidence in women by the society and by themselves, curtailed freedom to travel and the risk of being exposed to (sexual) violence (Bezhani 2001: 4). Exposure to domestic violence has been a worrying issue for many years (Amnesty International 2006: 4, 13), although this is hardly unique to Albania. However, here the wider public considers it as 'normal, as a means of education and a form of communication within the family', while law enforcement authorities widely condone such acts (Amnesty International 2006; Ekonomi *et al.* 2006a: 14; Minnesota Advocates for Human Rights 1996). As expected, the situation is compounded in rural areas (UNDP-Albania 2005: 78; Van Hook *et al.* 2000: 353). Violence is especially condoned by the public when the woman is thought to have brought shame to her family through behaviour particularly related to her sexuality and any assertion of independence which challenges patriarchal authority (Nixon 2009).

While violence is often associated – at least in the Albanian public discourse – with poverty and low levels of education, the highest levels of Albanian society are not immune to it. Top political figures have continued to display violent verbal and physical acts in public spaces. Many of these acts have taken place during live broadcasts of parliamentary sessions in the national mass media. It is interesting to note that some of the most brutal verbal insults aimed to 'dishonour' the opponent have involved swearing aimed at his female relatives! This masculinist, brutal and violent political environment remains the exclusivity of men, with few exceptions, as the figures show (Ekonomi *et al.* 2006b). In the 2005 parliamentary elections, only 10 out of 140 elected members of parliament (or 7 per cent) were women. This was one of the lowest rankings in Europe. After the 2009 elections this number more than doubled to 23 (or around 16 per cent) – the highest in these post-communist decades – but only after the introduction of a legal requirement for a 30 per cent quota for women's participation in party lists. Although the speaker of the parliament has been a woman since 2005, this has hardly affected how debates are conducted amongst elected MPs. Some parliamentary sessions end up resembling the US 'Jerry Springer show', with all the macho threats and acts of violence, as well as titillating verbal abuse, including from the prime minister. Otherwise, only one of the 16 ministerial posts is held by a woman as of 2010. Equally, all of the political parties have been traditionally headed by men. Representation at local level is even lower – only 1 per cent in the 2004 and 3 per cent in the 2007 local elections (Amnesty International 2006: 9; UN-Albania 2004: 6, 38). Potential disenfranchising of women voters has continued to take place through the practice of 'family voting', observed in as many as 30 per cent of voting centres during the 2007 local elections; the practice also continued in the 2009 parliamentary elections (OSCE/ODIHR 2007).

Things Change Slowly...

In other spheres many features remain the same, with only slight moderation. For instance, marriage continues to be universal, as is the early birth of the first child, whilst there is generally still a preference for sons over daughters (Gjonça *et al.* 2008; Murzaku and Dervishi 2003). According to the patrilineal logic, if children are considered as insurance against old age, only sons are valuable since daughters are 'lost' to their parents upon marriage; their care duties shift towards their in-laws upon joining the family of their husband; it is usually the youngest son of the family (together with his wife) who has the responsibility for looking after *his* parents in their later years. But the post-communist transformations and especially migration are affecting these customs too. According to statistics, the rate of divorce doubled between 1990 and 2006 from around 10 to around 20 per 100 marriages (INSTAT 2007a: 12). Likewise, the marriage age has increased – more so for women than for men – due to limited availability of marriage partners as a result of mass emigration.

The 2001 census also recorded around 700 couples who co-habited (INSTAT 2004b: 98). However, we suggest that this phenomenon has been on the increase in this last decade, accompanied by a change in perceptions in society about such a form of family formation. Murzaku and Dervishi (2003) note a number of typologies for such arrangements. First, there are college students and professionals who co-habit either because of changing behaviours and attitudes towards partnership, often borrowed from examples from the West gleaned through the media, or as a test for an eventual marriage, a type of 'unofficial betrothal'. Second, there are the affluent businessmen from provincial towns who buy a second home in the capital or nearby Durrës and co-habit there with college students; some may even have a wife and children in their main home. Third, divorced women, especially when they have young children, and who have escaped rural conservative communities, find it hard to make ends meet in the city and thus turn to cohabitation with more affluent and somewhat older men for support. Fourth, some successful professionals may prefer cohabitation in order not to share their wealth with their partner in the case of divorce. Finally, cohabitation was also abused by some men who used it as a transitory phase to transfer women from their homes through 'marriage' towards prostitution, often by a follow-up migration abroad (on non-traditional family formations in post-1990s Albania see also Sokoli 2006). By and large, some of these new living formations are considered as 'shameful' for Albanian women, although opinions in major urban centres have been changing. On the other hand, there is no slander for men who do the same – particularly for male migrants who often use co-habitation with foreign partners as a way out of the difficult first few years of settling in the host country.

Conclusion

This chapter has discussed migration, remittances and gender relations in Albania, focusing mainly on the post-communist period. Although not a new phenomenon, contemporary migration from Albania displays a highly dynamic character; by 2010 there are nearly 1.5 million Albanians – or 45 per cent of the country's resident population – spread around the world. The most significant migrant communities are situated in neighbouring Greece – more than 600,000 – and Italy with around 400,000 Albanians, followed by the USA and the UK. The dynamism of Albanian migration has also been reflected in the participation of women in these flows, as well as their role in them. Albanian migratory processes are highly gendered; migration started off as a male-led phenomenon, but a higher gender balance has since been achieved. Despite a measure of gender equality achieved under communism, Albania remains (and in some respect has become more so since 1990) a deeply patriarchal society. This feature has shaped Albanian migratory processes and their constitutive aspects, especially remittances. The latter have been the main plank supporting the Albanian economy throughout two post-communist decades. Remittances have been crucial for the survival and poverty alleviation of many individuals and families as well. Although remittances have been a fairly widely researched aspect of Albanian migration, the vast majority of these studies have been 'gender-blind'. The limited existing evidence suggests that men dominate the remittance process through the sending and receiving of these vital capital transfers as well as through decision-making on their use. Some differences are noted between northern and southern areas, with the latter being more open to more equitable gender relations. In the next chapters we explore these relationships in more depth and discuss them in light of our research data.

4

THE GENDERED TRANSNATIONAL HOUSEHOLD

This is the first of four chapters which are devoted to presenting our research findings. Its focus is the Albanian transnational household spanning Albania and Greece, considered from a gender perspective. We start by outlining the profiles of our remittance-receiving respondents and their migrant family members in terms of their gender, age, education level, marital status, occupation; and for the remittance-senders living in Greece, duration of migration, and where possible, geographical location. This sets the scene for a more detailed analysis of the typology of transnational households within which remittances are transferred at both ends. We identify three main types: first, the extended family residing in the village, whose adult son (and much less often, daughter) works in Greece and sends remittances to his parents; second, the nuclear family (wife and children) residing in the village whose husband/father works in Greece and sends remittances to his wife; and finally, the older parents of migrants, who reside in the village on their own and whose adult children and their families live and work in Greece – remittances are usually sent by sons and received by fathers. Other, more exceptional typologies are also mapped out. The last part of the chapter discusses the various ways in which transnational households linked by remittances maintain their family cohesion across the Greek-Albanian border.

Profiles of Migrants and Transnational Households

In this section we discuss the profiles of migrant households in the study villages and their migrant family members in Greece. We rely primarily on information from our household questionnaire in Albania, and hence build much of the discussion around a series of tables, but we also draw on our smaller sample of in-depth interviews. Following our methodology of a 'village-outward' approach, we start the discussion of the transnational households in the villages of origin, and extend it to Greece and back again.

Demographic Indicators

The demographic picture that emerges from our survey and interview data suggests a number of things. First, when we look at the age-groups on both sides of the border we see two parts of a single 'puzzle'. In the villages, our respondents are more numerous in the older age-groups – almost half of them are above 55 years old (Table 3). Exactly the opposite is the case amongst migrants in Greece: here, the majority are in the working-age brackets. According to our survey data 84 per cent of the principal male remitters are between 19 and 45 years old (Table 4). The four female remitters are also in this age-group. These findings are corroborated by other and larger statistical databases such as the 2001 Greek census, data from regularisation programmes in Greece and the Greek Labour Force Surveys (see Baldwin-Edwards 2004a). For instance, according to calculations of valid – as of October 2007 – residence permit data provided by the Greek Ministry of Interior, 72 per cent of Albanian permit-holders were in the 19–50 age-cohort (Maroukis 2008: 56–7). Those 51 years and older comprised barely 5 per cent of this population.

The second demographic indicator – respondents' sex – reveals a broadly similar mirror-image picture: women are in the majority in the Albanian villages, whilst men dominate as migrants in Greece. We must emphasise here, however, that such results are partially affected by our methodology and research project requirements, whereby we collected questionnaire data on primary remitters. Although we found from our qualitative data that women remitted too, they were seldom considered as primary remitters by their families; this was considered as men's 'duty'. Looking more closely at Table 3 we see that women are in the majority as respondents – and therefore as remittance administrators – in the age-groups between 16 and 55. The weight of this group is boosted by the presence of wives of male migrants in nuclear families. This is even more evident for the age-groups between 26 and 45, but especially for the 36–45 age-bracket where, of 53 respondents, only one is male. If we use remittance-administration as a proxy for gendered decision-making within the family, our results suggest that the more patriarchal model of decision-making is stronger in older ages – around 60 per cent of decision-makers in the age-group 46–55 are women, but this share falls by half to around 30 per cent for the next age-group of 56–65. This table would suggest that male emigration is emancipatory for women who remain in the villages, because they are now administering the household finances. However, our in-depth material suggests that this is not necessarily the case. Not only do

Table 3 Respondents in the villages by age-group and sex

Age-groups	Count	%	Female	Female % of age-group
13–18 years	2	0.6	2	100.0
19–25 years	8	2.3	7	87.5
26–35 years	36	10.3	34	94.4
36–45 years	53	15.1	52	98.1
46–55 years	84	24.0	54	64.3
56–65 years	84	24.0	27	32.1
66–75 years	71	20.3	20	28.2
76 + years	12	3.4	6	50.0
Total	350	100.0	202	57.7

Source: Authors' survey

Table 4 Age-groups of remitting male migrants

	Sons			**Husbands**			**Other males: F-father B-brother G-grandson**	
Age-groups	**Count**	**% of all migrants**	**% of sons**	**Count**	**% of all migrants**	**% of husbands**	**Count**	**% of all migrants**
19–25 years	56	16.0	23.6	2	0.6	2	1G	
26–35 years	125	35.7	52.8	19	5.4	19	1B	
36–45 years	47	13.4	19.8	45	12.9	45	2F+3B	
46–55 years	8	2.3	3.4	31	8.9	31		
56–65 years	1	0.3	0.4	2	0.5	2	1F	
66–75 years				1	0.3	1		
Total	*237*	*67.7*	*100.0*	*100*	*28.6*	*100.0*	*8*	*2.3*
Missing, N/A	113	32.3		250	71.4		342	
Total	350	100.0		350	100.0			100.0

Source: Authors' survey

men continue to hold on to a high degree of decision-making even when they live abroad, but women often feel overburdened with all the responsibility of the household and looking after the children and their education (see also the recent study by UNICEF 2009). We come back to the analysis of these gendered remitting patterns in the following chapters.

The third demographic indicator is education. Using primary remittance senders as a proxy for migrants and remittance administrators as proxy for the local population, our survey data suggest that those who remain behind in the villages have lower levels of education than migrants (Tables 5 and 6).[1] This is also in line with other large-scale surveys and studies in Albania (e.g. Azzarri and Carletto 2009), as well as more widely, since migrants are generally positively selected amongst the population. In our case, this is not unexpected as the older family members will undoubtedly also have lower education levels, as will females who are in the majority as remittance-receivers in the village. In addition, we also need to bear in mind that many of these 'residual' family members – at least men – may be returnees, since Albanian migration in the 1990s was of such a scale that very few families were not directly or indirectly touched by it.

However, in the villages, there are some interesting differences in education levels between the three ethnic groups. As we mentioned in the opening chapter, the study villages were of particular interest to us because of their ethnic and religious composition. The majority of the population is made up of ethnic Albanians, most of whom are – at least nominally – Muslim, but there is a minority of Christian Orthodox. In addition, there is a small group of Christian Orthodox who claim Greek citizenship – although not always ethnicity – through pre-war transnational ties to Greece. And finally, there is a significant community of Roma and Evgjit, some of whom declare themselves to be Muslims. The first two groups are broadly represented in our survey according to their population shares in the study villages (Table 7). The Roma and Evgjit communities are somewhat over-represented in our survey; they constitute an estimated 7 per cent of the total population of the study villages, whereas in the survey they made up 11 per cent. This numerical presence in our study resulted from our particular interest in these groups – the most marginalised in the country and locally – and their migrating and remitting patterns.

Coming back to the education of respondents, the survey data suggests that the Roma and Evgjit have the lowest levels of education when compared to the other two main groups (Table 8). The Christian Orthodox are the most educationally advanced in that they have zero levels of illiteracy, and higher levels of secondary and university education as a share of their population. The Muslims have higher levels only at the lower and primary compulsory education. The Roma and Evgjit are the most disadvantaged in that their highest level of education is eight years of compulsory schooling, whilst illiteracy is the highest of all three communities at around 10 per cent. A further breakdown of the data for compulsory education reveals that more than a third of this sub-group has attended only four years of schooling. Levels of education continue to be low for children – most of them have an average of three or four grades of education (whilst the average amongst the rest of the population surveyed is double that). Similar concerns have been raised by previous studies on Roma in Albania carried out by international organisations such as the World Bank (De Soto *et al.* 2005), the European Roma Rights Centre (ERRC 1997), and the UNDP (UNDP-Albania 2006). Such lower levels of education amongst Roma in Albania reflect their marginal position in society, and suggest rather poor prospects for the younger generation to improve their situation.

The interviewees living in Thessaloniki presented a varied picture of ages and education levels, but which broadly mirrored the data presented so far. The principal migrants and their spouses had generally completed either eight years of compulsory education or 12 years of primary and lower secondary education. Four interviewees had completed upper secondary vocational training (for zoology, construction or plumbing), and so had two of the female spouses. However, all the children of migrants who were born in Greece or had arrived there at a young age – i.e. the second and 1.5 generation – were enrolled in the Greek education system.[2] One young woman had completed a university degree, whilst several other young men and women were taking vocational degrees at institutes of higher education. The parents we interviewed expressed their pride at how well their children were doing at school and how parents' own dreams were being realised by their children. They had high expectations for them and proudly told how their children were taking piano and English language lessons, and how they spoke Greek without an accent (see also Gogonas 2007). The latter was emphasised as a sign of high ability, but it was also deemed necessary for being able to integrate better in school, the labour market and society more generally. Many saw education as a way for socio-economic upward mobility, by being able to access better-paid and stable jobs. Whether these expectations will be translated into real job opportunities commensurate with education levels remains to be seen.

Table 5 Highest level of education completed by respondents in villages

Education level	**Count**	**%**
None	10	2.9
Primary and lower secondary (8 years)	272	77.7
Upper secondary (12 years)	65	18.5
University (16 years)	3	0.9
Total	350	100.0

Source: Authors' survey

Table 6 Education-groups of remitting male migrants

	Sons			**Husbands**			**Other males: F-father B-brother G-grandson**	
Education	**Count**	**% of all migrants**	**% of sons**	**Count**	**% of all migrants**	**% of husbands**	**Count**	**% of all migrants**
None	2	0.6	0.8	3	0.9	3		
up to 4 years	4	1.1	1.7	3	0.9	3	1F	
5–7 years	10	2.9	4.2	4	1.1	4		
8 years	154	44.0	65.0	64	18.3	64	2F+2B	
9–11 years	8	2.3	3.4	6	1.7	6		
12 years	55	15.7	23.2	20	5.7	20	2B+1G	
university	4	1.1	1.7					
Total	*237*	*67.7*	*100.0*	*100*	*28.6*	*100.0*	*8*	*2.3*
Missing, N/A	113	32.3		250	71.4			
Total	350	100.0		350	100.0			100.0

Source: Authors' survey

Table 7 Ethnicity and religion of respondents in villages

Ethnicity/religion	Count	%
Albanian Muslim	254	72.5
Albanian Orthodox Christian	58	16.6
Roma and Evgjit	38	10.9
Total	350	100.0

Source: Authors' survey

Table 8 Education of respondents in villages by ethnicity and religion

Highest level of education completed		Albanian Muslim	Albanian Orthodox Christian	Roma & Evgjit	Total
None	Count	6	0	4	10
	% of ethnic/religious group	2.4	0.0	10.5	2.9
	% of Total	1.7	0.0	1.1	2.9
Primary & lower secondary	Count	195	43	34	272
	% of ethnic/religious group	76.8	74.1	89.5	77.7
	% of Total	55.7	12.3	9.7	77.7
Upper secondary	Count	51	14	0	65
	% of ethnic/religious group	20.1	24.1	0.0	18.6
	% of Total	14.6	4.0	0.0	18.6
University	Count	2	1	0	3
	% of ethnic/religious group	0.8	1.7	0.0	0.9
	% of Total	0.6	0.3	0.0	0.9
Total	Count	254	58	38	350
	% of ethnic/religious group	100.0	100.0	100.0	100.0
	% of Total	72.6	16.6	10.8	100.0

Source: Authors' survey

Employment

The pattern of employment for migrants, according to the responses given by their family members in the village survey, is very similar to that of Albanian migration more generally (Table 9). Considering that almost all the principal remittance senders in the sample are men, the majority of them (almost 60 per cent) work in the construction sector (see Illustration 3). This includes those working in skilled jobs such as carpentry, laying tiles, rendering, painting, decorating etc. The next most important share is those who work in the agricultural sector, almost 30 per cent. This is not at all surprising given that 20 per cent of the sample's migrants work seasonally in Greece, and this work is primarily in agriculture. A number of migrants who worked in agriculture also did construction jobs as and when these became available. The next most important sector was manufacturing, although far behind the other two sectors at around 3 per cent. This consisted of small-sized factories manufacturing wood, PVC, small food processing firms etc. The category 'other: semi-skilled' includes those (men) working as mechanics, plumbers, cooks, bakers and self-employed carpenters. The four women remitters, on the other hand, worked respectively in domestic care, hotel cleaning, as a cashier in a supermarket, and in a factory. Most of the spouses of the male migrants also worked in domestic cleaning and caring, the hotel and restaurant sector, agriculture and manufacturing, whilst some stayed at home to look after the children and the household.[3]

Table 9 Job done by remitter in Greece

Job	Count	%
Construction	207	59.1
Agriculture	102	29.1
Manufacturing	10	2.9
Other: semi-skilled	15	4.3
Other: low-skilled	16	4.6
Total	350	100.0

Source: Authors' survey

This picture did not match exactly with our fieldwork material collected in Thessaloniki due to the fact that, in urban environments, agricultural work is excluded. The male interviewees in Thessaloniki worked in construction, manufacturing, as plumbers, cooks and electricians in that

Illustration 3 Albanian migrant workers in Thessaloniki, 2006

order. Women, on the other hand, worked mostly in cleaning and caring. Some stayed at home to look after their young children and the households; one worked in a garment factory, another in a confectioner's.

Our findings show four things. First, they confirm the strongly-gendered character of the labour market in Greece, in that both men and women work in what are considered as strongly male and female sectors of employment respectively. Second, these labour market niches are affected by nationality as much as by gender. The construction sector in Greece is nowadays dominated by Albanian migrant men, while their female counterparts are the most numerous as live-out domestic carers (Maroukis 2008). Hence the gendered segmentation of the labour market in Greece is reinforced by the intersection of gender with nationality. This 'traps' Albanian workers in those employment sectors which are 'assigned' to them; at the same time it 'liberates' Greeks from having to do these tough, unpleasant and low-paid jobs.

Third, the survey results reveal that, despite the fairly high levels of education that most migrants possess, their employment is overwhelmingly in unskilled jobs. We need to emphasise, however, that besides some vocational training observed amongst a few interviewees, the education that most rural working-age adults had received in Albania was of a general and theoretical character, and to some extent quite linked to work in agriculture. It was thus not suited at all for urban and more capitalist economies such as that of Greece. During our focus-group discussion with key stakeholders in Thessaloniki, amongst whom were also leaders of Albanian migrant organisations, we learnt that such deskilling was overwhelming even amongst migrants who held university degrees. Besides the migrant status, this deskilling is also affected by the fact that Albanian degrees and other paper qualifications are not recognised in Greece (and other EU countries).[4] Furthermore, as mentioned earlier, the types of job available to Albanian migrants in Greece were in the low-skilled and manual employment sectors (see also Barjaba and King 2005; Lianos 2007). On the other hand, those who came from rural areas generally gained skills, which helped them improve their position in the labour market.

This brings us to our fourth remark: the gradual improvement in the labour market position over the years (Labrianidis *et al.* 2004; Hatziprokopiou 2006). Other researchers suggest that, compared to the host population, Albanians in Greece seem to move more slowly upwards in the occupational ladder (Lyberaki and Maroukis 2005). From a gender perspective it seems that such an improvement has been faster for men than for women. One reason behind this is that women's jobs are more stable than men's, given the increasing need for care and domestic services as the native population ages rapidly and Greek women increasingly work outside the house. Meanwhile, the welfare state remains weak and not much gender redistribution of reproductive work takes place within Greek households.

However, although Albanian migrant women are becoming *de facto* breadwinners in the family alongside their husbands, they have much lower rates of independent social insurance than their male counterparts. For example, their presence in the IKA (Greek Institute of Social Insurance) statistics for domestic work employment is very low, which contradicts findings from fieldwork surveys and qualitative studies, including our own here. Maroukis (2008: 62) suggests that this results from the tendency Albanian migrant women display to register themselves on their husband's social insurance booklet, rather than have their own. Whether insured in this way, or completely uninsured, migrant women become dependent on their male relatives (i.e. husbands) for their health, welfare provision and even for their very legal status in Greece (Vullnetari 2009).[5]

To put these findings into a broader perspective, we can clearly see how Albanian migration to Greece fits within the 'Southern European model of immigration' (King 2000b). Albanian migrants are concentrated in gendered and nationality-specific labour market niches, work often for low wages and informally, and undergo deskilling, all of which can lead to exploitation and social exclusion. It is clearly a 'win situation' for the host country – Greece – which develops itself through the 'free' supply of migrant labour at a minimal cost. It seems that migrant women bear a significant weight of this development, through their unpaid reproductive labour, and their wage work, both of which are overwhelmingly in the domestic sphere. Albanian women are thus protagonists of 'counter-geographies of globalisation' (Sassen 2000), both as migrants and when remaining behind in the rural areas of origin, as we shall see presently.

Back in our study villages in Albania, employment patterns among our respondents were typical for less-developed rural societies. Table 10 presents selected sources of income for the rural households surveyed. This table, supported by field observations in the villages, suggests a number of things. First, as expected, the most common activity is agriculture: a third of households engage only in farming, while many others combine it with other activities. In the majority of cases farming is at subsistence levels, although some families were able to produce commercial quantities. Second, the majority of households made use of a combination of income-generating sources – most often agriculture and one or more additional activities. The latter included livestock (milk cows and sheep), pensions and Economic Aid (EA – a kind of welfare payment for poor people), fruit orchards, and wage work such as in agriculture, construction, transport, and food processing. A handful of individuals were employed in the local administration or were self-employed as carpenters, electricians, mechanics and carpet weavers. In a few cases the family had a modest non-agricultural business, which most often was a small grocery shop, a bakery, a transport vehicle, a tractor, and in one case a fuel station (one pump and a small one-room building). All of these were family-run small businesses which benefited from the unpaid labour of one or two family members – a picture very similar to what has been observed by other researchers in rural southern Albania (Nicholson 2004b). Most of these activities and businesses were set up and many continued to be supported by remittances, especially from Greece.

The third observation is that 4 per cent of the households surveyed had no income locally whatsoever – they simply relied on remittances. Such reliance was also very important for the 7 per cent whose only other income was an old-age pension – in the majority older people living on their own or looking after grandchildren of emigrant sons and daughters.

Finally, a number of those who emigrated seasonally did so in order to put together some capital for setting up their own orchard or livestock farm, which would – they hoped – be sustainable on its own in the long run, thus reducing the need to re-migrate. In other words they emigrated in order to stay put. We will come back to this when we discuss uses of remittances in Chapter 6.

Table 10 Principal income sources for rural households

Source	Count	%
Farming	115	32.9
Old-age pensions	25	7.1
Old-age pensions and farming	65	18.6
Old-age pensions and rent from land	12	3.4
No income	14	4.0
Mixed other	119	34.0
Total	350	100.0

Source: Authors' survey

Thus, in line with the NELM, migration in this context is just one part of a complex portfolio of economic strategies, not only aiming to maximise benefits but also to minimise risks against failure (of crops), and to face sudden shocks such as illness and death in the family. As we shall see later, all members of the family are involved – albeit in asymmetrical ways and degrees – in these activities and in decision-making.

Such livelihood strategies are also reflected in the way that households organise farming when this is combined with migration. For example, in nuclear households where the husband was away in Greece for most of the year, the household invested generally in subsistence farming. Typical crops would be those which were less labour-intensive such as wheat and alfalfa, which the wife could manage to look after besides her other tasks in the household. Here is a typical example. Elsa (47) lives in the village with her husband (56) who is a seasonal migrant, and their youngest son (14). Their other two sons of 24 and 21 work in Thessaloniki; the eldest has been there for almost ten years and is now regularised, whereas the youngest is undocumented and has been repeatedly deported back to Albania. At the time of the interview the family had decided that the father should now stay in the village as he is becoming too old to migrate. The parents will concentrate on farming, while the elder sons will continue to remit from Greece. Elsa explains:

> Until now we have planted only wheat, because they were all away [in Greece] and I couldn't look after the fields on my own. Wheat and alfalfa for the cow… This year my husband will stay here [in the village]. So we will plant onions and beans [to sell]… We'll try our luck with these… Well, we decided for him to stay because our sons told him: 'no need to come here [in Greece]' –

> he is getting older now – 'work there [in the village] as much as you can, and if you can't, just stay at home'.

When respondent families were larger and comprised three or more generations, a range of produce was planted, but there was an increasing tendency nowadays to set up apple orchards. Even though only around 9 per cent of respondents reported receiving part of their income from apples, many more had invested in such activity and expected to receive the 'fruit of their labour' in the next couple of years. This next example is of such a large family. The interview was held at the home of the family and although the wife of the migrant (Asije 47) was the main interlocutor, others who were present – mother-in-law and daughters – chipped in with information.

> Now our family is made up of eight persons: my father-in-law (72), my mother-in-law (70), my husband (48), and four children (21, 18, 12 and 8 years old). We have always worked in farming, that is what we do here. We work a lot… We have 1 hectare of land with apple orchards and now we will plant another 0.7 hectares… We also grow onions, beans, wheat, barley, vegetables, we have two milk cows and a horse… My husband works seasonally in Greece, mostly in construction, so he brings good money… But we also have to work hard: me and my father-in-law work in the fields, our children come and help us after school in the afternoon, my mother-in-law does the house chores and prepares the meals… When my husband is not in Greece he ploughs other villagers' land using our tractor.

Spatial Distribution

Although we did not collect systematic data on the geographical location of migrants in Greece, we were informed of places that migrants lived, including the cities of Athens and Thessaloniki, the islands of Crete and Paros, as well as border areas near Kastoria and Florina. This is very much in line with the general trend of widespread settlement of Albanian migrants in Greece according to the 2001 Greek census (Rovolis and Tragaki 2006). Although some researchers argue that there has been no large-scale spatial concentration of immigrants within urban areas such as Thessaloniki (Hatziprokopiou 2004; Kokkali 2010), some of the key informants told us that micro-geography was important to some extent. For example, according to data from the Thessaloniki urban authorities, representatives of which participated in our group discussions in this city, 80 per cent of migrants in the municipality of Sikies, on the north-west periphery of the city, are Albanian and Georgian; the shares are almost equal between the two nationalities. Our sample in Thessaloniki was statistically too small to make any meaningful generalisations on this point.

As far as seasonal migrants were concerned, these migrated mainly to rural Veria, north-western Greece, and the border villages near Lake Prespa. Those who followed the latter route were the poorest of the village communities – often Roma and Evgjit families – who walked over the mountain to Greece in order to find work in agriculture there.

Especially older parents of migrants did not always know the exact name of the small town or village where migrants lived – they were told that they lived near big cities such as Athens or Thessaloniki, or in a particular island. Part of the reason was also because migrants had been very mobile within Greece, moving usually from rural to urban areas once they obtained a more regular immigration status. This mobility was to a certain extent accompanied by a degree of socio-economic improvement, which was reflected in the living standards – larger accommodation, furnished with mod-cons, a family car (which the men drove), savings in the bank, private lessons for their children, etc. In one instance the family had purchased their own apartment in Thessaloniki, whilst also having bought a house in Tirana. In another case the family had purchased part of the business in Greece – a small restaurant – where the migrant husband, his wife and their eldest son were employed. We found similar geographic and socio-economic mobility patterns amongst Albanian migrants in both Greece and Italy in our previous research (King and Mai 2008; Vullnetari 2008).

Duration of Migration

Our findings on this point once again confirm those from previous research on Albanian migrants in Greece in that the duration of their stay has been an important factor in their upward socio-economic mobility (Hatziprokopiou 2006; Lazaridis and Koumandraki 2007; Vullnetari 2008). In our survey, more than three-quarters (76.3 per cent) of migrants had been working in Greece for more than four years, whilst the share of those who had started to emigrate only recently is very low at only 3 per cent (Table 11). However, some of the migrants in the former group do not live full-time in Greece but work there only seasonally – a share of 20 per cent of the total sample; they effectively live between the two countries.

The length of stay points towards a maturing of the migrant population in Greece from this area of Albania. This is in line with the trend country-wide, but it is more pronounced in south-east Albania since it was here that some of the very first migration journeys started in 1990–91. The maturing is corroborated further with the material collected through in-depth interviews in Thessaloniki. All the migrants interviewed in Thessaloniki had

Table 11 Years principal remitter has been working in Greece

No. of years	Count	%
Less than 1 year	9	2.6
Between 1 and 2 years	29	8.2
Between 3 and 4 years	45	12.9
More than 4 years	267	76.3
Total	350	100.0

Source: Authors' survey

been there for more than four years. Typically, the males had emigrated since the early 1990s (one even in 1989), a migration which was initially characterised by its to-and-fro nature. Those who were married had their wife and children join them in Greece quite early on, whereas those who married later made a family reunification at a later time. All women interviewees in Thessaloniki and the female partners of male interviewees had emigrated to Greece as 'dependents', i.e. as the spouse of the male migrant. Only in one case was the fiancée already in Greece, having arrived there at an early age with her parents and siblings (i.e. she was a 1.5 generation migrant). Such a typology is typical of rural areas, if not of Albanian migration to Greece more generally, especially during the first post-communist decade (King and Vullnetari 2009b). The feminisation of Albanian migration, i.e. females' increased presence in migratory flows, during the later years of this decade is reflected in our research data. Thus, half of male interviewees had first emigrated to Greece between 1989 and 1992, another four had emigrated right after the chaos caused by the pyramid schemes in 1997, and the rest between 1999 and 2002. Only one young man had arrived in 2007. When it came to women, some joined their husbands in the 1990s, but the vast majority came to Greece after the first regularisation of 1998 (12 out of 15 spouses).

The case of Anita (23) and her husband Luli (32) below illustrates a number of the themes discussed in this section of the chapter. At the time of the interview, Anita had been living in Greece only for one year, when she joined her husband after their marriage in Albania. Although she holds a BA degree in agri-business and marketing from Korçë University, she now works as a house cleaner in Thessaloniki. Both non-recognition of her degree and her undocumented status have led to this outcome. Particularly the latter affects her life negatively: her freedom of mobility is limited and she spends most of her free time indoors or in fear of apprehension when she goes out; meanwhile, she has not been able to visit her family in Albania. In addition, she has become reliant and dependent on her husband, not least because she is uninsured as she works informally. All of these put her in a precarious socio-economic position and within the 'gendered geographies of power' (Mahler and Pessar 2001) she finds herself effectively imprisoned by the power that other people and institutions exert over her.

> *Anita*: When I came to Greece a year ago I entered through the passport control as if I had already been in Greece, but was just getting the entrance stamp on my documents… We paid €3,000 [to smugglers]
> *Luli*: I was personally with her, because if I didn't accompany her [as her husband] nothing would happen
> *Anita*: €3,000!
> *Luli*: cash in hand
> *Anita*: Why? Because we couldn't get a visa – they either want money [a backhander] for that, or they make it impossible. If we waited for family reunification, who knows when we would be together again… He [her husband] has been here [in Greece] for seven years with legal documents, paying insurance and all.
> *Luli*: I would never be able to earn the sort of money required for family reunification [€12,500 a year]. Even the average Greeks don't earn that much in a year.

Typologies of Transnational Households

Having set the scene through a discussion of migrants' and their families' profiles, we now continue with an analysis of the types of transnational household within which remittances are sent and received, and how decisions on their use are made. On the one hand this typology is set against the background of Albania's gender relations and patriarchal norms, and the subsequent roles and responsibilities that flow from them. On the other hand, the typology has also undergone various degrees of change as a result of migration, and also of the much broader socio-economic and cultural transformations during these two post-communist decades. These changes, however, do not always mean a liberalisation of cultural and social norms; indeed, at times they involve a strengthening of patriarchal values in some respects, especially in rural areas.

We first begin with the typology of households in the study villages before moving (metaphorically) to Greece for the remittance-sending parts of the transnational households there. In line with the aims of our research, and of the overall theme of the book, we are interested in the gendered dimension of this typology.

Remittance-Receiving Households

In the study villages three categories of gendered households were identified: those headed by women, those headed by men, and a very small number of households temporarily headed by children. Each of the main categories is subdivided into three types as follows:

Female-Headed Households

Type 1. This is a *de facto* female-headed household. The woman lives in the village with her children, while her husband spends most of the year living and working in Greece, returning to the village only for short visits. The husband remains the official household head even though he is away, but in practice the family unit is managed by the wife in the village. Generally the objective is to reunite the family in Greece, particularly if the husband has a steady job, a long-term staying and working permit and earns good wages. This household type was the most numerous amongst the female-headed remittance-recipient units in the villages.

Type 2. This is similar to type 1, but different because of the *temporality* of the role of women as household heads during the year. Here, the husband works only seasonally in Greece – up to six months in a year, but often for shorter periods – and lives in the village the rest of the time. Thus, the wife takes on the functional role as head of the household only for those months her husband is in Greece.

Type 3. In this household type the head is an *older widow*, who may be living alone or with her young grandchildren – often her son's children, and more rarely her daughter's – whose parents live and work in Greece. Usually, the children live in the village until they reach school-age, when they are taken to Greece to be enrolled in the education system there, except when the parents are undocumented. The widows may, in some cases, be living with grandchildren who are either orphans, or have lost one of their parents. In the latter case the other parent has re-married and lives with their new family in Greece, but the children from the previous marriage are not taken there so as to avoid intra-familial frictions with the new partner. At other times, the widow's household includes her daughter-in-law as well as the grandchildren, while the son is working on his own abroad. In these cases, either the migrant has not succeeded in fulfilling the requirements for family reunification, or the wife stays behind to look after the fragile and ailing mother-in law. Finally, within this rather varied type of household, the older widow may be living with her other unmarried sons and daughters, or divorced daughters.

Male-Headed Households

Type 1. The most typical household consists of *a multi-generational family* where middle-aged or older parents live with their children and grandchildren and where there is at least one migrant son who sends remittances from Greece.

Type 2. Elderly *widowers or couples* who are pensioners and who live on their own constitute another important format. All their children have migrated abroad (often to Greece but also to other countries) or internally to other urban areas in Albania. They live there together with their nuclear families and return to the village only for visits. Although on their own, the older parents in the village are the care 'responsibility' of the youngest son and his wife. Therefore, remittances are expected to flow in that direction – son and daughter-in-law to parents – and are considered a 'duty', while hands-on care is expected to be provided by this daughter-in-law when the parents fall ill. Often such remittances are labelled as 'pensions', as they are regular and in small sums, just enough to support the older parents. To some degree this label also reflects the determinants of remitting as an act of compensation to parents for the investment they have made in bringing up and educating their children (Poirine 1997). However, other sons and daughters may send some remittances, often labelled as 'gifts' or 'just for a coffee'.

Type 3. Very rarely is the *husband* the remittance-receiver, while the wife has emigrated and works alone in Greece. Although no such cases were reported in the household survey or in-depth interviews, we came across two such households during our field observations and group discussions.

Child-Headed Households

This final group is quite rare in the villages, and of a temporary character. However, it merits mentioning in order to highlight its occurrence, the context in which it takes place, and consequences for the children involved. The children are from Roma and Evgjit nuclear households whose parents emigrate seasonally to Greece – for periods ranging from several weeks up to three months. During this time, a teenage son or daughter leaves school in order to look after their younger siblings and do the household chores. Some remittances which parents send are administered by the children, generally with the assistance of relatives who live in the village.

Remittance-Sending Households

Crossing now over the border to Greece, we observe that the household typology here – this time of remittance-senders – is much simpler. There are three types, all headed by men.

Type 1. The most typical household is the *migrant nuclear family* with or without children, sometimes hosting temporarily a migrant male relative, usually the husband's brother. The migrant couple together with the brother (where relevant) remit to the husband's parents back in the village. Some money and more often clothes may be remitted to the wife's parents, although not in equal value to the remittances directed to the husband's parents.

Type 2. Less usual than the first, but important nonetheless, in this household type the nuclear migrant family is joined by the migrants' older parents (generally the husband's parents) to create *a multi-generational household*. The older man in the family in Greece is usually the formal household head, although he may not always make the highest monetary contribution to the family's budget, which is usually made by his son – the 'primary' migrant. At other times, only the older mother (grandmother to the couple's children) will join the nuclear migrant family, especially if she is a widow. These grandparents play important roles in the migrant household in Greece by providing child-care, doing the cooking and cleaning, while sometimes they may also bring in additional incomes from casual work (usually men). Another subtype is typically composed of three generations: the older age-cohort (in their early sixties) who were the first of the family to move to Greece and are often still in employment; their children who followed them later – now in their late twenties and early thirties; and the young babies born to the married son(s) in Greece – married daughters will have moved out of the household to that of their husband. Although situated in urban Greece, gender and generational roles within this type of household are perhaps quite similar to those in Albanian villages.

Type 3. Households composed of two or more *men who are on their own in Greece*, whether because they are unmarried, or because they migrate without their wives. They are often friends or relatives and share the basic household budget and other household chores. This is particularly the case for seasonal migrants living in rural Greece, many of whom are married, but also for single longer-term migrants, many of whom live and work in urban areas.

Our findings fit with the 2001 Greek census data, according to which 65 per cent of Albanian migrant households in Greece lived in some conventional form of family living arrangements – couples with or without children – whilst only 14 per cent lived in multi-member households but whose members were not related to one another by kinship ties (Baldwin-Edwards and Kolios 2008: 12–13).

We did not interview any female-headed households, although a number of our interviewees emphasised the gendered egalitarian nature of decision-making in their households. One exception was a female-headed household which was composed of two sisters – both of whom were highly educated – and a younger brother living in Thessaloniki. In an unusual way, the eldest sister had been the first migrant who had then supported the subsequent migration of her younger sister and then her brother in that order.[6] To some degree the low incidence of this type of household is related to the rural background of our sample. Our key informants in Greece, however, reported that according to their experience and knowledge such female-headed households now form a recognisable part of the Albanian migrant community in Greece. Some of them may be divorced and widowed women who live on their own or with their young children.

Transnational Family Cohesion Across Borders

Without a doubt migration, as part of the post-communist transformations of these last 20 years, has affected family cohesion, including gender and generational norms and relations within it. Unlike before, many such families are now reconstituted beyond as well as within Albania, spanning two or more countries. This section attempts to tease out some of the changes observed in our research.

Changes in Household Typologies

Most changes affecting the typologies presented in the previous sub-section relate to the situation in Greece. There is a temporal, as well as a socio-economic change. In the early 1990s, Albanian migration was dominated by men, who lived together in Greece for the time they spent there working. The living conditions were often precarious, and they lived crammed in rooms in very poor buildings, in rundown neighbourhoods with poor infrastructure (see for instance Iosifides and King 1998). In rural Greece, they lived in barns or sheds in the fields. After the 1998 regularisation programme, many were joined by their wives and children, or had children in Greece. The nuclear family then moved to more decent living situations. This was accompanied by, and in turn was also due to, a continuous regular status, better paid and steadier jobs, better knowledge of the language, but also changes within the Greek society itself vis-à-vis migrants.[7] Sometimes, a nuclear family would be the place where several other male relatives (brothers, cousins) and sometimes friends would find shelter. The only female would be cooking and cleaning whilst men went out to work in physically demanding jobs. This is still the case today to a certain extent, although there may be only one or two such relatives residing with the couple and their children. At other times, two or more brothers (and less so sisters) lived together with their partners and children in one household in order to cut costs and put some money aside for launching the separate household later on.

Thus, despite the challenges and hardships faced in Greece such as low pay, deskilling, precarious employment and social stigmatisation, Albanian migrants have managed to improve their socio-economic position in the host society (see also Hatziprokopiou 2006; Labrianidis *et al.* 2004). This is a clear example where both structure and agency are crucially interwoven to produce the lifeworld we study (Giddens 1984).

Over the years, and after regularisation and family reunification, the most typical Albanian household now in Greece is that comprised of the husband and wife, and their young or teenage children. Sometimes, elderly parents will join them for some months, or even one or two years – depending on their ability to obtain visas and staying permits – primarily so that the grandmother can look after the young children and the household, whilst the grandfather may find a job as a security guard for building sites. This enables both members of the middle-aged migrant couple to do paid work; another effect of the grandparents' presence is to maintain intra-generational family cohesion (see also King and Vullnetari 2006).

However, the elderly parents may be 'needed' only for some time, whilst the grandchildren are still young. This situation may not always work for all families, as some decide that the cost of living in Greece for all the household members may be higher than the income earned, especially if the migrant wife cannot find a well-paid job. Thus, it might be financially more beneficial that the elderly parents stay in the village in Albania, where the living costs are much lower than in Greece, and where €100 or €200 will go a long way in covering expenses. However, this discussion about how to 'arrange' the multi-generational transnational family is not only about economics, as 'happy families' are not always the norm (Baldock 2003). In particular, conflicts between mother-in-law and daughter-in-law arise – they are nothing new to the Albanian family. Part of the migration benefit considered from the point of view of young migrant women is their 'liberation' from the constant petty squabbles with the mother-in-law in Albania. The disagreements range across many issues: the way one cooks or furnishes the house, brings up the children, behaves with their husband, spends the hard-earned money, not to mention the desire for privacy (King and Vullnetari 2009b). While gender relations are crucial in understanding social reality, we must not neglect gender's intersection with age, social status and class. The example below illustrates this. Thus, *social location* – within gender relations at the *geographic scale* of families in this particular case – is saturated with power, but is in turn re-shaped through geographical re-location as the migration from Albania to Greece takes place.

For those young wives who were happy to follow their husbands to Greece to achieve family reunification and to 'escape' the oppressive and controlling presence of their mother-in-law, the subsequent reunification of the latter in Greece as part of the reconstituted multi-generational emigrant household may come as an ironic and unwanted event. On the other hand, for the older generation, to be 'abandoned' in the village by their migrant children (and the grandchildren too in many cases) is not what they had worked all their lives and raised children for; they anticipated a family-centred old age surrounded by their children and grandchildren whom they could fuss over, enjoy, and receive respect and support from (King and Vullnetari 2006). So for them, too, migration brings a sense of unwanted irony.

Kadrie is 78 years old and nowadays lives on her own in the village. Both her sons live with their families in Greece. Her principal income is her meagre old-age pension of 5,000 lek per month [€45], supplemented by some remittances that her sons bring with them when they visit or send with the other brother, whoever is visiting. This is about €100 three times a year. Some nephews who live in North America have sent her some medicine now and then, and some money as a present 'for a coffee' once or twice. Both her sons have bought a building plot in Tirana and plan to build a flat there together with some relatives, part of which they can then sell off to potential buyers, whilst at the same time securing a base for themselves in the capital. A few years ago she went to live with the youngest son and his family in Greece, but returned to the village after two years of mostly constant quarrelling and even physical fighting with her daughter-in-law. Now that they live apart, she misses her son and grandchildren, but has had to accept reality.

This example throws up a number of issues for discussion, one of the most important of which is care, the subject of the next sub-section and the last part of this chapter before concluding.

Care and Family Across Borders

In the preceding parts of this book we have emphasised the importance of family within Albanian society. It is within the family that care has traditionally been performed – mutual care between generations, and somewhat more asymmetrical care between genders. In the last two decades, many intra-family care practices have been adjusted to fit the migratory situations that the majority of households in Albania have gone through. In order to analyse these in a transnational setting as ours, we follow the classification of Baldassar (2007) and Baldassar *et al.* (2007), who build on the work of Finch and Mason (1993). According to this categorisation, different types of care – practical, financial, personal ('hands on'), emotional and moral support – are characterised by 'varying degrees and forms of communication and interaction' (Baldassar 2007: 276).

The families in both Albania and Greece maintain their links transnationally and thus transmit care in a variety of ways. First of all, there are the telephone calls, which are frequent, at least once a week (for a discussion of telephone calls as the 'social glue' of transnational life see Vertovec 2004). For instance, the vast majority of respondent families in the rural areas – more than 90 per cent in our survey – have mobile telephones, and a third have a landline. Usually, it is the migrants who make the call to their family in the villages – the opposite happens only on occasions such as birthdays or ill-health. Phone calls are used to take care of practical issues such as discussing the use of remittances and children's education, to transmit emotional and moral support during periods of physical absence, episodes of ill-health or death in the family, and to share joyful news and events together such as births, birthdays, baptisms and weddings. Phone calls bring closer especially families which are divided by the 'invisible borders' of visas and 'papers' (cf. Kapllani 2009), when migrants are undocumented in Greece and cannot visit their families, or when their family members in Albania are unable to get visas to visit them in Greece.

Visits do, however, take place. This is the second means of transnational interaction. Visits from emigrants to their parts of the family in Albania take place generally three times a year: during the Greek Orthodox Easter (March or April), during the Greek summer holiday (August-September), and for Christmas and the New Year (December-January). Those who live far away, for instance in Athens or in remote Greek islands, may visit less and often avoid the winter trip if they have young children. On the other hand, those who live nearby, especially around the border areas and as far as Thessaloniki, may visit even more frequently. Some migrants living in Thessaloniki make monthly visits, and effectively live between the two countries.[8] Other visits may take place for special life-course events such as weddings, funerals, births, or in case of the illness or funeral of a family member.

Clearly, migrants' visits are conditioned by Greek immigration regulations. The most common problem is the ease with which migrants can fall back to an irregular situation through no fault of their own (Maroukis 2008; also confirmed by our focus groups in Thessaloniki). The procedure for stay and work permit renewals is highly bureaucratic, cumbersome and has been plagued by alleged corruption and inefficiency of staff (Fakiolas 2003). It may take up to two years for the Greek authorities to renew a permit, from the time when migrants have handed in their applications with the relevant documentation. Even then, migrants are often given expired permits, or permits with less than a month's validity. This bureaucratic ploy leaves migrants separated from their families, trapped in Greece by the delayed return of their documents. This means that at times they are not even able to attend the funeral of their loved ones in Albania.

When they do occur, these visits are avenues when all forms of care are transmitted, including hands-on care and financial aid through remittances and gifts (Baldassar *et al.* 2007). There are visits in the opposite direction as well – usually of parents to their migrant children and grandchildren – but these too are conditioned by strict and demanding visa procedures.

The third way of maintaining transnational relations are 'proxy visits', i.e. migrant relatives and friends who visit the parents of other migrants who cannot or do not visit. These trips are occasions when money, objects, care and affection are transported between the two families, or between two parts of an extended family, on behalf of close relatives. The transmission of care interlinks here with the social aspect of remittances. Using this avenue requires strong relationships of trust, while at the same time being attractive as a low-cost transport channel. Moreover, the interpersonal character of this transmission mode means that the pure physical transfer of money or goods is accompanied by affection and status: caring for one's family, as dutiful sons/husbands should do, translates into high prestige within the community.[9]

Videos and voice recordings are less frequently used, except when occasions such as weddings or baptisms, and sometimes holidays, are recorded for family members in the 'other place'. They are more attractive amongst older family members. For migrant grandparents these home-made videos counter somewhat the isolation they feel in host countries, as they spend a lot of time alone indoors while the younger-generation migrants are at work or at school. For older parents in villages, it is one way to virtually 'visit' their children and observe the houses and cities where they live, the places where they work, and the celebrations they have with friends. The video-tapes and discs are transmitted during either personal or proxy visits.

Finally, information communication technologies and the Internet have become increasingly important means for retaining transnational ties and transmitting various forms of care, especially over longer distances when transnational communities span continents. They are particularly used by the younger generations, but also more middle-aged ones, and in a few cases even older grandparents. Moreover, mobile text messaging is much cheaper than telephone calls, and although it does not replace them, it is a convenient tool for short and quick communication on a practical issue, and even for emotional support.

However, it is the Internet which has spurred a spectacular rise in popularity and use over a short period of time of social networking sites such as Facebook, with entire kin, village and regional communities being transnationally re-created online (see Illustration 4). The village of Pojan has its own Facebook site with hundreds of participants. However, the Internet is less frequently used in rural areas, including our study villages.

Illustration 4 An Internet café in Tirana, 2009

For example, although there is an Internet café in Pojan, none of the surveyed households had an Internet connection at home; indeed many did not even know what the Internet was or what it meant. Computer ownership and computer-literacy are very low in rural areas, primarily due to the high cost involved in both. The mobile phone has helped link this 'periphery of the periphery' – to borrow Fuga's (2004) expression when describing rural areas in Albania – with the global world. To what extent the Internet will help make it part of the 'global village' remains to be seen.

Conclusion

This chapter has presented the first part of the research findings. We started with a discussion of the profiles of migrants and their families, thereby setting the scene for the analysis of gendered transnational households and the ways in which transnational links are maintained across borders. We have thus focused on what Gardner and Grillo (2002: 179) call the 'transnational domestic sphere'.

Migration in the south-east Albanian study area has been quite intensive over the two decades of post-communist transformation. This has impacted on the household composition in these Albanian rural areas as well as in Greece. Whilst single male households dominated much of the movement and living settings in Greece in the 1990s, the later migration of spouses and children to join the migrant men as a result of regularisation programmes changed this. The dominant household type amongst our interviewees as well as in the survey data is now the nuclear migrant family. This is a sign of the maturation and stabilisation of Albanian migration in Greece, reflected in higher standards of living than before, child enrollment in Greek schools, and in many cases, purchase of property and investment in business in Greece.

The data we have presented here on the profile of migrants in Greece and their family members in rural Albania enable us to draw a number of conclusions. First, the majority of migrants are in the working-age bracket, a finding which is very much in line with the profile of Albanian migrants generally, as shown by other research. Very different is the demography of the respondents in the villages, where two-thirds are aged above 46 years. Likewise, education levels are higher for migrants than for the locals, also because of the age differential. However, it is worrying that the Roma and Evgjit continue to have the lowest education levels and experience marginalisation, both in Albania and as migrants in Greece.

When we look at gender patterns within the age groups, we can suggest that women gain some degree of emancipation as they administer the remittances sent by their husbands. However, this is not a straightforward issue, as we shall see in the following chapters. Indeed, women's job progression in Greece when they also emigrate appears to be much lower than for men – they mostly continue to work in the cleaning and care sectors, as they have done from the time they emigrated. Men, on the other hand, do move to more skilled work either in a different or within the same sector of employment, such as in construction. Furthermore, women's emancipation as migrants is curtailed by the gender-biased immigration policies in Greece which regard men as primary breadwinners, as well as by the patriarchal nature of the Greek society itself, which regards work in the cleaning and caring sector as belonging to the 'feminised' informal realm of the economy (Vullnetari 2009).

There is reason for greater optimism, though, when we consider the second and 1.5 generation. Their education has become one of the key aspects of investment for migrant parents, who have high expectations that at least their children will one day live as dignified Greek citizens. Here too, however, optimism is dampened by the harsh immigration regulations, especially as Greek citizenship and the rights that derive therefrom are constructed around ethnicity, religion and blood ties (Triandafyllidou and Veikou 2002). Given that a large share of migrants – as we saw from the data presented here – have lived in this country for more than ten years, some even for almost 20 years, the Greek immigration and integration policies need to move away from considering them as temporary labourers. These policies need to address the contribution and rights of these Albanian migrants by accepting that a share of them have now made Greece their home and are there to stay. The second generation, by definition, have been born in Greece, and they are mostly younger children, up to teenagers. Greek migration and social policy also needs to accept the fact of their existence. Given the continued suspicion of 'foreigners' (however defined or socially constructed) – a reflection of the strong ethno-nationalist sense of 'Greek identity' – it remains an open question as to how the younger generation of Greek-educated Albanians will fare in the labour market. Whilst there is optimism in the aspirations of parents for their children, and in the latter's generally good performance in the Greek education system, this must be countered by two pessimistic scenarios. The first derives from the current economic crisis that Greece is – more than any other EU country – struggling to come to terms with. The other is more permanent and rooted in the clientelistic and ultimately corrupt way that Greek society functions, so that access to jobs (and other resources and rights) is conditioned as much by 'who you know' as by requisite qualifications.

Alongside the maturing and longer-term migration and its accompanying typology, we also found that other, more temporary, shorter-term and recent forms of migration were present. In these cases, men were the sole migrants, living in male-composed households in Greece during their stay there, whilst their families lived in Albania. Often the latter were headed by women who took the *de facto* position as head of the family. These migrant male households were often focused on return to Albania, which was reflected in more remittances and lesser associative life in Greece.

The most vulnerable were households where children and the elderly were left on their own, the former especially the case amongst migrating Roma and Evgjit minorities.

Finally, there is intra-family care, which has clearly undergone significant changes due to the pressures exerted, but also the opportunities presented, by migration. On the one hand, vulnerable individuals and households in rural areas can continue to count on the support of the extended family and the wider community. On the other hand, transnational care, whether practical, financial or emotional, is being transmitted in a variety of ways such as through telephone calls, personal and proxy visits, and increasingly the Internet. In the next chapter we focus more closely on one aspect of such care – remittances.

5

REMITTANCE FLOWS, PATTERNS AND PROCESSES: THE SHAPING ROLE OF GENDER

In this chapter we cut to the core of our research, namely the analysis of remittances and the way that gender shapes, and is shaped by, them. The key focus is on financial remittances sent by individuals within households. We start by discussing transmission channels, and continue with a gendered analysis of sums and remitting frequencies. This is followed by an examination of gendered remitting patterns within transnational households – who sends remittances and who receives them. We also pay close attention to the various changes in remitting patterns over the years since the early 1990s, and interpret these changes in the light of post-communist transformations over the same period and as linked to the evolution of migration and development patterns in the context of our research area. Throughout the presentation and discussion of research findings, we mix tabulated data from the questionnaire survey with quotes from interviews and focus groups.

Remittance Transmission Channels

The principal ways in which Albanian migrants in Greece used to transfer money home in the early 1990s was by bringing it home themselves, sending it via relatives and friends, or by paid courier – usually a taxi driver. Four reasons accounted for this. First, the migrants were overwhelmingly undocumented at the time and choosing formal channels such as banks was not really possible, and also quite risky. Second, the formal channels of transmission were themselves limited, very bureaucratic and not widely available to migrants. Third, the geographical proximity of the two countries meant that taking the cash by hand during visits was feasible, and even desirable. Fourth, migrants often worked seasonally in Greece only for a few months, and preferred to bring the cash with them when they returned.

However, these methods, especially the first two, had risks embedded in them. During the early 1990s, and again in the late 1990s, Albania was gripped by insecurity, political turmoil and reduced authority of the law. Especially after the arms depots were robbed in 1997 and thousands of light armaments circulated freely in the hands of the public, various gangs of brigands ruled the main roads, especially close to the border crossings to Greece (Vickers and Pettifer 1997). Returning migrants were especially their target since it was common knowledge that they brought back hard-earned cash. This was the point when the Money Transfer Operators (MTOs) saw lucrative opportunities for business and started targeting the Albanian remittance market by providing financial products and services. Later on, the Greek banks became aware of the potential of this market and entered the competition, which has, over the years, brought down transaction costs and transfer time. Karafolas and Sariannidis (2009) argue that the growth of the banking network in Albania, specifically the branches of Greek and Italian banks, has stimulated the growth of remittance transfers through the formal channels as a share of total sums sent. Let us look at how the situation presents itself at the time of our survey in 2008. Table 12 presents the basic data on this, drawn from results of the questionnaire survey. The percentage sums exceed 100 since more than one reply could be given to this multiple-option question.

Table 12 Transfer channels

Channel	Count	%
Hand-carry	321	91.7
Family/friend	95	27.1
MTO	36	10.3
Paid courier	10	2.9
Bank	6	1.7
Debit card	2	0.3

Source: Authors' survey

Hand-Carry

This is the most common method of sending remittances to Albania in our survey – mentioned by more than 90 per cent of questionnaire respondents. In-depth interviews in Thessaloniki also revealed that hand-carrying was still the most preferred method. This usually takes places when the remitter returns for visits, or at the end of the working season (for those who are temporary migrants). Several reasons account for such a high share of users of this mode of transfer. First, as noted already, there is the geographical proximity between the two countries, and especially between the origin villages under study in Albania and the key destination of Thessaloniki, Greece (refer back to Map 2). Second, the degree of regularisation amongst Albanian migrants, particularly for those coming from our research villages, has increased.[1] This has enabled migrants to travel more easily for visits to Albania, as explained in the previous chapter. Third, as migration matures, the male migrant is joined by his wife and children, leaving behind mostly older parents. As a result, amounts sent have declined for this type of migrant household and migrants consider that it is not worth putting the small sums they send, such as €100 or €200, through the banking or MTO systems.

The importance of this channel of transfer is confirmed by other large-scale quantitative research. First, the IOM's 2005 survey found that almost 70 per cent of their Albanian migrant respondents in Greece transferred their money to Albania by hand-carrying it themselves (de Zwager *et al.* 2005: 31). Second, the household surveys carried out yearly and more recently quarterly by the BoA come to similar conclusions. Around 83 per cent of respondents in the 2006 survey stated that their migrant relatives in Greece and Italy brought the money home themselves (Frashëri 2007: 72). In the follow-up survey of 2008 the share of hand-carrying was 32 per cent for the entire sample, but this time there was no disaggregation by country of destination (Rëmbeci 2009).[2]

Relatives or Friends

This is the second most important way of transmitting the cash to Albania – 27 per cent of respondents in the survey said that their migrant family member sent money this way. This share was about 12 per cent in the 2005 IOM survey (de Zwager *et al.* 2005: 31). The BoA surveys of 2006 and 2008 reported that around 20 per cent and 33 per cent respectively of all migrants (not only in Greece), sent money through this channel (Frashëri 2007: 72; Rëmbeci 2009: 118).

As migration has matured, the majority of migrants live in communities where they are surrounded by relatives, friends, or acquaintances from the same or an adjacent village. If a migrant is not able to travel to Albania for work or documentation reasons, they will often find some other trusted person who does. Particularly as Thessaloniki is quite close to southern Albania, there are migrants from these villages who travel back and forth constantly. At other times, migrants will go to the bus station where passenger buses leave to go to Albania every day, and may by chance find someone they know who is travelling to the village. Migrants and their families who participated in our research emphasised that no monetary payment was made to the person who transferred the money. Sometimes the sender would buy the transmitter a beer to say thank you', but most often 'the debt' incurred would be paid back through reciprocity.

Paid Courier

This is a less expensive option when compared to MTOs, especially as it does not require any documentation. There is a range of such paid couriers who transport money for a fee, e.g. taxi and bus drivers who usually do business between the two countries, and also businessmen who may have a small transport service firm doing the same route. The typical scenario is that a migrant will go to the bus station where buses leave for Albania and give the driver a package with the name of someone who will go to collect it at the other end, for instance when the bus arrives at the bus stop in Korçë. In the early 1990s Greek taxi drivers were quite privileged since they had the possibility to work on both sides of the border as they had documentation. This was considered as the safest way to transport money, in the absence of other feasible options and in the face of the threat that armed brigands posed. Albanian taxi drivers have taken over much of this business now. However, trust is at the base of these informal transactions, and often the drivers are either from the same village or area as the package sender, or are recommended by a friend or relative. The third group is constituted of small business owners such as shopkeepers, who go to Greece to buy their goods, and whilst they are there they also transport money, furniture or other goods for a small fee. The money arrives at the destination within the same or the next day, depending on the distance between the start and the end of the journey. The services are usually carried out for a flat fee of €5 or €10 for any sum remitted.

Only around 3 per cent of our respondents stated they received money this way nowadays. Both BoA surveys, as well as the IOM one also reported very low shares of use for this transmission channel (de Zwager *et al.* 2005: 31; Frashëri 2007: 72; Rëmbeci 2009: 118), which appears to have been more important in the past than it is now.

There is one important point to note about the three informal remittance transfer methods mentioned thus far. Whether hand-carried, sent via relatives or friends, or consigned by a bus or taxi driver, the conveyors of the cash are almost invariably men. Clearly sending remittances is a 'male thing', not just because of the symbolic association between men, money and 'business', but also because those who operate taxis, buses and lorries are, inevitably in this part of the world, men.

Money Transfer Operators

Money Transfer Operators/Companies (MTOs/MTCs) are one of the most important channels for remittance transfers worldwide, especially when distances between origin and destination countries are significant. Together with banks they form what many call the formal or official channels of remittance transfers. The world's two largest MTOs are also present in Albania, namely Western Union (WU) since 1998, and MoneyGram (MG) since 2004. They operate either through their own branches or through local partners and by 2005 they had captured nearly 80 per cent of the total formal remittance transfer market in Albania (Kring 2007: 15). WU alone accounted for almost 80 per cent of formal transfers between Italy and Albania (Hernández-Coss *et al.* 2006).

Although competition in the remittance market – most notably from the banks – has affected fees charged, these remain relatively high. According to research carried out by London-based Profile Business Intelligence (PBI), in 2005 a transfer of €150 between Greece and Albania cost €14.50 through MG and €15.25 through WU, both for deliveries within 10 minutes.[3] According to the MTOs' own promotional material, these fees remained the same in 2008, i.e. around 10 per cent by WU and 7.5 per cent by MG per transferred amount (see also Karafolas and Konteos 2010: 968). However, migrants we interviewed reported that they paid fees between 10 per cent and 20 per cent for money they had sent with WU.

Despite the high cost, around one in ten of the survey respondents said that they received remittances through an MTO. This was a higher share than those using banks – as we shall see later. The 2005 IOM survey found a slightly higher share amongst migrants in Greece using MTOs – around 12 per cent (de Zwager *et al.* 2005: 31). In contrast, the BoA surveys of 2006 and 2008 mentioned earlier reported lower shares – around 5 per cent of their respondents (Frashëri 2007: 72; Rëmbeci 2009: 118).[4]

There are three main reasons why MTOs are preferred by our respondents. First, the speed and the reliability of transfers. Money sent through WU or MG is with the recipient within 10 minutes, or an hour at most, whilst only a few banks in Albania offer real-time transfers. The respondent households used the MTO channel especially if they needed money urgently, either because they were poor and had no resources to fall back on, or because a particular urgent need such as an illness or death had arisen. As one of our respondents put it, it was used when the transmitter wanted to be sure that the money would arrive 'absolutely' within the same day.

Second, the higher degree of accessibility for both migrants and their families was important. MTOs and their small-business partners operate longer working hours, which enables migrants to make transfers even after they finish their work for the day. Moreover, the wide geographical spread of their network of agents and outlets means that migrants and their families can send and receive money as close to where they live as possible. In this context, especially important are the partnerships with agents which operate in rural areas, such as with the national post office in both Albania and Greece (working with the WU), or exchange bureaus and newsagents for MG. For instance, a WU agent started operating in one of the study villages from mid-2008, whereas there were no banks in rural areas at this time.

Finally, the simplicity of procedures and lack of bureaucracy were seen as highly relevant to the particular living circumstances of migrants. MTOs usually require only an ID to make transfers, irrespective of migrants' legal status in the host country. In contrast, Greek banks often offer services – and certainly the least expensive ones – only to senders who hold an account with them. Such an account is usually possible only for those with a regular migration status, and many other additional documents are needed such as pay-slips from employers, income declarations, guarantees etc. (Karafolas and Konteos 2010; for Italy see Piperno 2005). Even when migrants have a legal status in the country, they may continue to work in the informal labour market, as we saw earlier, where pay-slips and other such documentation are impossible to obtain. This affects migrant women in particular, who work overwhelmingly in domestic and care services on an informal basis.

Especially for families living in extreme poverty in the villages such as the Roma and Evgjit, receiving money via an MTO ensured a much-needed regular income supply. For instance, most of our respondents would explain that there was no need to pay so much for the MTO transfer when the family in the village had enough to get by until the migrant returned home for visits. For Roma and Evgjit households, this is not the case. It appears thus that the poorest pay the higher prices. Others used MTOs when transfers were needed regularly, for instance when the migrant parents had left their very young children to be looked after by grandparents in the village, and sent small amounts each week in order to ensure that there was money to cover their needs at all times. MTOs were used especially in two other cases: when the migrant lived far away from Albania, such as in the islands near Turkey, and/or lived in small rural communities where relatives or people from the same area of origin were absent; and especially when this was combined with the undocumented status of the migrant. 'They live far away in Crete and are undocumented', said the elderly mother of a migrant son. Her son had been living in Greece with his wife for seven years, but since they did not have papers, they could not visit Albania. Furthermore, they did not have friends or acquaintances where they lived, leaving WU as the only possible option for sending their money. Although expensive, it ensured that the mother had a regular income each month, to look after her two young grandsons – the children of the migrant couple – who lived with her in the village.

Banks

The final transmission channel reported during our research was banks. However, results were not straightforward in that while the use of banks to remit to families in the villages was still limited, a higher share of respondents held bank accounts. In addition, in-depth interviews revealed higher use of banks to transfer larger sums for investment. Let us look at each of these elements in turn.

The household survey in the villages of origin found that only 2 per cent (six) of our respondents received remittances through banks, of whom only two used the debit card facility.[5] Several historical, psychological and practical reasons help explain this low use. First, despite the increased network and role of banks in the country, Albania remains a largely cash-based society. There were only a very few banks during the communist period: it was considered that, in an economic system which condemns surplus capital as the fruit of exploitation, their services are not essential to the populace. Opening a bank account then was highly bureaucratic and only a handful of privileged people had accounts for their savings; wages and all other transactions were in cash. The transition to neoliberal capitalism and a market economy was accompanied by reforms in the financial sector as well. In 1991 a two-tiered banking system was introduced, with the Bank of Albania designated as the central bank with supervising and overseeing powers over the activities of all second-tier commercial banks, as well as of the Micro-Finance Institutions (MFIs) and MTOs (Bitzenis and Nito 2006: 96). Gradually the national banks were privatised, whilst new private banks entered the market, mostly from abroad. By 2010 there were 16 commercial banks licensed to operate in the Albanian market, the majority foreign-owned; Greek banks have a significant presence. Yet, the Albanian banking system lags behind those in the wider Balkan region. By 2005 cash payments still accounted for 95 per cent of all retail transfers (Hernández-Coss *et al.* 2006: 11), while during 2009 almost 96 per cent of all bank transactions were simply cash withdrawals (BoA 2010: 101).

The second reason for the low use of banks is the legacy of the pyramid 'savings' schemes. As we saw in Chapter 3, these mushroomed during the early- and mid-1990s as a result of the underdeveloped official banking system in the country on the one hand, and the increasing need for capital in a rapidly expanding economy, on the other (Jarvis 2000). Interest rates of up to 50 per cent were offered but could not be sustained, and as the schemes collapsed in early 1997, half of the country's population went bankrupt. But the psychological scars of this occurrence have lasted longer than the material and monetary damage. It has been difficult to rebuild the trust in banks and the recent global financial crisis has not helped. Ironically, Albania was spared the woes of credit-based societies and the cash-based character of the economy helped it to weather the storm. However, its reliance on remittances – particularly from Greece – does not bode well, as we shall see in the following chapters.

A third factor has been the limited accessibility of these banks. While most of the population still lives in villages – although that has been rapidly changing due to large-scale internal migration – all banks are concentrated in urban areas. They are often perceived as highly bureaucratic, costly, inflexible and slow (Hernández-Coss *et al.* 2006; Kring 2007). Especially for migrants in Greece, the limited opening hours of banks are inconvenient, as migrants work well into the evening each weekday and often on Saturdays too.

Furthermore, as de Zwager *et al.* (2005) reported, until the mid-2000s banks had shown little interest in migrants and their remittances. However, this has been changing, due in part to increased awareness about the lucrative remittance market. The various research and actions from the Albanian government and international organisations such as IOM and the World Bank that followed IOM's 2005 research have certainly had their impact. By the end of 2008 the cost and time of money transfers through banks had been reduced significantly, while products tailored to migrants' needs were on the rise. For instance, the IOM research found that it took up to a month to transfer funds between countries and the costs were 'relatively high' (de Zwager *et al.* 2005: 27). Later DFID-funded research concluded that improvements had been made and the transfer time had been reduced to between two and five working days (PBI 2005: 10–11). Another IOM-led study also reported that transfer times had fallen to between two and four working days (Kring 2007). Our research revealed that, by 2008, various banks that serve the Greece-Albania 'remittance corridor' had reduced transfer times to two to three working days, and, for some products within the same bank, even instantaneously. As for the cost, our material suggests that these have also reduced drastically with some banks offering transfers of up to €12,500 for just a €1 fee! In addition, various banks have designed financial products targeting migrants and their families, such as mortgages linked to remittances, loans, micro-credits for businesses, joint debit cards for members of the same family who live in Greece and Albania, and so on.

The majority of the research participants who had used banks had experienced a significant improvement in the service, which they rated now as uncomplicated, more flexible in requirements for documentation, and professional. Access to banks in Greece remained problematic for undocumented migrants, however. Although we noted reports that having a regular status in Greece was no longer a requirement for opening bank accounts, the issue for undocumented migrants remained the inaccessibility of their money if they were caught by the immigration authorities and deported back to Albania.

The worldwide campaign to 'bank the unbanked' has reached Albania too (cf. Orozco 2007). Increased awareness and falling costs due to better competition have encouraged more Albanians to start using banks. Thus, our second key finding in this context is that despite banks' limited use for remittance transfers, a higher share of participants had accounts. Almost 50 respondents or 14 per cent of the survey sample responded that they held their savings in a bank account; whilst seven respondents or 2 per cent of our survey had received a business loan from a bank. Of both these categories, only one family had a savings bank account *and* a loan and was thus counted twice in these statistics. The IOM (de Zwager *et al.* 2005: 31–2) survey reported some interesting data on remittance households (sending and receiving) cross-tabulated with bank account possession, and broken down by region in Albania. For the Korçë area, those who received remittances had a much higher bank account prevalence compared to those who did not – around 40 per cent and 4.5 per cent respectively. The situation amongst migrants in Greece was much better; 74 per cent of the IOM respondents residing in Greece held bank accounts. Although we cannot provide figures on the latter, given that our research in Greece comprised a statistically small sample, this pattern was confirmed in the in-depth interviews. However, bank accounts of migrant couples were often held in the name of the husband. This is affected by the nature of work that men and women respectively do in Greece, as discussed in the previous chapter. While most Albanian migrant women receive their wages from domestic work in cash, their male counterparts who work in the more formal sectors of the economy are sent theirs via bank transfers. But it also reflects gender relations within Albanian society, certain features of which are reclaimed, if not reinforced, through migration.

The final, but most significant finding in this sub-section on banks, comes from in-depth interviews in the villages and particularly with migrants themselves in Thessaloniki. This is that banks may not be used to transfer the smaller amounts of €50–€200 remitted every two to three months, but they are overwhelmingly preferred to hand-carry and other methods for larger sums. Often the transfer takes place from the account the migrant held in Greece to another account he (they are indeed usually men) held with the corresponding bank or branch in Albania. Consequently, such transfers were not captured by our survey since they did not pass through the 'hands' of family members in Albania. The migrant was always the manager of these funds. Their significance is not only in the sums transferred – up to €100,000 – but also in their use: it was reported that these monies were invested in property (e.g. buying flats or building houses in urban areas), as starting capital for a business, saved in banks, or passed on as loans to relatives who needed capital for their businesses. In the latter case, the money was transferred directly to the account of the relative. Here are two illustrative quotes. The second one explains how the various remittance transfer channels are used and for what purposes.

> I have personally used the bank [for transfers] to buy a home there [in Tirana], so I sent the money by bank… This investment cost me around $100,000 [€80,000]… The transfer didn't cost me anything because I had the money in a bank account here [in Greece] and I sent the money to the account I have with the same bank there and withdrew it in Tirana [Berti, 47, migrant in Thessaloniki].

> I give my parents €100 every month, not because they need it, but because I fulfill my [filial] duty… We are used to the same traditional way [laughs], put the money in the pocket and take it to *mother* every month, or send it through relatives and friends, as you know… Whereas for larger sums I send them by bank. It's a good thing that the ABA [American Bank of Albania] has opened a branch here [in Thessaloniki] as well, which has lower transfer costs for money… For instance it cost me €15–€20 to transfer around €5,000–€10,000 recently through ABA. Whereas at NBG [National Bank of Greece] which has been one of the first banks to have branches both in Greece as well as Korçë and Tirana, you paid something like €40 per transfer… I have only used WU for very special occasions when I needed the money to arrive in Albania *absolutely within the same day* [Gimi, 30, migrant in Thessaloniki].

Two things regarding the gendered aspects of these quotes can be highlighted in conclusion. The first is that the interviewees – the remittance-senders – are men, who constituted the overwhelming majority of senders in our survey. In fact only four of the 'principal remitters' nominated by the survey respondents (remittance-receivers) were women – hence 98.9 per cent of remittance-senders were men. The second point to make is that, where smaller sums are concerned, they may be consigned to the migrants' mother rather than his father, as the former is the one who manages the daily household economy.

Amounts and Frequency of Remittance Sending

More than half of the survey respondents received remittances every three to six months (Table 13). This is a clear pattern of remitting if we combine it with the times when migrants visit their family members in Albania – usually three times a year, as mentioned earlier in this chapter. The sub-group of seasonal migrants who work in Greece for up to six months a year is also included here; most of them bring their remittances when they return home at the end of the working season. The next most important group is that of migrants who remit once a year. This pattern may reflect the maturing of the Albanian migration in Greece, whereby migrants and their families have settled there, and only their older parents have remained in the village – hence fewer visits per year and less remitting. Around 10 per cent of respondents reported that they receive remittances as and when needed by the household in Albania.

However, even when one category of frequency was chosen to represent the reply, in fact the remitting pattern was not always clear-cut as frequencies varied from month to month, and from year to year. Frequency also depended on the income of migrants and their cost of living, as well as other unexpected expenses. For instance, in the month when migrants have to pay their quarterly bills, they may not remit at all. And of course, there is also the payment for all the paperwork for their stay and work permit, which is a substantial drain on migrants' earnings.

A gendered breakdown of the data reveals that households administered by wives receive remittances significantly more frequently than the other types of household (Table 14). Although the wives also receive the majority of money every three to six months, like the other household types (generalised in the table as 'not-wife'), unlike them they receive remittances once a month and every two months nearly twice as much as the other group.

Much like the frequency, the amounts sent also vary per family; they depend on the situation within households, and they change over time. Factors which influence sums remitted include whether the migrant is single or married and with children, whether the family is with him/her in Greece, on their legal status in the host country, on the type of job the migrant does and the earnings the migrant household has, and not least on the orientation of the family towards a future in Albania or Greece.

The survey data show that the sums remitted per year from Greece to rural households in Albania continue to be significant. The estimated total

Table 13 Remitting frequency

Frequency	Count	%
Twice a month	3	0.9
Once a month	27	7.7
Every two months	31	8.9
Every three to six months	194	55.4
Once a year	58	16.5
Less than once a year	2	0.6
As needed by the household	35	10.0
Total	350	100.0

Source: Authors' survey

Table 14 Cross-tabulation of frequency of sending remittances with remittance administrator

How often sends remittances	Wife	Not Wife	Total
Twice a month	2 (2.0%)	1 (0.4%)	3 (0.9%)
Once a month	13 (13.0%)	14 (5.6%)	27 (7.7%)
Every 2 months	12 (12.0%)	19 (7.6%)	31 (8.9%)
Every 3 to 6 months	61 (61.0%)	133 (53.2%)	194 (55.4%)
Once a year	3 (3.0%)	55 (22.0%)	58 (16.6%)
Less than once a year	0 (0.0%)	2 (0.8%)	2 (0.6%)
As needed by the household	9 (9.0%)	26 (10.4%)	35 (10.0%)
Total	100 (100.0%)	250 (100.0%)	350 (100.0%)

Chi-square (df 6) 26.05, $p< .001$

Source: Authors' survey

amount of remittances per year that the survey respondents receive stands at almost €1 million, with an average of around €2,600 per household. This figure is slightly higher than the average assessed by the IOM survey – €2,173 per household received in the Korçë region in 2004 (de Zwager *et al.* 2005: 42). Whilst this may point towards an increase in remittances over the last four years (when most research had predicted an opposite trend), the discrepancy is partly accounted for by inflation; or it may be due to methodology, not least the 20 per cent share of remittance-oriented seasonal workers in our sample versus none in the IOM study. Indeed, around 60 per cent of our survey respondents sent up to €2,000 per year, and 80 per cent sent up to €4,000 per year (Table 15). In another survey carried out in 2007 – this time amongst Albanian migrants settled in the Emilia-Romagna region of Italy and originating from Tirana and Elbasan in Albania – an average of €2,400 was sent to each recipient family (Colleo and Perrelli Branca 2008: 11). Although remittances from Italy are estimated to be higher than from Greece (Rëmbeci 2009: 122), our findings and this study may reflect particular 'remittance corridors' that might be somewhat different from the general country-wide trend.

A more detailed examination of our data by recipient group reveals interesting results. The smallest annual amount remitted is €50 whilst the largest sum is €12,000, both of which are remitted to parents (Table 16). This means that this group of remitters includes migrants (sons) who send some 'coffee' money (euphemism for small amounts) to their elderly parents whilst they are focused on life with their nuclear families in Greece, as well as young single men, who intend to have these remittances saved for the creation of their own family in the future. The average amount of remittances sent to wives (€3,150) is much higher than for the other groups (€2,500), for fairly obvious reasons. Sums sent to other relatives such as brothers, sisters and grandparents are, as expected, the lowest. Gedeshi *et al.* (2003a: 33) came to similar conclusions in their study of eight rural communes in the Korçë region. They found that emigrants whose wife and children lived in Albania sent an average of €3,740 a year, more than twice the amount remitted to older parents at €1,440 a year. The above finding is also corroborated if we compare wife-headed households with other remittance-recipients (Table 17). We observe that in the latter group of households remittances show a higher concentration in the sums of up to €2,000; when the wife is the administrator, however, remittance sums show more variety and are mainly concentrated in the higher amounts.

Table 15 Frequency distribution of categories of yearly remittances

Remitted sums per year (in Euros)	Count	%
less than 1,000	66	18.9
1,000–2,000	139	39.7
2,001–4,000	76	21.7
4,001–6,000	44	12.6
6,001–8,000	19	5.4
8,001 or more	6	1.7

Source: Authors' survey

Table 16 Descriptive statistics for remittance amount per year – entire sample and by remittance administrator

Sample	Count	Mean	Std. Dev	Min	Max
Entire sample	350	2,595.8	2,144.2	50	12,000
Remit admin is wife	100	3,151.5	1,973.6	250	9,000
Remit admin is father	143	2,518.4	2,115.9	150	10,000
Remit admin is mother	98	2,226.0	2,325.1	50	12,000
Remit admin is 'other household member'	9	1,677.8	868.2	800	3,500

Amounts are in Euros.

Source: Authors' survey

Table 17 Cross-tabulation of remittance amount per year with remittance administrator

Remitted sums per year (in Euros)	Wife	Not Wife	Total
Less than 1,000	5 (5.0%)	61 (24.4%)	66 (18.9%)
1,000–2,000	35 (35.0%)	104 (41.6%)	139 (39.7%)
2,001–4,000	38 (38.0%)	38 (15.2%)	76 (21.7%)
4,001–6,000	14 (14.0%)	30 (12.0%)	44 (12.6%)
6,001 or more	8 (8.0%)	17 (6.8%)	25 (7.1%)
Total	100 (100.0%)	250 (100.0%)	350 (100.0%)

Chi-square (df 4) 32.51, $p<.001$.

Source: Authors' survey

Gendered Patterns of Remittance Sending and Receiving

As our findings so far have shown, the process of remitting in the Albanian context is a very gendered one. This is partly conditioned by the patriarchal nature of Albanian society, which in turn has shaped migration patterns and continues to shape relations within transnational spaces and households. In this part of the chapter we turn our attention to a very important issue, but one which has received little attention in research so far – the profiles of remittance senders and receivers. The profiles of the various sender–receiver dyads that we set out below may seem unduly detailed and repetitive in format. But, in a sense, this is precisely the point. Our purpose is to accurately illustrate the many varieties that these pairings take, in order to challenge the way that so many remittance studies overlook the micro-dynamics of intra-family transactions. As we have pointed out more explicitly in a recent paper (King and Vullnetari 2010), looking at whether women or men are 'better' remitters, or whether one sex sends, or receives, or uses more wisely, more or less remittance amounts, are not the right questions. The gender dynamics of remittance transfer need to be unpacked in detail in order to understand precisely what is going on.

We start by focusing on remittance senders – first men, then women. In the next chapter, we pick up the remittances at the receiving end and examine how they contribute to the development of the migrant-sending areas.

Male Remitters

From the long-term migrant to his wife and children in the village.

In this first type, the family is nuclear with young or teenage children. The father will be working in Greece and visiting home regularly, whereas the wife will be living in the village looking after the children and the household. Remittances sent to this type of household are amongst the highest in our survey. Here follows a typical example. Flutur (47) lives in the village with her two teenage children, while her husband works in Greece. He visits three or four times a year and usually brings his remittances home with him. Flutur explains:

> It's about €500 per month… Then it depends how things go, he may bring it once every two or three months, sometimes once a month, sometimes he sends the money with someone else. But that was more in the beginning, because now he brings it when he visits us.

From the seasonal migrant to his wife and children in the village.
This is a similar type of household to the one above, except that the husband works in Greece only seasonally – up to six months in a year. During this time he may visit once or twice. He generally brings his money with him upon return, but if the economic situation of the family is poor, he also sends it via friends or MTOs.

A significant share of the villages' male population engages in seasonal migration to Greece, usually working in agriculture. They are often composed of those who are not able to obtain longer-term permits for Greece, and those who do not want to go through the tedious and uncertain process of obtaining these permits. The majority of these migrants have been working in Greece since the early 1990s, going back-and-forth. After the 1998 regularisation they decided to keep their base in the village and continue working there in farming, or run a small business. However, remittances from Greece continued to be a lifeline and such seasonal work migration provided the only avenue to combine both aspects of a transnational livelihood strategy.

Seasonal migrants go to Greece following two different routes: documented and undocumented. The first one involves a process of applying through the Greek consulate in Korçë where the migrant can obtain a single-entry visa valid only for one month, once the application for migrant workers by a potential Greek employer has passed through the lengthy route of the Greek bureaucracy (for a detailed description of the procedures, see Maroukis 2008). Upon the migrant worker's arrival in Greece, the visa is then extended to the maximum of six months, allowing him to work there. These permits are tied to employers, i.e. the migrant is only allowed to work for the sponsoring farmer. However, when there is no work in this farm, he may go to work elsewhere, on neighbouring farms and even in better-paid urban jobs, provided that the sponsoring farmer consents to this. Most seasonal migrants in this group work in Veria, north-western Greece, in the apple and peach orchards, which are a speciality of this region. Only a few of them moved to work elsewhere when there was no work in their primary arrival area. Many did not have the necessary networks to help them find a job or provide accommodation during these short periods of time. As such, they tended to return home before the six months were over.

The undocumented route is taken by the poorer families who do not have the necessary capital to pay for the visa process, the necessary network of friends and relatives who can find sponsoring farmers and help with other obstacles in the process, and who may be discriminated against because of their ethnicity such as the Roma and Evgjit. Consequently, working conditions are more precarious and the pay is lower for this group, which consists primarily of the above-named minorities. Most of them walk over the mountain to reach the Greek villages of the Prespa Lake area near the Albanian border. There they are usually employed by elderly Greeks in their small family farms, which often cultivate beans. The migrants may work for one or two months, or until the Greek immigration authorities apprehend them and deport them back to Albania.

Temporary migration has been recently promoted by international development agencies as a solution to the migration–development issue, as the archetype of a 'triple-win' situation. Cloaked under the buzz-word of 'circular migration', this movement is primarily aimed at addressing the needs of countries in the Global North for cheap labour in certain sectors of the economy such as agriculture, without the strings (of integration) attached. As target migrants, the individuals involved are presumed to remit or bring back home the vast majority of their earnings, supplying these origin countries with much-needed exchange capital. Migrants themselves also win because they improve their economic situation and are also not separated for long from their families. Or so the argument goes. This 'perfect immigrant', to quote Hahamovitch (2003), fits the wish of the Global North to 'open their markets [for managed work] without opening their borders'. However, as Hennebry and Preibisch (2009) show through their analysis of temporary programmes in Canada, where the majority of 'circular migrants' are rural Mexicans, migrants are far from clear winners.

Back in Albania, we also see that earnings of temporary migrants are amongst the lowest and the work is precarious and casual – they do not work every day and often work only three to four months a year. The pay is based on the number of hours worked. It is therefore very difficult for a seasonal migrant to be able to bring back good money. They earn around €18–€20 for a 10–12 hour working day, or around €350 per month. Overall, they may bring back €1,500; some, however, manage up to €3,000. Usually, the migrant will send money back home via friends, often about €150 or €200 once a month and then bring the rest of the money with him when he returns at the end of the working period.

> The money, [he brings it] when he comes himself at the end… He brings around €2,000 [Monda, 45, living in the village].

> He [her husband] used to go to Greece without documents, then for the last two years he has been going through work visas. Last year he stayed six months, and the year before that only five months… Last year he brought home €2,800… He sent some once, I can't remember how much it was, through C… [who is a local businessman and imports from Greece]… We didn't pay him

> because he is a relative… He wasn't earning a lot, only €25 per day… He worked in agriculture, and the Greek employer would also give him food, but he had other expenses: paying for his cigarettes because he smoked, buying a telephone card to call us, or perhaps even a beer when he went out with his friends… So the money gets spent… He brought less money the first year, because he only stayed five months then, and he earned less, about €20 per day. I think he brought home about €2,200 then, all at the end [Ana, 44, living in the village].

From the migrant to his wife, children and parents.

The receiver is usually the father, except when the latter is very ill or has died; in these cases the recipient is the mother. She may also involve the migrant's wife in the administration of this money. The migrant's wife and children may be staying behind for two main reasons. First, because the migrant is unable to arrange family reunification with her and the children – he may have casual work, or may not earn the required income. But the wife may also remain behind in order to look after her husband's elderly parents who are in need of care, especially when he is the youngest son. Here are two examples of remittances sent to multi-generation recipient households:

> My husband left as soon as the borders opened. My kids were young then, I was 27 years old and I had two old women at home – my mother-in-law who was in her 70s and my husband's aunt who was in her 80s; she [the latter] was suffering from Alzheimers… We had to sacrifice, we needed money… I then went two-three times to work in Greece with my husband and once we took the children with us; we worked and they went to school… But I had to return because my aunt's health deteriorated and then eventually she died. Then we went back to Greece again with my husband and returned after a while. I had my mother-in-law to look after, who could I leave her with [she is now in her early 90s]?… My husband continues to work there [in Greece] [Besnike, 47 years returnee from Greece].

> There are four of us in the family. I am the household head, then there is my wife (67), our daughter-in-law (22) and our granddaughter [from a deceased daughter] of 14… Of course remittances [from his son, 30] are important for us. The only other income we have is from our pensions – 15,000 lek a month [€130] and subsistence farming… He sends €300, €500, €1000 every three months, it depends… [Selim, 71, father of a migrant son].

From the migrant son to his parents, when the son is single.
Usually, it is the father who receives the remittances, unless he has died, in which case he is replaced by the mother. The household may include other unmarried sisters and brothers of the migrant. Remittances from single young men can be quite substantial, since they usually live in cheaper and shared accommodation with other single men or families of relatives, and do not have a family of their own in Greece. However, there are also occasions when all the money is spent abroad on renewing the staying permit, as well as on other outlets such as gambling, going out with friends and paying for sex, leaving very little or nothing to be sent back home. There are also occasions when the son may be in prison in Greece, for one or other reason, in which case there are no remittances.

> I don't send the money by post or any other means, I go there [to Albania] myself. I go there once a month and take €1,000 or maximum €1,500 each time [Genci, 23, migrant in Thessaloniki].

> In the beginning I used to send home almost all my earnings from Greece. But as time went by and I became older this has changed. Now I send around €200–€300 every two months. The rest I put in my bank account… My other brother who lives in Athens sends money as well… I would send it via WU and when my sister was at university in Korçë, she would receive the money… Now I send it through friends and they give it to my father [Andrea, 24, migrant in Thessaloniki].

From the migrant son and his wife to his parents.
The sender is usually the son and the receiver is usually the father, except when the latter has died; in which case the recipient is the mother. When the migrant son and his wife live in Greece together with their children, the sums sent to his parent(s) are drastically reduced, and become very infrequent (see also Duval and Wolff 2010: 84). It is recognised at this stage that the migrant's primary responsibilities of care and economic support are towards his own nuclear family in Greece. The parents will be sent what can be spared. Furthermore, living expenses in Greece increase as the family grows and expands, children attend school and grow up. Moreover, the cost of living in Greece has become notoriously expensive in recent years. In contrast, the living cost of elderly parents in Albania is minimal – besides the basics such as food, utility bills and health, their other most important expense is taking care of life-cycle and kinship events for occasions such as births, weddings, ill-health and funerals. We discuss these in more detail when we analyse the use of remittances in the next

chapter. Remittances are brought back when the migrants visit their parents – usually three times a year – but they may also be sent with other siblings, relatives or friends, especially if these live in the same city. The sums are around €100–€150 each time.

From migrant brother to another sibling.
We came across four cases from the questionnaire survey in which the brother remitted to his siblings – to a brother in three cases and to his sister in the fourth case. We say a little about each of these cases in order to illustrate the variable nature of the reality of remittance dynamics. In the first, both brothers were single, in their early 40s; one lived in Greece and the other in the village. The one in the village lived in a house which was uninhabitable, with the roof and walls caving in. Both brothers spent most of their time drunk, and it was thanks to some relatives they had in Greece that the brother who lived there managed to find any work at all and earned some money. Some of this was sent to his brother in the village. He worked as a shepherd and remitted around €800 per year.

In two further cases, a married brother lived in the village with his wife and children, and received remittances from a younger brother working in Greece. Their parents died when they were young and they had tried to help one another – one by offering a family setting to the other, and the other by helping through remittances.

In the last case, the brother lived with his wife in Greece, and remitted to his sister in the village. After the death of her husband she had moved back to her parental home where she lived with her teenage daughter and elderly parents. As the brother is the youngest son, he and his wife are responsible for the financial and day-to-day care of the elderly parents. A compromise has been reached that the daily care is taken over by the widowed sister in exchange for her and her teenage daughter living in the parental home and receiving support through remittances from the brother and his wife. Another brother lived with his family in Greece and helped occasionally, but the youngest one was the principal remitter. The sister received between €3,000 and €4,000 per year from the brothers.

It is clear from these examples that motivations to remit are complex. Following Lucas and Stark (1985), remitting in the latter three cases is a perfect example of *enlightened self-interest.*

From migrant parents to their children.
As mentioned in the previous chapter, some poor Roma and Evgjit parents migrated together leaving their children behind. They could not afford or otherwise be able to obtain documents, which left them with the only

other option of walking over the mountain to Greece. They worked in bean farms in border villages of the Lake Prespa area for two or three months, during which time their eldest teenage child was left in charge of the household and other younger siblings. When grandparents or other close relatives lived nearby, they helped the children in their everyday tasks, and on how to spend the meagre remittances sent by the parents. The remittance sender was usually the father.

From the migrant grandson to his sister and elderly grandmother.
We came across only two such cases – both in female-headed households – when the principal remitter was the grandson. The household consisted of an elderly widowed grandmother and two or three teenage grandchildren from a son or daughter who had died. The remaining parent of the children had re-married and lived with the new family in Greece. In both cases the teenage grandsons had emigrated to Greece, but lived separately from their fathers, although the latter supported them to find jobs etc. The granddaughters lived with the grandmothers in the village. Although some remittances flowed from the grandsons and other older migrant sons, both families lived in poverty, their only other source of income being the grandmothers' meagre old-age pension of 5,000 lek [€45] a month. Both granddaughters were reaching 18 and one was already engaged to a man from a coastal town, while match-making talks were ongoing in the case of the second. Marriage was seen as the only option which offered the young women protection and security, especially if the grandmothers fell ill or died.

Within the *gendered geographies of power* framework these young women are 'effectively imprisoned' by power, first in their own families, then upon marriage in their husband's household (Mahler and Pessar 2001). Their social location – near the bottom of power hierarchies within the family – is just as important as gender in producing such forms of gendered power relations.

Female Remitters

From the migrant to her husband and children in the village.
We came across only two cases in our research when the wife had emigrated and she was the principal breadwinner supporting her husband and children in the village through her remittances. The work of the women in Greece involved a mixture of farm work and care services in rural areas of south-western Greece. This pattern of migration and remittance transfer is absolutely atypical of rural Albania. Earlier IOM/ILO (Kring 2007) and BoA (Frashëri 2007: 72) surveys in Albania

both reported that less than 1 per cent of their sample comprised wives who had migrated and remitted to their husbands. Most of the recipients in these other surveys, however, lived in the coastal towns of Durrës and Vlorë.

From the migrant daughter to her parents when she is single.
Once again such cases are very rare as independent female migration from rural areas continues to be frowned upon, especially for young single women. We came across only two such cases in our research. We describe each one in turn.

In the first case, the single daughter was 25 years old, had completed eight years of compulsory education and worked as a sales assistant in a supermarket in Greece. She remitted €200 each month to her family in Albania through paid couriers, and when she visited herself. The recipient was the mother, indicating the existence of parallel 'female remittance channels' identified in Smith's (2009) research in another part of Albania.

In the second case, already mentioned briefly in the previous chapter, the single daughter aged 26 lived in Greece with her younger sister of 22 and brother, 18. She was the first to migrate and her sister and brother joined her later in that order; their parents and grandmother remain in the village. Although possessing a nursing degree from Albania, the eldest daughter worked in a factory in Greece as her qualifications are not recognised there. Both her sister and brother worked in typically gendered employment sectors – she in a garment factory, he in construction. Between the three of them they remitted €2,000 a year which the eldest daughter gives in instalments to their father when they visit their family three or four times a year.

From the migrant daughter and her husband to her parents.
Married daughters bring small sums during visits to their own parents in the village. These are labelled as 'presents' or 'just for a coffee'. According to the Albanian patrilineal customs, daughters are not required to support their parents after marriage – this remains the duty of sons, especially the youngest son. As such, a daughter's remittances are considered as temporary or as a one-off gift (Smith 2009). The questionnaire survey did not record sufficient information on this remittance typology, partly because it was constructed to solicit information on the primary remitter, and less so for other remitters. However, the in-depth interviews revealed a complex web of relations and negotiations about these particular types of transfers. We illustrate with two examples, starting with Irena (37). She lives in Thessaloniki with her husband and two young sons. She was not

working at the time the research took place as she was looking after her new-born baby, but she used to work in a pizzeria. Whilst her husband has been working in Greece since the early 1990s – first in agriculture and then in construction – it is only in the last five years that Irena has joined him there. Prior to that she continued to live in the village to look after his frail parents, until they died of old age. Thus, there are no remittances to be sent in that direction. On the other hand, some money – around €20 each time – is sent now and again to Irena's parents. They live with her brother and his wife according to tradition, and therefore Irena's money is considered as a present, or as she put it, 'just for a coffee'. She explains:

> So it's not worth sending that [€20] through the banks. I usually send it with my nephew, or my sister, or my brother, or my brother-in-law, whoever goes there, or when we visit… When I was working, besides money we would buy them clothes, we took them food when we visited etc… My sister [who is also in Greece] helps them much more than I do, because she works herself. Her children are much older than mine and they also work.

Unlike in this example where Irena's remittances to her own parents were based on largely altruistic motives – she will not inherit from them and has no social obligation to support them – in the following case remitting is motivated by enlightened self-interest (Lucas and Stark 1985). Here, the married daughter sends higher remittances to her parents because they are looking after her young daughter of four. She was in her early 40s and had been living with her husband in Greece for over 10 years, working as a domestic cleaner, while he was employed in construction. She brought €1,000 each time on her visits to the family during the Christmas and New Year period, and in August. She did have a younger brother, but as he was still studying at the local university, he was not – yet – expected to support the family financially. There was only this one instance in our questionnaire survey where the married daughter was the principal remitter.

From the migrant sister and her husband to another sibling.
We came across at least three such cases during our research. In the first instance the sister and her husband helped her brother with a sum of €500. The money was sent via WU from her husband to her brother, thus reinforcing the male remittance channel. In the second instance the migrant couple helped with finances and machinery to start her brother's business in the village in Albania. The sums involved had been significant.

In this case, the money, which was a loan, was sent through the bank, whilst the machinery was bought in Greece and transported to Albania. Alket, 42, the remitter's husband, explains:

> When her brother called my wife and asked her for help with his business, she didn't tell me about this for four days. She tried to beat around the bush, saying: how would you feel if we helped my brother, because he is in difficulty [*ka hall*]? This is where we had some friction. Because I am planning to buy a house here [in Greece]. And the moment when I find the right house and I will need the money here to pay for it, I will not have enough money. They [his brother-in-law and his family] are not able to repay me back the debt. I am not saying this because I don't love these people, I love them, but when I will be in difficulty, then we might quarrel and become enemies. You will be filled with hatred after that [the non-repayment of debt] because you will be let down… So he knows I have been here for such a long time, and we have put some money aside, and he asked for help… So I got together with my other two brothers-in-law [who also live in Thessaloniki] and bought the machinery he needed for cutting marble [to make fireplaces, headstones etc]… We paid cash… they cost €9,000. We then booked a van to take them to him, which cost another €600, and finally I sent him €15,000 through the bank as capital. I sent that to his bank account…

Note how the gendered roles in private and public spheres are played out. Negotiations within the family reflect the wives' strong and decisive role as they try to win over their husbands to help their brother in Albania. Once this has taken place, it is the men who do the actual act of physically transferring the money or buying the machinery.

Finally, in the third case of this typology, the poorer sister in the village was supported by her two married sisters in Athens. This help was mostly in-kind, although very small amounts of money had been sent to her now and then.

We did not come across other types of female remitters, but some of the stakeholder interviewees in Greece brought to our attention the existence of some older divorced or widowed women who remit to their children and grandchildren in Albania. One example was given of a migrant woman who remitted to her son in Albania who himself worked as a nurse, but was unable to sustain a decent living from his salary in the public sector. We suspect these remitting mothers are very much in the minority. None of the BoA or IOM surveys we cited earlier identified this category of senders in their findings.

Table 18 displays the general pattern of remitters – overwhelmingly males. Table 19 sets out some of the more unusual remittance dyads which our data revealed and which we have explored in this section of the chapter.

Table 18 Principal remittance senders

Remitter	Count	%
Son	238	68.0
Husband	100	28.6
Brother	4	1.1
Father	3	0.9
Daughter	3	0.9
Grandson	1	0.3
Sister	1	0.3
Total	350	100.0

Source: Authors' survey

Table 19 Unusual patterns of remitting

Remitter	Recipient
Father	Son
Father	Daughter
Daughter	Father
Daughter	Mother
Brother	Brother
Brother	Sister
Sister	Sister
Grandson	Grandmother
Wife	Husband

Source: Authors' survey

Conclusion

This chapter has revealed very interesting and important findings, some of which are similar to previous research while others chart new territory. One thing can be said with certainty: that the relationship between senders and receivers of remittances within transnational households, and their reasons for choosing one particular remitting channel over another, are complex and multifaceted. The combination of qualitative and quantitative data gathering and analysis has brought forth this complexity of relationships not only between genders, but also between generations and within them.[6] Although there is a dominance of men in these relations – as senders of remittances when young and as receivers of remittances when older – women's position is for certain far from straightforward. Whilst they are by definition the receivers of remittances in nuclear households when their husbands are working abroad, they are not far behind men when their sons send them remittances.

Most of these remittances continued to be sent informally, although the use of banks has been on the increase, especially for large sums. We shall discuss policies later, in Chapter 7, but it is worth mentioning here that there is increased awareness in the banking sector of the potential of remittances as good business. Competition and this re-orientation have brought benefits for migrants and their families in terms of lower transfer costs and time, as well as better and more services tailored to this target group. Considered historically, over the last 20 years things have changed and improved significantly: transfer channels, sums, uses, not least household composition and therefore also remitting patterns.

6

REMITTANCES AND DEVELOPMENT

This chapter follows closely on the previous one. Now, though, we take the story one step further by building on the remitting patterns discussed in the previous chapter, and extending the analysis to include various facets of development deriving from the inflow of remittances. We consider development as a process which includes social and human well-being, besides the traditional economic growth indicators.[1] We start by discussing the uses of financial remittances, highlighting a number of observations specific to our study which are often overlooked in the mainstream literature on remittances and development. Here, we pay particular attention to well-being and social development. We then continue with a consideration of non-monetary remittances, namely socio-political, technological and in-kind transfers. Finally, building also on the previous chapter, we analyse the effects these various types of remittances have on gender relations within transnational households, as well as on communities of origin in Albania.

Uses of Financial Remittances

From a development point of view, the way in which monetary remittances are used is perhaps even more important than how much is sent or how often (Nikas and King 2005). Our survey results on remittance uses – presented in Table 20 – are generally self-explanatory. We can easily observe that the vast majority of families use them to cover their daily living expenses, as well as to improve their living conditions, particularly through better accommodation and purchase of household goods (see also Illustrations 5 and 6). Such a finding is very much in line with previous studies on remittances in Albania (see Colleo and Perrelli Branca 2008; De Soto *et al.* 2002; de Zwager *et al.* 2005; Duval and Wolff 2010; Frashëri 2007; Gedeshi *et al.* 2003a; King and Vullnetari 2003: 48; Kring 2007; Nikas and King 2005; Rëmbeci 2009). However, we want to single out a number of observations for further comment.

Table 20 Principal uses of remittances: percentages of respondents citing each category

Category of use in rank order		%
1.	Current household expenditures (food, clothing, utilities etc.)	95.0
2.	Life-stage events (weddings, births, funerals, religious celebrations etc.)	82.0
3.	House improvement (new dwelling, repair of existing one)	55.4
4.	Purchase of household goods (furniture, electrical appliances, small generators to substitute failing electrical supply)	55.4
5.	Medical expenses (medicines, doctors' fees)	54.3
6.	Investment in farming	33.7
7.	Contributions to social security to ensure pension rights	30.9
8.	Savings for household needs, such as health emergencies	23.7
9.	Education of young family members	22.9
10.	Paying back debts unrelated to migration (informal borrowing from friends, credit from shops, loans from banks to finance business investments such as farm improvements)	15.1
11.	Paying back migration-related debts (visas, smugglers etc.)	12.3
12.	Leisure and holidays	6.9

Source: Authors' survey

Life-Cycle Events

Survey respondents seem to place a high importance on life-stage events, which rank second in the table. In the literature cited in the previous paragraph, much of which reports the results of earlier surveys and qualitative generalisations, life-stage events have lower-ranked importance. However, our survey results may not come as a surprise when contextual factors are considered. First, our respondents live in rural areas, where traditional social and cultural norms remain important for families and individuals. Observing such events means not only strengthening one's social network, but also one's social status in the home society.[2] Second, experiences of poverty include social elements as well as economic ones (Tahiraj 2007). Escaping poverty means not only feeding and clothing oneself, but also being able to afford to organise and participate in such life-cycle events – the contrary would result in social isolation. An Evgjit father of a migrant son put it this way during a discussion we were having with him and members of his family in one of the villages:

> ... you need to be able to follow these things [*të hyra të dala* – relatives' visits and life-cycle events], otherwise you bring shame on

> your family [*të ka syri turp*]. It's not just about eating and drinking, it's about paying someone respect… Poverty isolates you from others around you (Dane, 53).

Third, as Albania has been slowly incorporated into the global consumerist culture, events such as weddings are more than just about celebration – they are opportunities to display one's wealth. Often migrants sacrifice a great deal while abroad – where they are often placed in the lower ranks of host societies performing the least qualified jobs and facing social exclusion – in order to retain or gain higher social status in origin communities. This '*status paradox of migration*' as Nieswand (2008: 189–94, cited in Hemming 2009) has coined it, is analysed by Hemming in the Albanian context. The latter argues that the act of displaying wealth is a way for 'the underpaid construction workers and waiters, assembly-line workers and fruit and vegetable pickers' to escape their grim lives in their host countries and create an inflated reality in Albania which gives them status and prestige (Hemming 2009: 584).

Leisure

In the migration–development literature using remittances for leisure is generally considered as 'conspicuous consumption' or an 'unproductive' use of such transfers. Instead, we have chosen not to use a 'Northern' lens here and thus refrain from making such narrow economically-oriented judgements. Remittances are private transfers and we agree with Guarnizo (2003) that the choices that migrants and their families make are rational, given their personal and family circumstances and the broader social and cultural structures in their home country. Moreover, is the opportunity to enjoy leisure time and activities not one of the ultimate goals of well-being, especially important after months and years of family separation? If families and individuals manage to achieve this, we ought to consider their migratory projects as successful, rather than judgementally scorning them for displaying 'irrational' behaviour.

In our rural areas of research around 7 per cent of survey respondents reported using their remittances for this purpose, which often involved going to a restaurant for a meal with the family during the migrant's visits in the village, or spending some holiday time by the coast in Albania. Such leisure activities (quite modest, to be sure) are related to increased affluence through remittances, which has in some ways re-shaped power positions and inequality within these rural communities, where some are now accessing 'privileges' that only a handful had been able to enjoy in earlier years (for similar findings in Morocco, see de Haas 2007a).

Debts

In contrast to the small group who use remittances for leisure, another group of people – who find themselves at the opposite end of the remittance spectrum – use them to cover their debts. Around a third of our respondents fell into this category – paying off either migration-related or non-migratory debt. This concerns some very poor households who have to borrow money or credit to cover their daily living expenses during most of the year and pay it back once the migrant sends remittances. The borrowing is usually informal – from family and friends, as well as buying on credit from local shops (in Albanian known as '*me listë*', literally translated as 'on the list'). Roma and Evgjit households were significant in this group, indicating their poorer and more marginalised position in society. These communities were also the most represented amongst those who used remittances to cover migration-related debts such as paying smugglers, transport to Greece, or visas for those able to obtain them (see also De Soto *et al.* 2005).

Besides the poorer families, another group which used remittances to pay off debts consisted of those who had received formal loans from banks and MFIs to finance a (usually agricultural) business. In one instance a household had around 100 sheep which they had bought using a bank loan. The wife and daughter-in-law looked after them in the village, while the husband and the son worked as shepherds in nearby Greek villages and their remittances were used to service and pay off the loan. Their migration was a typical case of 'migrating to stay', i.e. they were migrating in order to ensure the sustainability of their livestock business, so that they could continue living in the village without having to migrate again.

Agriculture

Around one third of survey respondents used their remittances to support various agricultural processes – our fourth specific observation. Table 21 specifies in more detail some of the activities on which the money was spent. We see that 62 per cent of those who had used part of their remittances in agriculture (34 per cent of the total sample having invested in agriculture) had invested in setting up or expanding apple orchards, which have become one of the commercial specialities in this part of the Korçë area, due both to an established tradition of apple production in this region, and to the particular combination of soils and climate in the elevated, flat valleys. Generally, investments in agriculture reported in the survey and interview data ranged from the small farmer who sold some milk from his one cow in order to diversify the family's income, to the more sophisticated apple, onion and potato growers and livestock farms (mainly sheep and some ox breeding, but also some pigs). We illustrate this with an interview excerpt from Asije, 47:

> We all work here and mostly use our income from here for everyday needs. What he [her husband] brings back we put aside to use in the apple orchard and for the children's education… At least a quarter of what he brings [between €5,000 and €10,000 a year] goes toward the apple orchard.

As Asije highlights, the farms and businesses sustained by remittances generally rely on the unpaid labour of family members, a feature in previous research (Nicholson 2004b). However, some farmers who cultivated large areas of land hired day-labourers during the most intensive periods of work, such as planting and harvesting. In two cases the numbers were between 25 and 50 workers at a time, whilst usually it was less than ten. The majority of these day-labourers were women; farmers preferred them because of the perceived higher quality of work they did when compared to men. Many of them were Roma and Evgjit; as the poorest living in the neighbourhood, they were therefore readily available for low-paid, casual work in the fields.

The above clearly illustrates the trickle-down effect of remittances for non-migrants and rural areas of origin more widely. We could thus argue that the effects of remittances on development of origin areas and countries are, overall, positive. However, as we shall see in the next parts of this book, this is not straightforward.

Table 21 Categories of remittance uses in agriculture in rank order

Investing in agriculture		% of subsample
1.	Set-up or sustain apple orchards (buy the fruit trees, pesticides etc.)	62.5
2.	Purchase of fertilisers and seeds	31.7
3.	Renting – and in few cases purchase of – agricultural land	23.3
4.	Purchase of livestock such as sheep, cows and pigs	13.3
5.	Purchase agricultural machinery	5.8

Source: Authors' survey

Illustration 5 House of a non-migrant family, south-east Albania, 2008

Illustration 6 The difference remittances make, south-east Albania, 2008

Social Well-Being and Development

This theme is often overlooked by most research, although it is very important for migrants and their families. Indeed, according to Table 20, more than half of our survey respondents reported using their incoming remittances to cover medical expenses,[3] around a third to pay for social security contributions and around a quarter to finance the education of younger family members. The IOM/ILO surveys found that between 8 and 12 per cent of their surveyed households in coastal Albania used remittances sent from their relatives abroad to finance education (Kring 2007), whereas the BoA reported that 16.4 per cent of remittances sent by respondents in their household survey was used to cover education and medical expenses (Frashëri 2007: 74). This would suggest that remittances, and therefore migration, have a positive effect on social development.

Our qualitative material and key informant interviews broadly confirm this suggestion, specifically on the issue of education. Children in such remittance-receiving households could focus on their studies, instead of providing labour for the family's farm. Also fees, books, clothes and other such needs were better met through remittances. But there were also some mixed results. Three illustrative examples are instructive here. In the first one, we met the father of a migrant son who lives in Greece. As the father was too embarrassed to let us in the house because they were very poor, we sat talking to him on the balcony. He kept the household going and supported his ailing wife with the work he did in his agricultural plot. All the remittances that his son sent from Greece went towards the education of the two younger siblings – brother and sister – who attended the local university. In the second case, the remittances of the father from Thessaloniki financed the education of his daughter, also at the local university. Interestingly in this particular case, his son had not wanted to continue higher studies because of peer pressure. He had wanted to earn his own money and, against his parents' wishes, had joined his father in Greece. However, as he was undocumented, he could only find work occasionally, and had to spend most of his time indoors for fear of being apprehended. In the third and final case, two brothers living in Thessaloniki and Athens supported their younger sister to study at the university in Korçë. 'Almost half of my remittances were spent for this purpose', confirms Andrea (24), the youngest brother.

These three cases reflect at first sight a reinforcement of patriarchal gender relations through the process of migration and remitting, i.e. men emigrate and provide money, women stay behind in the village. However, migration can also reshape such gender relations by empowering women through the higher education opportunities that remittances provide – arguably their agency is thus enhanced. In contrast, some of the migrant men may simultaneously be disadvantaged by migration as their social and physical mobility is restricted by broader structures both of global capitalism and the Greek institutions. Recalling Hugo's (2000) conclusion, migration can be 'an empowering experience [for women and men] … influenced by the context in which migration occurs'. In our study context, as we shall see presently, the social location of these young women in rural areas confers on them disadvantages and barriers. Although highly educated, the gendered power dynamics that structure Albanian macro or state-level institutions restrict their agency (Mahler and Pessar 2001). This in turn impacts on personal and local development in the long run. As Andrea says, although his sister is now a qualified teacher, she is unemployed – as were a number of other highly-educated young women we came across in the study villages. Practices of nepotism, alleged corruption and lack of public investments in social infrastructure are all impediments to translating this educational investment into long-term personal and local development.

Some recent studies which have analysed data from the 2005 ALSMS also cast doubt on another aspect of the link between migration, remittances and education, similar to our second example above. Thus, Dabalen and Miluka (2010) argue that migration negatively impacts on education of migrants' children who remain in Albania. They suggest that this may be due to the expectation for younger people to join the migrant parent abroad; the effect was much stronger for children whose parents lived in Italy compared to those in Greece. Trako's (2008) findings concur. She argues that remittances decrease the likelihood of school attendance for children between 12–17 years of age in recipient households. On the one hand, expenditure on education was lower amongst households receiving remittances than those who did not, while they also had a lower proportion of children enrolled in school. Besides expectations for migration, Trako suggests that the result might also be due to lower parental input as one parent – usually the mother – is overstretched trying to take care of various things on her own, as well as the potential withdrawal of children from school in order to work at home.

Some of the women we interviewed expressed similar feelings of being overburdened by these various tasks – not least their children's upbringing – which they had to do on their own while their husband was away in Greece. However, children's schooling in our study sample continued to be important.

Non-Agricultural Businesses

Similar to previous research, the share of respondents reporting such uses was quite low at 3 per cent. Its importance, however, became more evident through field observation and in-depth interviews with selected returnees and local stakeholders. Businesses set up with remittances consisted primarily of small grocery shops, some bars, cafeterias, hairdressing salons, a few warehouses, one petrol pump station, and transport vehicles such as minivans and heavy-duty trucks – not very different from what previous ethnographic research has noted over the years (Nicholson 2004a; 2004b). However, the majority of them are registered in the name of the husband. For instance, of the 38 registered businesses in Pojan only seven were headed by women, and of the 29 registered in Zvezdë only five were headed by women. Our local key informants cautioned us about these figures, suggesting that in an estimated 80 per cent of cases women actually did most of the work, as well as the accounting and administration. Since the husband was registered as the only person working in the business, he was also the one who was insured through the compulsory premium system for self-employment; *de jure*, these women were employees who worked in the informal economy.

Indeed, some of our respondents would ironically note that such women are simply 'employees' of their husbands, as the husband is the one in charge, whilst they only clean the shop and sell the products. In such cases the word *argat* was used, which in Albanian has negative connotations of servitude and exploitation inherited from the semi-feudal Ottoman times. Nowadays this word is generally reserved for day-labourers who work in manual and low-status jobs.

Internal Migration, Re-Migration and Onward Migration

Remittances from Greece had also financed other types of potential migration, such as internal moves to urban areas, namely Tirana, Durrës, Korçë and Pogradec. Tirana and Durrës are the two main cities forming the economic core of Albania. The former is the capital and by far the largest urban centre in the country. Durrës is the country's main port and beach resort. Korçë and Pogradec are provincial towns and local growth centres for south-east Albania. In the majority of cases the money was used to purchase or build property – building plots, apartments and houses. These were intended as an investment for the migrants' old age, for themselves if they returned to Albania before retirement, or as an asset for their children's future.[4] Only 3 per cent of our survey respondents reported such use for their remittances, but we were able to gain more insights from our in-depth interviews and group discussions with migrants and key informants in Thessaloniki. The reason we were not able to capture the full magnitude of such investments was because generally the sums did not go through the 'hands' of those remaining in the villages. As mentioned earlier, these remittances were often sent direct via bank accounts between

Greece and Albania. It was usually the migrant men who were in charge of the process, from making the transfer to investing it in Albania, although women were closely involved in the decision-making process.

Finally, remittances and return had gone hand-in-hand with re-migration or onward migration, for example to Italy or further away. Thus, some remittances from Greece had been used to facilitate a move which could potentially produce better social and economic outcomes (King *et al.* 2003). In turn, remittances sent from these other countries were invested locally too. For example, one young man who had used his earnings from Greece to facilitate his onward migration to Italy, was sending remittances from Italy which were being deployed in building a pig farm in the village.

Non-Monetary Remittances

In this section of the chapter we look at three – less researched, but highly important – types of transnational household transfers: socio-political, technological and in-kind remittances.

Remitting Gender and Democracy – Social Transfers

Whilst most of the literature has focused overwhelmingly on financial remittances, the social dimension of the impact of migration on origin communities has been neglected and rarely explored systematically (Goldring 2003; Hugo 2005; Piper 2005). This can be analysed from two perspectives: on the one hand, monetary remittances have a social and cultural as well as an economic impact on these sending areas. This is reflected not only in the use of monies sent, but also in the ways in which such transfers shape ideas, perceptions, norms and roles within origin societies. We have analysed this aspect in the preceding sections of this chapter and will continue this as we discuss gender roles a little later on. The other dimension is the transfer of what are referred to as 'social remittances' which, according to Levitt (1998: 927), are the 'ideas, behaviours, identities and social capital that flow from receiving- to sending-country communities'. From a development perspective, social remittances are key to understanding migrants as agents of social and political change, as well as the ways in which migration affects change for those left behind (Nyberg Sørensen 2005). Indeed, social remittances might even be more important than financial transfers in the long run (Kapur 2004). Once again, there is a connection between social remittances and the patterns of utilisation of monetary remittances; for instance a switch might occur from wholly consumption-oriented expenditure to investment in business as a more 'entrepreneurial' spirit develops amongst the wider migrant or family network. On the other hand, changes brought about by social remittances might be necessary to ensure that monetary remittances continue to flow in (Nyberg Sørensen 2004: 17).

In the last two post-communist decades there has been an emergent Albanian transnational social space, articulated around migration routes and 'remittance corridors', especially encompassing Greece and Italy (Chiodi and Devole 2005; Maroukis 2005a; 2005b).[5] This consists of a web of transnational links and practices some of which we detailed in the previous chapter in the context of the transnational Albanian household spanning Albania and Greece. We can briefly mention here the telephone calls, migrants' visits, 'proxy' visits, return migration, and the Internet which serve as transmission channels for various types of remittances, especially from migrants in Greece to their relatives and friends in Albania. 'Reverse' remittances may also flow in the opposite direction through these same channels. These ideas, practices, identities and knowledge that migrants transmit or bring with them, impact on gender and generational roles, ethnic identity, class and social status, as well as on demography, political and social participation, and human rights in Albania.

As a result of living abroad, migrants develop certain expectations in relation to what constitutes democracy, how local and central governments have a duty to serve, be transparent and accountable to the people, what professional ethical standards are acceptable across various industries and services, what adequate infrastructure and environment look like, and so on. In a recent study of such transfers from Mexican migrants residing in the US to their origin communities, Pérez-Armendáriz and Crow (2010) confirm that migrants 'remit democracy', as they put it. In other words, they play an important role in helping to strengthen democracy in their countries of origin through the diffusion of democratic ideas and behaviours.[6] However, in such discussions the host country – Greece in our case – is also important. As Greece is far from the beacon of democracy in the world – in fact many facets of its democratic culture are quite Balkan-like – political remittances flowing back to Albania are therefore limited too. On the other hand, certain migrant groups' own historical developments may restrict such political engagements even when they find themselves in the 'thick' of political action. An example from recent events in Greece can be called to help here. As we write (May 2010), Greece has been gripped by violent strikes and protests against the government's austerity measures to cut back the country's giant deficit, which will cost many their jobs and livelihoods. Many migrants have taken to the streets alongside their Greek colleagues to call for justice as these processes unfold. A recent article in one of the Albanian migrant newspapers in Greece lamented how the Albanian community was numerically the least represented in such protests. The author of the article condemned his compatriots for their passivity, choosing to watch the action from the comfort of cafeterias around Omonia Square (where the protest was being held) instead of joining in (Gjoça 2010). He also pointed to another sensitive issue: how much do these migrants feel that these protests and the issues with which Greek society is grappling belong to them? In other words, it reflects to some extent also their low level of socio-political integration in their host society. For Albanians in Greece, this minimal political participation is by no means entirely their own fault, as the ethno-religious hegemony of Greek national identity, with its xenophobic reliance on *ius sanguinis* or 'blood law' as the key criterion of national belonging, hardly welcomes them with open channels to be politically and democratically active in the host society (Triandafyllidou and Veikou 2002).

Remitting Skills and Technology

A much acknowledged, but less conceptually explored and less-well understood dimension of non-monetary remittances is also the transfer of technical knowledge and skills, or 'technological remittances', to use the term coined by Nichols (2002) and Goldring (2003). We encountered such remittance types during our research and noted their important developmental impact on the study villages, especially in construction and agriculture. Indeed, many words used in the construction industry in south-east Albania are Greek, as are the architectural designs of most new houses built around the villages.[7] As most male migrants work in the construction sector in Greece, when they improve or build their own homes in Albania they apply skills and techniques they see in their work processes there (Dalakoglou 2009).[8]

As far as agriculture is concerned, the investment of skills and knowledge is particularly evident in the growth of apple orchards. Many – especially seasonal – migrants work in apple and peach orchards in rural Greece where they have acquired a number of skills, such as pruning, spraying and watering techniques, related to this farming sector. They have in turn introduced these in their villages of origin in Albania by creating and expanding their own apple orchards there. We use Besmir's case to illustrate. A plumber by profession, Besmir (24) migrated to Greece as soon as he completed his vocational course in Korçë at the age of 18. Although he did manual and casual jobs in the first few months of his arrival there, he soon found skilled work as a plumber and was able to start earning well. As he lives in Thessaloniki and has a regular migration status, he travels frequently to visit his family in the village. During these visits he brings back money which is invested in the family's apple orchard. The 1.2 hectare orchard is now set with an extensive watering system which Besmir installed using knowledge he had gained in Greece. In their study of Albanian migrant workers in Greek agriculture, Labrianidis and Sykas (2009: 408) found that almost all of their respondents had successfully applied their experience gained from work in the Greek countryside to their own farm undertakings in Albania. Our own field observations and interviews with key informants in the villages and in the Korçë Regional Development Council confirmed this technological transfer for the migrants who worked in agriculture in Greece.

The expansion of apple orchards in rural south-east Albania is due to three main reasons. First, they provide an opportunity for higher household incomes; second, they require less intensive labour than other farming processes (although more financial capital);[9] and third, this activity is considered as semi-skilled in the farming jobs hierarchy, in stark contrast to the back-breaking work needed for row crops. Painstaking and stooping work on field crops is largely associated with hard labour in socialist cooperative farms, and thus has a certain stigma attached to it – especially by rural youth (Vullnetari 2008). Ironically, many such young people – almost always men – go to work in rural areas of Greece, which have themselves suffered massive outmigration of their youth towards Greek cities, precisely because of this disaffection with farm work and conservative rural societies (Cavounidis 2006: 108; Kasimis and Papadopoulos 2005). Andrea's (24) experience below illustrates this well, and is very typical of his generation. Note how he makes a distinction with the older generation of his brother (who is 39) and with similar work in rural Greece.

> My brother used to work more in agriculture. I can tell you with conviction that I did not like working in agriculture at all. When I was asked to do that, I always argued first with my parents, and even when I went, I did things the other way round. Instead of cutting down the weeds, I would cut the beans and such things… Not intentionally but I didn't know… and was not interested to learn. So my parents then had no choice but to send me home saying I was no good at it and that I was causing more damage than making good. It wasn't just me; many other friends of mine were the same… It wasn't intentional, it just was very boring. You simply worked; I didn't understand why I was working in the first place… There was no income… True, many Albanians work in Greek villages near the Albanian border, and they do exactly the same jobs there as in Albania. But [the difference is that] they are paid there. They don't work just to survive [*për të nxjerrë bukën e gojës*]. They get paid [wages].

Finally, we note in this category also the role that migrants can play as advisors and intermediaries for further investment and marketing. Besmir's case is again instructive here. From his work at a supermarket in Greece he has made potential business contacts, which he wants to explore for expanding his family's apple business through exports to this particular chain of supermarkets in Greece. In another one of the study villages similar connections had enabled villagers to start exporting their beans to Greece, which ensured a good income for them, as well as work for non-migrants locally.

Lemons, Water Pumps and Medicine: In-Kind Transfers

In-kind remittances are goods that migrants send or bring to their families of origin. They often reflect the family's material needs and can act as signifiers of emotional care towards members of the family and friends. In the Albanian context they have been transformed in size and nature over the years. Many of those familiar with the Albanian migration scene may recall the early 1990s cross-border movements and the cars, vans and buses loaded with impossible volumes of bags, furniture and domestic appliances. One such example is described in Dalakoglou's (2010) recent article which features – among others – a door tied to the roof of a migrant's car returning from Greece to visit his home in Gjirokastër, south Albania. This is some way more sophisticated than a television set transported on a donkey reported at another border crossing point near Saranda in the early 1990s (Reuters 2003).

According to Misja (1998), the ratio of in-kind to monetary remittances was almost equal in the early 1990s, and gradually evolved in favour of financial transfers to a 3:1 ratio by the end of that first post-communist decade. De Zwager *et al.* (2005: 21) estimated in-kind remittances to be at the level of one sixth of monetary transfers by the mid-2000s.

Half of our survey respondents replied that they received one type or other of in-kind remittances. The statistical ranking of responses was for clothes, food, medicine and electronic appliances, in that order. Fewer households reported that they had received jewellery, computers and computer-related products, non-agricultural tools and machinery and agricultural tools and machinery. Food is usually brought back when migrants visit and is designated not only for the family members, but also for the visiting migrants to use during the time they are in the village. Explanations given were that some products from Greece were of a higher quality (at a particular time of year), as Albania is considered a dumping ground for expired solid and other food products. Sometimes the migrants had become used to a particular product or cooking ingredient which they could not find in Albania. And at other times, some types of food such as oil were simply cheaper to buy in Greece than in Albania, since those sold in the Albanian shops are Greek imports anyway. Clothing brought back was both new and second-hand.

The impact of such remittances becomes wider when we incorporate our qualitative data, according to which migrants sent in-kind remittances not only to their immediate family members, but also to other extended kin as well as friends and acquaintances. Urim, 50, who has lived in Thessaloniki for more than a decade, explains:

> Besides money, we also send clothes, because they are cheaper here… I also buy some medicine for my mother here because she has problems with her blood pressure… Food…When we go we stay there two or three days and take food with us, especially so we can use ourselves whilst we are there. Not that there is no good food there [in Albania]; food there is usually tastier without a doubt. But, we buy it here [in Greece] because it is sometimes cheaper. For instance, the tomatoes may be more expensive there at this time of year, the lemons or olive oil are usually cheaper here… I have also taken water pumps there, and heaters, because they are cheaper here…

Other interviewees had similar stories to tell. We present two more quotes here, which reflect the diversity of such items:

> My husband also brings back food, clothes for the family, for me, medicine for the older parents… He has brought long-life battery lamps, our water pump… He has sent these [the heavier items] with some people who travel with their cars and he pays €20, €25–€30, it depends [Elda, 34, wife of migrant living in the village].

> He [her son] brings parts for the tractor, for the combine-harvest machine, when needed. He bought the combine-harvest machine over there [in Greece] and drove it here himself… Driving for three days from Thessaloniki… [Zana, 41, mother of migrant son].

Reading these quotes, which reflect typical opinions expressed in many other interviews, we cannot but be amazed at how food (and other items) in Albania can be more expensive than in Greece (or other developed countries). One of the strong arguments for the development potential of remittances is that their real value in the origin countries of migrants is much higher than where they are earned. Evidently, it is not always so.

Albania is illustrative of how the new conditions of economic globalisation impact both at a macro level, but also at the more micro-scale of families and individuals. Post-socialist neoliberal policies left the country wide open for penetration by global forces, to some extent thus reproducing old and creating new forms of colonial dependency, such as with Italy and Greece respectively (Mai 2003). Most of Albania's trade is with these two countries. Imports – which form the bulk of this trade – are financed by remittances from migrants working mostly in these very same countries. The irony is that most of Albania's imports are foodstuffs, which are later sold at soaring prices, while Albanian farmers trade their produce for a pittance, often even throwing it away completely after it has been left in stock to waste. Under such circumstances, the real value of remittances is not much higher in Albania than where they are produced. As we shall see later, Albania's asymmetrical economic structure and its reliance on remittances are not conducive to long-term sustainable development.

Coming back to our in-kind remittances, their discussion is also interesting in the context of our research and this book's focus on issues of gender and development in Albania more broadly, as they seem to be the type of remittances most sent by women. In her fascinating research on gender, migration and kinship ties among transnational households in central Albania and their migrant members in Greece and Italy, Erin Smith (2009) shows how migrant women found it difficult to transfer money to their own parents and other kin; these were generally reserved for the men's relatives, according to Albanian customary norm. Thus, sending or bringing material goods – especially clothes – was one way to make up for this asymmetric remitting pattern. Similarly, in our research married daughters more often sent in-kind than monetary remittances. Items such as medicine, television sets, fridges or washing machines were mentioned. Married sisters living in Greece also sent such in-kind remittances to their married sisters living in the villages, as Elona (40), an interviewee in one of the villages, relates:

> I have two sisters in Athens… They help me a lot, all the time… They mostly send me things for the house… They almost never send me money, but even with these things it's a great help. I don't need to spend money and go and buy them… Small things, big things, whatever is needed for the house… if they want to send me something, they send it by bus… the Athens-Korçë bus… They pay the driver around €10 for this… Then my husband goes to Korçë in a taxi and collects it… because they won't bring it here to the village.

Let us now examine more closely the social dimension of monetary and non-monetary remittances; we do this by focusing on the interplay between these and gender relations. This is the subject of the next and final section of this chapter before concluding.

Remittances and Gender Relations

Previous studies have shown how the effect of remittances on gender relations in Albania has been a reinforcement of traditional and patriarchal relations, since the majority of those who send and receive remittances are men, and the majority of decision-makers are also men (King *et al.* 2003; 2006). This earlier research derives mainly from the British case, where migrants come from the rural fastnesses of northern Albania. Our findings in this book suggest a more diversified picture, which is to a certain degree related to the origin of the sample in south-east Albania – historically a more egalitarian society than that in the north and north-east of the country. However, some changes are due to the evolving impact of migration, as we shall see.

First, the combined financial and social remittances have ensured a higher standard of living and easier home-making. Many migrant houses are now equipped with an indoor kitchen, at times fitted with the best mod-cons, indoor water supply, key domestic appliances such as fridges and washing machines, indoor bathrooms and more comfortable furniture. This has made women's daily household work much easier, although it is not always the case; in poorer households women continue to wash clothes by hand, often outside and in the cold of the winter, and cook in small and cramped outdoor kitchens. The following interview extract draws the contrast between the extreme frugality of the past and the consumer mentality of the present:

> Of course there is a difference. Before I used to wash the dishes with sand, now I use Test [local brand name of washing-up gel, but which in parts of Albania is used as a name to refer to all washing-up liquids]… But not the best type, but that which is cheaper… I am still quite frugal as I have suffered much poverty in the past… Before we had only maize flour to cook with, now we use that only for nostalgia… If we don't like this TV we go and buy another one. If this fridge is not good, we go and get a new one… The same with the cooker and so on [Hajre, 64, mother of a migrant son].

Second, and linked to the example above, we note the gendered typology of remittances not only by what type was sent more by men and women – financial and in-kind respectively – as discussed earlier, but also how men and women allocated them in their everyday use. For example, men in our research preferred to use financial remittances in order to establish or expand the family's business – usually an agricultural enterprise – while women were keener to improve the living environment of the family. Once again this pattern seems to fit closely with the overall gendered norms and roles within the context of the patriarchal Albanian society. Two examples follow. First, Zana (41) and Petrika (46) live in the village with their 18-year old daughter. Their 24 year-old son works in Thessaloniki and remits money home regularly. When asked how they use their remittances, Zana and Petrika explained:

> *Zana*: I want to buy/make things for the house, they [her husband and her son] only want to spend it on metal [machinery]. And so we also quarrel sometimes…
> *Petrika*: Well, when something is necessary, e.g. for farming, a spare part for the machinery or something like that, we will get that one first… So who decides?… We still retain our tradition to a certain extent.
> *Zana*: For instance, all these years that they started with the machinery I haven't added anything to the household. Now we have prioritised agriculture: one time it's the tractor that needs a piece, next time is the combine-harvest machine, the other time the car and so on.

The second example is from Asije's family, whom we met earlier. The excerpt is a conversation where the various women who participated in the interview present their views:

> *Asije* (47): In our family it is my father-in-law or myself who receives these remittances [from her husband]… Then it is my husband and my father-in-law who decide what they will be spent on…
> *Ilda* (18): There are three generations in our family and we all have different ideas. I want books for school for instance, or I need this item of clothing which I must absolutely have. Whereas mother says that we need this and that for the house. Whereas granddad says that we need this and that for the apple orchard. And so a certain disagreement arises amongst all of us, but of course this doesn't escalate…
> *Granny* (72): Everyone has their own ideas.
> *Ilda*: We all try to meet our own needs, although it is the eldest in the family, for instance, who administers things in our household, and

who *knows* where this or that money should go, so that all are satisfied in the end.
Asije: So in the end, it is the head of the household that gives the final verdict.

Our third observation is that, in female-headed households, women felt they had gained a certain degree of empowerment. On the one hand, this was due to their role as administrators of remittances and household finances in the absence of their migrating husbands. This is not to say that decision-making on how remittances were used was a straightforward process. Often husbands continued to retain an important role there. On the other hand, empowerment was also experienced through withdrawal from work, when the husband could remit to the degree that his family could have a decent life without other income sources. Thus the wife stayed at home and looked after the children and the household. It is important to emphasise here that what work was available locally was of the lowest-paid, unskilled and hardest type – in the family's agricultural plot, as a day-labourer in local farms, or in the food-processing and garment factories situated in the nearest town; not exactly empowering! Analysing their data from a country-wide survey in the 1990s, Konica and Filer (2005: 10) suggest a similar effect of remittances in recipient households, i.e. increased remittances made women less likely to work.

Such re-enforcements of typical patriarchal 'male breadwinner' and 'housewife' roles in the family were further shaped by ideas flowing into these rural areas through Brazilian soap-operas shown regularly on day-time television. The power of mass media in shaping expectations and behaviours has been examined in the past in Albania, but in a very different context – with reference to the role of Italian television in shaping Albanian migration to Italy (Mai 2002).

Fourth, we want to make an additional observation on the gendered dimension of remittances, migration and education, which takes us back to our discussion earlier in this chapter on the uses of financial remittances. Describing the effect of monetary remittances on social development, we argued that children's education had generally benefited from these transfers. But we also cautioned of mixed results on the wider and longer-term impacts. One of the mixed impacts we briefly touched on was the differentiated outcome for young women and men. Some remittances enabled some young women to stay on in education after completing the compulsory stage between the ages of six and 15. Attending further education potentially increased their chances of being more independent and mobile later in life, whether through employment or by marrying into a higher-income household. We illustrate with an interview excerpt from Zana and Petrika:

> *Petrika*: well, recently when we planted the onions we hired five or six *argatë*... Now that the hoeing needs doing, we will hire some more, it depends on the need.
> *Zana*: especially this year, because our daughter is in her final year [of secondary school] and needs to study much more. Last year I used to take her with me to the field to help us, but this year I will let her study.

Note here the multifaceted dimensions of remittances. The couple's migrant son who remits has himself completed secondary school, and is now supporting his sister's education. This year is crucial for her as her results will decide on a place at the university, an aspiration for many young rural women as a way out of rural areas and out of poverty. In addition, the trickle-down effect of remittances is felt by the hired day-labourers, who – as we mentioned earlier – come from some of the poorest sections in this rural society.

However, a few caveats are in order here too. Higher education does not necessarily translate into a job, and certainly not into development for the local (rural) areas. During our research we met a number of young women who had graduated from the university but who could not find employment, due to a combination of nepotistic practices in public service recruitment and lack of investment in such services in rural areas. Once out of school, these women had only limited occasions to go out and associate with their friends, especially as no entertainment opportunities exist locally for them except for informal chats over coffee in each other's houses. The predominant mentality in rural areas equates young women with the family's 'honour', thus making their emancipation and liberation possible only within the 'protective' patronage of the family (see also Nixon 2009). Older women – mothers and grandmothers, not to mention mothers-in-law – are part of this social pressure as much as men. Within the geographical scale of rural communities and all the way up to the level of Albanian society more broadly, gendered power is expressed and exerted from those placed higher in the hierarchy of power – men and older women – over those placed at the 'receiving' end of it.

Our female interviewees in the villages and in Thessaloniki expressed their frustration at these gender perceptions and attitudes, especially the pervasive traditional norms which limit their mobility. Asije, 47, and her two daughters (18 and 12) explain, intercutting one another to produce practically a single-voice narrative:

> *Asije*: well, men, for the moment men are at the head in the villages
> *Ilda*: because women's emancipation has not reached the level it should… Social pressure is very strong [*të vret shumë opinioni*]
> *Bruna*: because the village is so backward, women's rights… are not here yet
> *Asije*: emancipation is very much delayed

Later on in the discussion it was the youngest, Bruna (12), who seemed to be the most outspoken on the issue. As we were discussing the wider prospects of the village, she interjected: 'this is a cursed place… it's such an ugly place that I can't find words to describe it to you'. Irena (37), who lives in Thessaloniki and visits her relatives often, insists that 'they [villagers] won't change'. As a result, many young women aspired to find liberation and emancipation abroad through emigration. When their father was in Greece they hoped for a family reunification, and when they were much older the prospects of marriage with a successful migrant were sought. But as Anita (23) had discovered, all was not what it seemed:

> There, in Albania, there is that mentality that when you get engaged, when you get married, if your husband is in Greece, he is expected to take you there with him no matter what… They think Greece is… But when you come here, it's very different from what I had imagined it… First of all I have no documents, so every time I go out in the street I am scared of the police… Then other difficulties, a new life, difficult job and even when you work hard no money is left over… If I knew all of this before, I would have not come here.

According to Hugo's (2000) scenario which we discussed in Chapter 2, Anita should have been empowered through her migration to Greece, as she is far from her family and is earning her own money. While these are important factors in this process, they need to be combined with the other factors that Hugo writes about, most crucially legal protection. The latter would reduce her social isolation and enable her to engage with her family on her own terms.

Rising expectations and aspirations followed by further migration, as a result of financial and social remittances, have taken place amongst young men as well (cf. Massey *et al.* 1993). Almost all the young men who had emigrated to Greece in their teens emphasised that their motivation for doing so had not been poverty, but their desire not to be 'left behind' socially: like their migrant peers they too wanted to have their own money and buy things for themselves; like them they too wanted to share in the experiences that others talked about. A final quote from Andrea (24) again:

> This was a time and an age when I spent the money on trinkets [uses the Greek word *kazeleki*]... The money wasn't enough as I also started smoking, so my pocket money wasn't enough. My family couldn't support me more, but my requirements increased... I looked at my peers or older guys who came back from Greece [on visits], I saw how they had a good life. So I also decided to go... My father wanted me to continue in school. At the same time I didn't want to because I didn't feel good in myself, compared to my peers who had left Albania... The day I left my father wasn't at home... I only told my mother [that he was leaving].

Recalling our earlier analysis in Chapter 2 of the 'migration hump' and root causes for migration, it is clear from the example above that poverty and penetration of foreign capital do not fully explain certain types of migratory flows. Social factors and the 'demonstration effect' of migration need to be taken into account in order to deepen our understanding of the dynamics of gendered geographies of power, not least how migration impacts development in areas of origin.

Conclusion

This chapter has examined the complex and multiple ways in which migration, gender, remittances and development interact. While most of the literature on remittances focuses on financial flows, their social dimension is hardly discussed. Furthermore, a number of other non-monetary flows are brought back or transmitted by migrants, which play an important role in the transformation of rural areas of origin. Decision-making about their use is an equally complex process, whereby women have a degree of power, albeit not always visible from outside. In spite of this, the degree to which women are empowered by migration as individuals within households is not very high. In fact, many women whose husbands had migrated experienced being overburdened with the tasks of single-handedly looking after their children, their home, and often being involved in income-generating activities such as agriculture or factory work. On the other hand, their household work was facilitated enormously by the accessories and comforts which financial and in-kind remittances had provided, such as the modern indoor kitchen, the fridge or the washing machine.

In other cases remittance capital has been invested in repairing village houses as well as in businesses. The growth and prosperity of the agricultural sector in this area is partly due to deployment of remittances – financial and technological – as money and skills are employed into the local economy.

However, it is of great concern that many families and individuals continue to struggle to survive, are often perpetually in debt because of lack of income-generating activities, or suffer physically and mentally from family separation. Development, not just economic, but human, which includes all aspects of one's life, development as availability of opportunities and as freedom (Sen 1999), is out of reach for the majority of the population. Especially the elderly and children, but also many households more generally, live in insecurity and poverty. Obstacles can be found on both sides of the border – in Albania and Greece. In Albania, issues of a structural nature, such as public policies and practices, limit the full potential of local development at best, and undermine it at worst. In Greece, the perpetual insecurity of legal status in the country and the draconian immigration regulations exhaust and frustrate even the most persistent and courageous of migrants. Yet, there is resilience – although it comes at great personal and family cost: the human cost of migration.

7

MIGRATION–DEVELOPMENT–REMITTANCES–GENDER: WHAT ROLE FOR POLICY-MAKERS?

Following the analysis of the previous three chapters, which has been mainly at the micro-level, we now move our discussion one step further and examine the multiple relationships between migration, development, remittances and gender from a local, regional and national perspective. The principal axes of our analysis remain remittances and gender, structured now around two threads. First, we discuss the relevant policies which have been proposed or implemented so far in Albania, and specifically in our research area. Second, we draw on expert opinion based on in-depth interviews, informal conversations and focus-group discussions with key stakeholders in Albania and Greece. We pay close attention to the potential for development in the rural areas of origin, where remittances can theoretically and practically be used to generate sustainable livelihoods. We include in this discussion some of the key factors that could ensure the optimal use of such remittances for investment, as well as the ways in which gender shapes such entrepreneurial activities.

Macro-Level Policies in Albania

Public policy-making in Albania in the last 20 years has not only been a matter for the Government of Albania (GoA), but has been highly influenced by international development organisations, otherwise known as the donor community, the civil society and NGOs. Also important as a wider framing discourse or meta-policy has been the process of moving towards membership to the EU, known as 'rapprochement' or accession.

Development

The National Strategy for Development and Integration (NSDI), covering the period 2007–2013, is the most important development strategy in the country and acts as a roadmap that sets out Albania's national development and EU accession priorities until 2013. EU accession has become extremely important in framing Albania's priorities, particularly migration and development matters. Albania signed the Stabilisation and Association Agreement (SAA) with the EU in June 2006, which came into force in April 2009. The SAA provides a framework of mutual commitments on a wide range of political, economic and mobility issues. More specifically, it focuses on enhanced regional cooperation, the establishment of a free-trade area with the EU within ten years, political dialogue and a gradual approximation of Albanian legislation to the EU *acquis*, in particular in the area of Justice and Home Affairs, including migration. Emphasis on the latter is on combating irregular migration and promoting 'managed migration flows'. The country's progress is monitored through yearly reports produced by the European Commission. Albania's approach to the EU was furthered on 28 April 2009, when the government formally applied for EU membership. At the same time, the country became a member of NATO, spurring enthusiasm for a renewed interest in the field of FDI. However, weak law enforcement and high actual and perceived levels of corruption remain important impediments to business development. As of 2009, Albania still ranks 95th out of 180 countries in the Transparency International Corruption Perceptions Index – ten points lower than in 2008. This is the lowest index in South-East Europe except for Bosnia and Herzegovina, and is significantly below the OECD average.[1]

Returning to the NSDI, this strategy is based on converging 20 sectoral and 11 cross-cutting sector strategies, including regional development, migration and gender equality. The inter-sectoral Strategy for Regional Development (2008–2013) aims to achieve sustainable socio-economic development and a reduction of regional socio-economic inequalities by coordinating the actions of public institutions at central level, such as ministries, with other local institutions and stakeholders throughout the country. Development strategies are also approved at a regional level and each region has its own Regional Development Strategy (RDS), carried out with the support of the UNDP.

Two of the most important institutions in terms of policy and practice on economic development in Albania are the Ministry of Economy, Trade and Energy (METE), and the Albanian Investment Institute (ALBINVEST), a quasi-governmental organisation created in 2006 under the supervision of METE. The Institute's mission is to promote development in Albania by compiling and making available information on policies, strategies, programmes and projects for private sector development and investments; improvement of the country's image abroad; and stimulating and promoting products and services in the foreign market.

Migration

The Albanian Government's policy on migration during communism was focused on closely-managed internal relocations and a ban on international moves. Exit from the country without a permit was considered as high treason and punished severely: there was a shoot-to-kill policy at the border and if caught alive, the individual was jailed for up to ten years, while his/her family was internally exiled. This was combined with heavy militarisation of borders and increasing isolation of the country. Consequently, there were very few who managed to escape during this period. On the other hand, internal movements were also highly controlled by a web of rules and regulations forming what Sjöberg (1994) calls the 'anti-migratory system'. Its aim was to keep urbanisation to a minimum, whilst retaining most of the population in rural areas.

The collapse of the communist system in the early 1990s meant borders – at least on the Albanian side – fell with it too. Suddenly, it seemed as if the entire country was on the move, either going abroad or relocating internally (Carletto *et al.* 2004; 2006). Yet, it was not until 1993 that the Albanian parliament passed a law which granted Albanians the right to such moves. Subsequent years showed a similar trend in policy-making on migration: trying to catch up with what was taking place on the ground. Planning was associated with the 'evil' communism that the country was trying to leave behind and was, thus, anathema. The various governments ruling the country between 1991 and 2003 treated emigration primarily as a means to export unemployment and import wealth through remittances. In this vein, three bilateral agreements were concluded with Germany in 1991, Italy in 1996 and Greece in 1997. After the first group of around 1,000 Albanians did not return from Germany upon completion of their one-year contract, the agreement was not renewed with this country. The other two agreements aimed to meet labour demands in the agricultural sector of both neighbouring countries. Statistics for all three programmes are lacking, but it is estimated that only a limited number of Albanians benefited from them (GoA 2005a).

Although the political programmes of various Albanian governments proposed policies to defend migrants' rights abroad, push for regularisation and strengthen consular services, these were broadly rhetoric to attract votes during electoral campaigns (ACPS 2002: 10). In reality, migrants were generally treated with institutionalised contempt. Not only have consecutive Albanian governments a less than inspiring record when it comes to concrete and practical achievements for protecting their citizens abroad from discrimination and exploitation, but their relations with these migrants themselves have also been exploitative. One such example is the 'migrant tax', as it is known in colloquial parlance – a €1 a day tax that Albanian migrants had to pay on their foreign-registered vehicle during the time they visted Albania. This very unpopular and unreasonable fee, paid on exit of the vehicle from the country, was scrapped only in 2006. Even more negative were experiences of consular services both in Greece and Italy, which were a mirror-like reflection of what was on offer in Albania itself: alleged corruption and nepotism, inadeqacy, indifference, verbal and even physical abuse; and all these 'services' for disproportionally high fees.

It was not until 2004 that a concerted effort was put together in the preparation of the National Strategy on Migration (NSM), encouraged and in turn supported by international organisations such as the EU and IOM. The strategy, covering the period 2005–2010, was approved in November 2004 and launched during a multi-stakeholder meeting in early 2005. Its implementation was envisaged to take place through a National Action Plan (NAP) on migration, also approved in 2005. In line with EU and SAA priorities, *migration management* is at the core of the strategy and is envisaged to be achieved through four main objectives:

- *mobility* – expanding legal channels for emigration, e.g. through seasonal work programmes and circular migration, and encouraging return;
- *development* – addressing the root causes of migration, enhancing remittances and reversing the 'brain drain' by encouraging a 'brain gain';
- *protection* and *support* of the diaspora (migrants abroad) through advocacy for their rights and actions against abuse, improvement of Albanian consular services for citizens abroad, support for the creation and consolidation of migrants' diaspora organisations in host countries;
- *integration* – developing further the legislative, policy and institutional framework with regards to emigration, return and readmission of Albanians and Third Country Nationals (TCNs) and immigration of TCNs aiming to bring Albania closer to the EU (GoA 2005a; see also Geiger 2007).

The Ministry of Labour, Social Affairs and Equal Opportunities (MOLSAEO) was put in charge of the implementation of the strategy and its action plan. More specifically, the Directorate for Migration Policies is the responsible entity within this ministry for migration policy and migration management. However, a number of other line ministries such as that of Foreign Affairs and Interior, as well as other institutions, would be involved.

Implementation has so far been problematic. According to a progress report of the European Commission (2008), the coordination and monitoring plan for the NSM's implementation was finalised only in May 2008 – more than three years after the adoption of the strategy. The report further adds that 'preparations for the implementation of the strategy on migration are continuing, although slowly'. In other words, more than half way through the period during which the strategy should have been on track, the relevant governmental structures are in their preparatory phase! Thus, it comes as no surprise that the level of implementation has been very low, as an independent think-tank in Tirana found during their research (Onorato *et al.* 2007). The NAP on migration stipulated a total of 66 measures, 63 of which were scheduled to be implemented, or at least start being implemented, before the end of 2006 (GoA 2005b). The authors of this monitoring report concluded that by early 2007 only 17 of the 63 *measures* (27 per cent of the total) were carried out, 12 of them (19 per cent) were partially carried out, which means that more than half were not implemented as required in the document. The rate for failing to carry out the *actions* stipulated in the plan was even higher at 77 per cent. More concerning was that, of the 15 ministries consulted within the framework of the study, eight of them had no idea even of the existence of the NSM and the NAP, let alone of their content. Some went so far as to completely dismiss these documents as 'useless', since they were the product of another government which was no longer in power. Finally, of those ministries that were aware of these documents, there was a serious lack of coordination and collaboration (Chaloff 2008).

Furthermore, the Albanian government does not consider the NSM as its own product; rather, as something pressed upon it by external actors such as IOM and the EU (Chaloff 2008). In his powerful critique of the role of external actors in Albania's migration policy, Geiger argues that IOM's double role in this context is not altogether free from conflicting interests – as a 'quasi-local "external" actor but also [as] a "quasi-governmental institution"' (Geiger 2007: 129). Indeed, the country's NSM was formulated with the assistance of IOM on behalf of the GoA. IOM went on to become 'the technical support unit of the Albanian government [...] responsible for the elaboration' of the NSM (quoted in Geiger 2007: 129); in addition, IOM has guaranteed Albania's readmission process towards the EU. IOM for its part also perceives itself as the leading agency on migration-related initiatives in Albania. Indeed, most, if not all, programmes on migration in Albania are initiated, implemented or otherwise technically supported by IOM.

IOM represents just one of several global institutions which are the main regulators of global mobility and global economy, along with other international actors such as the World Bank, whose 'view from the North' drives academic and especially policy discourse (Glick Schiller and Faist 2009). Power – as the driving-force behind our 'gendered geographies' model – is all too obvious here. Led by such forces, managed migration has become the new 'development mantra', whose narrative portrays a 'triple-win' situation. Never mind that the degree to which the parties involved 'win' is rather asymmetrical, where host countries remain of course the priviledged actors, accumulating power to turn off the tap of immigrants as they see fit. But origin country governments too are empowered by this process, as they are pressed to 'manage' their own potential migrants, in what some regard as 'remote control migration' (Guiraudon and Lahav 2000; Zolberg 2003).

Remittances

Remitances from emigration have long been considered one of the key instruments for the country's development, as we have also argued in preceding chapters of this book. The recognition of their importance is reflected in the creation of a separate national action plan on remittances as part of the NSM, which was based on an important piece of IOM-funded research (see de Zwager *et al.* 2005). However, here too there were delays and the NAP on remittances was not approved by the Council of Ministers until November 2007. The NAP consists of eight measures to be taken by a range of actors including various ministries, the BoA, INSTAT and the National Albanian Post Office. In a nutshell, the measures relate to the:

- improvement of data and best practices on remittances;
- expansion of banking services in Albania and improvement of collaboration of Albanian and Greek and Italian banks with regard to remittance-based services offered;
- expansion of capacities of other financial institutions such as the MFIs in Albania, but also the Albanian Post Office to transfer remittances or improve this service where it exists;
- improvement of legal status of migrants in Greece and Italy to facilitate their legal employment and access to the banking system in these countries;
- improvement of knowledge and access of migrants before migration, whilst in host countries and upon return, of various financial services related to remittances, savings and investment;

- increased capacities of the Albanian government and migrants' organisations in host countries to collaborate in co-development initiatives between these countries.

In other words, the focus seems to be primarily on channelling remittances through banks and other financial institution, and very little, if any, on practical steps related to their use.

True to its word, IOM initiated a number of projects on remittances following its seminal 2005 research, once again with the financial support of the EC, and of the Italian government in particular (see reports from Abazi and Mema 2007; Balliu 2007; Kring 2007; Meka *et al.* 2007; 2008). These reports reflected the aims of the NAP outlined above, i.e. their focus was on the financial sector, its composition and capacity to transfer remittances. In parallel action, the BoA itself started to carry out its own remittance household surveys – first yearly and then quarterly (see Frashëri 2007; Rëmbeci 2009). These examine a range of issues including the uses of remittances by households. Finally, the World Bank and the European Bank for Reconstruction and Development (EBRD) have also commissioned research or convened multi-stakeholder meetings (see e.g. Hernández-Coss *et al.* 2006).

To date, however, no monitoring reports have to our knowledge become available to ascertain the level of success that the NAP on remittances has had, not least the usefulness of such an approach. As the NSM comes to an end by 2010, such monitoring will be greatly needed for future policies. For instance, in spite of some achievements, some of which we were able to identify through our research – such as lower transfer costs, larger sums being remitted through the banks, etc. – there continues to be a lack of easy-to-understand and accessible information available to migrants and their families. This lack of information – related to transfers, credit facilities and investment opportunities in areas of origin – is particularly acute in rural areas, and especially affecting women. Thus, it is not very clear if the positive outcomes we mention in our findings result from the actions of banks themselves and increased competition, or because of sustained and well-implemented government-led transnational action.

Furthermore, a gendered analysis has been lacking in all of these reports and research initiatives, which seems odd in the face of the numerous gender-related initiatives in the country, often involving the same organisations and actors (Nixon 2006).

Return Migration

A third pillar related to migration policy in Albania and linked to the wider migration–development debate, is that on return. Albania is one of the few countries, and the first one in Europe, to have signed a Readmission Agreement (RA) with the EU *en bloc*, for non-voluntary return of its own citizens and those TCNs who have transited through Albania to reach the EU. Signing the RA was a prerequisite for the SAA (Article 80). The RA was ratified by the EU parliament in September 2005, although it took three more years for individual EU country parliaments to sign the SAA itself. The provisions for the Albanian nationals within this RA came into force in May 2006, those for TCNs in 2008 (IOM 2006a; 2006b). There are fears that the lack of capacity for implementation and indeed the very terms of this RA might turn Albania into a 'readmission trap' or a 'revolving door' for TCNs (Long and Celebic 2006: 30). Once again, no monitoring reports have become available to date, and no specific attention has been paid to how gender shapes such returns. In fact, there is a widely-accepted presumption that most irregular returns will be male migrants who have travelled abroad for work, whilst repatriated women generally fall in the 'trafficking victims' category. Services are thus tailored with these pre-fixed categorisations in mind.

Gender

In terms of gender, the most important policy document is the National Strategy on Gender Equality and Domestic Violence (NSGE-DV), covering the period 2007–2010. Once again, MOLSAEO takes the lead in gender-related issues as well, where it cooperates with local and international NGOs implementing projects, and international agencies which provide most of the funding for them. Perhaps due to the patriarchal relations in Albanian society (i.e. aiming to counterbalance these), gender policies and projects almost always equate gender with women. While several organisations carry out gender-specific projects, most are gradually transiting towards a system of mainstreaming gender into wider projects such as those on development, democracy and environment (UNDP-Albania and SIDA 2004: 11).

In spite of progress in this area, Albania remains far behind other countries as far as gender equality is concerned. By 2009, the Gender Development Indicator for Albania was 0.80, giving it a rank of 68th out of 177 countries (EBRD 2009: 15). Finally, the NSM, the NAP on Migration and the NAP on Remittances all fail to consider gender as an analytical category (Nixon 2006).

Having examined in some detail the policy environment, initiatives and (lack of) achievement on issues of development, migration and gender in

Albania itself, we now widen the discussion to analyse power dynamics at a broader geographical scale expressed across the transnational terrain spanning Albania and Greece.

Albania–Greece Relations

Background

Relations between Greece and Albania were quite antagonistic for decades. This long-running tension was primarily related to the vexed questions of southern Albania ('North Epirus' for the Greeks), of the Greek minority living within the present-day borders of Albania, and of the Albanian-origin Cham population and their rights to property within the present-day borders of Greece (Konidaris 2005). To complicate matters further, Greece identified Albania first with the Ottoman Turkish occupiers of the eighteenth century, by reason of the religion of most Albanians (although the majority are only nominally Muslims); and second with its other enemy the communists, and the country where many Greek refugees, guerrillas and communists sought shelter during the later part of the Greek Civil War of 1946–49 (Vickers 1995).

The hostile and frozen relations of the decades that followed were thawed somewhat in the 1980s, as Greece was one of the first countries with which communist Albania started to negotiate bilateral agreements, albeit primarily in the cultural domain (Vickers 1995: 211). As communism collapsed in the former Eastern-bloc countries around Greece, and as Greece became a full member of the EU and of the European Monetary Union, its role also changed. From the early 1990s Greece became the 'North' of its Balkan neighbours who aspired to join the EU, whilst continuing to play the 'Southern' partner vis-à-vis more developed EU members (Labrianidis *et al.* 2004). It is in this role of the 'North' and EU member that we see Greece today in all its dealings and cooperation with Albania, from implementing its own bilateral cooperation programmes, to heading multilateral ones on behalf of the EU.[2] The close cooperation between Albania and Greece in the field of economic, social and international relations has led researchers to coin this state of affairs as a 'closed circuit'. Here, bi-directional flows of people (migrants from Albania to Greece and investors in the reverse direction), money (profit from investment versus remittances), goods (imports and exports and in-kind remittances) and services, as well as the flow of ideas and skills, link both countries in complex and tangled ways (Labrianidis *et al.* 2004).

The institutional bases for relations between the two countries have been established through the Friendship, Cooperation, Good Neighbourliness and Security Agreement signed in 1996. Greece has been an important trading partner of Albania, but only second to Italy, which dominates the Albanian foreign commerce by far. For example, between 2002 and 2006, Italy accounted for around 73 per cent of Albania's exports and 28–35 per cent of its imports; Greece's respective figures were between 10–13 per cent for exports and between 16–22 per cent for imports (INSTAT 2007b). In 2009, Greece continued to retain its second place, accounting for nearly 15 per cent of Albania's imports – versus 26 per cent from Italy – and around 7 per cent of Albania's exports – versus 60 per cent to Italy (BoA 2010: 17–18). In 2004 Greece came first in the list of foreign investors in Albania, with invested capital of more than US$ 500 million, representing almost 30 per cent of total FDI in the country. More than 200 Greek companies are active in Albania in the sectors of telecommunications, petroleum, banking, construction, the food industry and textile manufacturing. Although second in ranking – after Bulgaria – as the most important investment destination for Greek companies in terms of number of projects, Albania still accounted for only 3 per cent of the total *value* of FDI invested by Greece (Labrianidis *et al.* 2004: 1198). This important role was retained well into the late 2000s, when Greece was the second largest foreign investor in Albania, and its fourth biggest donor (Germenji 2010: 57).

Migration and Co-Development Policies

Having been the country most deeply affected by Albanian emigration, Greece's role in the financing and implementation of various programmes on migration and development in Albania has been important; although once again second to Italy's (for a summary of Albanian-Italian cooperation in this area, see Colleo and Perrelli Branca 2008). The development aid given by the Greek government is managed and distributed through Hellenic Aid, whilst other funds given by the EC are managed through a variety of projects, the most important of which are the INTERREG I, II, III, and IV on cross-border cooperation. Indeed, IOM's various studies on migrant readmission, remittances and irregular migration have been heavily financially supported by the Greek government.

Throughout our research we did not find any evidence of co-development policies or programmes on migration and development that were being jointly carried out between Albania and Greece, not only at local, but also at national level.[3] True, all projects implemented within the EU frameworks – mostly through the CARDS and AENEAS programmes – link migration and development, at least theoretically. However, in practice two things are observed. First, the majority of external funding goes to those projects which focus on combating irregular migration – through border controls, training of border police etc.; and to those which aim to combat trafficking of women and children – mostly through repatriation, accommodation in shelters and awareness raising campaigns (Geiger 2007: 125).[4] For example, the Greek government through its Hellenic Aid channel has been funding a significant number of projects in Albania, including in the Korçë region, targeting women and children as 'victims of trafficking and exploitation for prostitution and begging'.[5]

Second, where development is concerned this is not an end in itself, but a means to reduce or 'eliminate' further migration, in line with the thinking that more developed areas will not produce migrants. In fact, as recent research shows (de Haas 2010), the evolution of a migrant-sending country from a very poor to a less poor state does not reduce migration; often it increases the potential for further migration. As the channels for legal entry remain quite narrow, this migration potential turns into 'irregular' migration. The results in recent years have been an increased rate of expulsions from Greece and increased payments to smugglers – around €2,000–€3,000 for a one-entry and up to €5,000 for a two-year Schengen (EU) visa (Kanellopoulos and Gregou 2006: 27–8).[6] Our qualitative material presented in the previous chapters testifies to this. Initiatives in this framework focus mainly on increased border surveillance and training government officials, especially the border and migration police and the judiciary.

Third, some projects deal with the return and reintegration of apprehended 'illegal' Albanian and other third-country migrants. For example, the Greek Ministry of Interior led and coordinated the jointly EU-Greek funded AENEAS project between Albania and Greece which focused precisely on the return of Albanian and other irregular migrants, and training Albanian border police and civil servants from the Albanian Ministry of Interior to deal with the consequences of the RA implementation.[7]

Finally, the bilateral agreement on seasonal labour migrants signed in 1997 is still active, serving as it does the needs of the Greek economy for migrant labour in agriculture. This is an option taken by many migrants from rural areas, often as a way to keep themselves out of poverty, although sometimes the remitted cash is invested in small-scale agricultural enterprises, as we have seen. However, the procedures to obtain such visas are cumbersome, bureaucratic and take very long (for a detailed description see Maroukis 2008: 9). Moreover, as we saw in the previous chapters, the pay is low and living conditions are often primitive for this kind of work. For these reasons, this remains a narrow channel of legal migration. Precise figures are not available, but some researchers suggest around 7,000 Albanians held such visas during 2003–04, the majority of whom worked in agriculture (Baldwin-Edwards and Apostolatou 2009).

In short, the migration–development cooperation with the EU, in particular that with Greece, in reality reflects a largely host-country agenda: stemming unwanted migration from Albania while addressing labour needs for sectors such as agriculture (for similar conclusions in Italy see Chaloff 2008).

Diaspora, Civil Society and the Life of (Transnational) Projects

Within the framework outlined above, a number of initiatives were carried out in our research area and the Korçë region generally. Once again, gender was often equated with women and dealt with in the framework of anti-trafficking or anti-domestic violence projects, whilst migration was dealt with as a matter of border security (for Greece). Although the level of awareness of the benefits of migration locally – especially in terms of financial remittances and skills – was very high, its inclusion in local development programmes was almost non-existent. It was acknowledged that these were in principle private transfers and could not possibly be touched. On the other hand, collective transfers were almost non-existent as were the transnational links between migrants and their areas of origin at the institutional level.

Organising the Diaspora in Greece

Collective action has been rather limited amongst Albanian migrants in Greece until recent years, for a number of reasons. First, there is the recency of this migration dating only since the early 1990s, with no previous accumulated migratory experience in this country. Second, the legacy of coercive collectivisation as well as of elaborate methods of spying – everyone was presumed to spy on everyone – during the not-so-distant communist past, has certainly played a part in the level of distrust Albanians have towards each other and towards community voluntary organisations. This is in contrast to the high degree of trust placed on family members, forged during the years of communism as well as through the turmoil and insecurities of the post-communist transformations (Lubonja 2001; Murzaku and Dervishi 2003). Third, migrants have had to deal with a high degree of exploitation, discrimination and marginalisation, which has allowed little space for their social capital to develop. This is particularly the case in Greece (Gropas and Triandafyllidou 2005). The fact that almost all migrant organisations there date from around 1998 – which is also the year of the first regularisation – is quite telling in this context. Finally, matters of a more practical nature are vitally important; most migrants work long hours in order to make ends meet. This is particularly the case for women who are usually employed as domestic helpers and carers, in addition to looking after their own families and households in Greece.

However, things are changing. By 2008 there were an estimated 100 Albanian migrant organisations in Greece (besides those of ethnic-Greek migrants), 80 per cent of which were based in Athens. This reflects to a certain extent the concentration of the Albanian community geographically, but also the opportunities and spaces for such activities. The majority of these organisations are small and there has been a certain drive in recent years for their regrouping under 'umbrella-like' arrangements. Thus, by 2008 there were two such entities: a) *The Albanian Migrants' League*; and b) *The Federation of Albanian Associations*. Each of these comprises of around 25 migrant associations. There are, however, other organisations which are not members of these 'umbrella' groups.

Many organisations suffer from disputes amongst and sometimes within themselves, as we found from our interviews and informal conversations with a number of the leaders, from debates in the major Albanian migrant newspapers published in Greece, as well as during one of our focus-group discussions with stakeholders in Thessaloniki, which became quite rowdy as a result. These antagonistic relations stemmed either from personal rivalries or deeper ideological factors (read: political persuasions). This is a classic example of transnational political activity, or 'reverse' social remittances, i.e. home-country politics are transmitted from Albania to the immigrants in Greece. Indeed, branches of the three main political parties – the Socialist Party, the Democratic Party and the Movement for Social Integration – have been created in Greece, and are often used as vehicles for garnering migrants' support during electoral campaigns back home.

In the last five years there has been an increase in organisations which base their membership on the town, village or region of origin of migrants. Most of these organisations have a core membership around a network of people who are family-kinship related, and especially in larger organisations the management is dominated by men in their 50s. Besides such hometown-type associations, there are also other groupings organised on the basis of professional interest, particularly of writers and artists.

However, in contrast to other migrant organisations, the Albanian ones almost always focus on cultural issues and the preservation of Albanian identity. Fearing cultural uprooting, these organisations provide particularly for the socialisation of the second generation through Albanian language classes. Albanian migrant organisations which advocate civil, legal and human rights for this community in Greece are rather few, as are those which focus on women's issues or have a female majority on their board of trustees and directors.

Participation amongst our interviewees in Thessaloniki, or returnees in the study villages, in any formal organisation was very low. The exception was a very small number of migrants who held ethnic-Greek documents and at times claimed Greek ethnicity as part – thus not exclusively – of their overall identity. These migrants often attended meetings at the Epirote House federation in downtown Thessaloniki (for more on the various Albanian migrant organisations in Thessaloniki see Hatziprokopiou 2006: 213–17). They had been issued with an ethnic-Greek membership card which, prior to the 1998 regularisation, also served as an identification document and was used to acquire jobs, housing and prevent deportation by the police back to Albania. However, none of the migrants we interviewed were involved in village-based organisations. Furthermore, no one had participated in collective action to support public works or other types of collective activities back in their origin village. A few of the interviewees were also key community figures and they were not aware that such activities existed amongst migrants from these study villages. Fatmir, 42, who has been in Greece since 1989 explains:

> I don't know of any initiative of collective remittances [after we explain to him what these are]... And I have never heard of them personally... There are many reasons [for this absence]. It depends on one's budget, it also depends on the trust. We don't have trust. If you give the money to someone, but who do you give it to? If we all collect that money and go and do it ourselves there, would we have time? No.

Others had bitter experiences of cooperation, like Urim:

> This has not happened and will not happen. For instance I invested some money to repair our street in the village and the families there [whose houses are by the street] told me they would give me their share of the contribution. But at the end of the day I ended up paying everything myself... I bought some hard spread – about two or three truck-loads. It wasn't very expensive, about 15,000 lek [€120], but at the time this was a lot of money. 15,000 lek is not nothing. And they kept promising me, but no one gave me the money... So things like these will not happen... First, no one has come up with any idea, but also I am not very optimistic that it would work... Not because it is not worth it, but because some migrants say: 'it's not like I go there often'. It's the indifference. And then distrust... I don't think it's about the money, as all these

migrants from Pojan who live here [in Thessaloniki], if each gave €100 something could be done…

However, an interesting transnational virtual space of association is slowly emerging with the wider spread of Internet use and social networking sites such as Facebook. A Facebook site for Pojan has been created online with hundreds of member-users, mostly migrants who reside in Greece, Italy, North America and other host countries, although some are also based in the village itself and in the towns around. It will be interesting to observe for future research whether such virtual transnational spaces made possible by the advent and the rapid expansion of the Internet, can become the seedbed of social collective action that benefits origin societies.

The Social Life of Rural Projects in Albania

Coming back to civil society in our study area, through our mapping exercise we identified around 80 local NGOs registered as having their office in the Korçë region, primarily in the Korçë district.[8] In the commune of Pojan itself the following associations existed at the time of our research: the Farmers' Association, the Beekeepers' Association, the Apple Growers' Association, the Bean Growers' Association, the Potato Growers' Association, the 'Vëntrok' Water Users' Association (this is a national association, which has the right to manage the waterways and has leased these for 50 years), the Women's Association, the Association Roma Active Albania and the Association of Orphaned Children and Youth of Korçë.[9] A number of women had been members of a credit union they did not even know the name of, and which was also defunct for all intents and purposes. We use the word 'existed' rather than 'operated' here, because many of these organisations existed only on paper, and only a handful were active. This was due to a combination of factors including disagreements amongst members, lack of funds, lack of managerial experience, lack of training opportunities and because some had simply been implanted from outside in one short-lived donor-funded project or another (see Sampson 1996 for a powerful critique of civil society in Albania).

Whilst the NGO sector has mushroomed in Albania since the 1990s when the communist ban on such independent associations was lifted, the sector has continually been plagued by fierce competition over funds (Misha 2006). The competition is not only amongst local NGOs, but also with more experienced and powerful ones from abroad, as well as other larger organisations such as IOM. As a result, most EU (and other) funds for Albania are disbursed through foreign NGOs which in turn are required to have one or more local partners. These are either founded for the specific project, or brought on board from the existing pool. However, such involvement is very asymmetrical with the local partner often doing the legwork – collection of data through surveys or interviews, or implementation of services – and the international partner controlling the budget and the planning of the project. Moreover, most NGOs' agendas are donor-driven, making it thus very difficult for sustainable and consistent activities (Misha 2006). This 'humanitarian colonialism', as some have dubbed it, is hardly unique to Albania. However, Albania, along with other post-communist countries, has provided fertile ground to experiment with models that have (often not) worked elsewhere in the Global South.

On the other hand, the NGO sector itself has more broadly become a kind of elite club, attracting highly-paid, highly-skilled and highly-educated (often at masters level) individuals who come from, or have settled well, in urban areas; the rest of the population are the 'target' groups and 'beneficiaries' and are rarely consulted on services provided *to* them. In one example of a project implemented in the study villages, an urban-based women's NGO was funded by a Scandinavian government development agency, through an Austrian-based private company which managed the project, to 'educate' rural women on how to keep their village clean by separating different kinds of waste. Patronising attitudes aside, rural women were deemed to be the target group, since they are the ones who perform these chores in the family and society, thus reinforcing their 'natural' role as housewives.

Migrant organisations in host countries, particularly Greece in our case, were also generally taken on board as the 'token' partner. To paraphrase one of our academic stakeholders in Greece, migrants are generally approached as a target group and not as a partner with whom the project should be designed and developed. As the leadership remains in the hands of Greek partners, who 'use' migrant women and men as beneficiaries of the project, the scope for the latter to develop their skills and integration remains limited.

Finally, there was some transnational cooperation between the University of Korçë and its counterparts in Greece, but these initiatives were again very limited.

Facilitating Factors, Impediments and the Future

As has been clear from our account throughout this book, remittances constitute an important element not only in the lives and economies of individuals and households in Albania, but also of the local community at large. Indeed, everyone commented on the significant improvements that have been noted as a result of migration and remittances at the local level. However, some negative aspects could also be observed. There is, for instance, a significant degree of inequality in these rural areas between migrant and non-migrant families. Although our questionnaire survey does not allow us to capture this, we were able to confirm it through observations on the ground, as well as in-depth interviews with families which had access to different types of migration. The Roma and Evgjit communities remain the most marginalised in that respect, although some Albanian families lived in dire poverty too. Money is of course not everything and the human and emotional costs of migration were only too obvious during our conversations with those remaining behind. Family separation, especially when migrants could not travel back because of lack of documentation, was a major sacrifice that could only be rationalised (if at all) as the necessary price to be paid for a better financial future.

Although a significant number of households have left the villages for good, these rural areas are far from abandoned and present considerable potential for development initiatives. For instance, many of our research participants saw great potential in the large-scale farming of a number of fruit and vegetables. The increase in cultivated areas of apple orchard had resulted from local experience, whereby households that could use such income-generating activities were earning decent sums of money, sometimes equalling those brought from Greece. Since this type of agricultural work is considered more skilled, it is less stigmatised by at least the middle-aged villagers. The psychology around agriculture is also changing and there is more interest in farming on the part of those who can consider themselves landowning farmers and employers. There are signs of the reclaiming of a pre-war status as well-off farmers who are part of the landowning class. These farming enterprises, however, need significant capital injections before they can run on their own.

As production of these fruits and vegetables expands locally, so does the potential to invest in agro-businesses that use these produce as core materials. As such, examples were given of cooling storage warehouses where produce could be collected and stored for sale internally in Albania and even for export; fruit-processing factories for making jams, pickles, compote; expanding existing or increasing dairy processing factories, etc. There are some initiatives which have started in this direction. However, these are all capital- and knowledge-intensive businesses, which are out of reach for most poor villagers. The most that the majority of the villagers were hoping to use their remittances for was to repair their house or build a new one. Not everyone intended to become an entrepreneur and employer. Many would be happy if there was employment locally they could take as day-labourers or contract workers.

However, there are certain areas that need to be improved if remittances are to be used optimally.

The life of people residing in the study villages has for centuries centred around farming and working the land. Agriculture continues to be the most important local income-generating activity, and the only one for some very poor families. However, this sector generally suffers from a number of problems. Structurally, there is a lack of insurance markets for produce; a lack of information on trading prices; lack of large-scale and mechanised farming; inefficient controls at higher levels for the quality of imported products such as pesticides; and competition from cheaper imported produce; to name but a few. The most difficult thing the farmers found was finding adequate markets to sell their produce, which is often left in stocks and wasted. As a result of WTO agreements, the Albanian market is periodically flooded by subsidised imports from neighbouring Greece and Macedonia, where farmers can benefit from large-scale farming, better mechanised processes, subsidies, and generally better institutional support. On the contrary, in Albania land is very fragmented in small plots, insecurity over land titles and ownership continues to affect future plans for investment, and there is a low rate of mechanisation. This is improving and in our study area we noted consolidation of land through the purchase and rental land markets. Progress is also being made regarding the types of crops cultivated, with an increasing number of farmers now concentrating on large-scale cultivation of especially beans, potatoes and onions. Coming from almost half a century of centralised economy and planning, farmers are only slowly coming to grips with the mechanisms of the market economy, understanding how markets work, and above all actively marketing their produce. Following forced collectivisation during communism, most do not contemplate cooperative-type collaborations, thus leaving individual farmers disempowered in the face of global market forces. Most cooperation is done at family and kinship level, usually during planting and harvesting, but this has not been extended as yet to collective trading.

Locally, although the fields in the area are some of the most fertile in the entire country, restricted access to water resources and dilapidated drainage and watering systems have constantly presented serious challenges to sustainable agriculture. Many who can afford to, have invested in deep wells locally, but because these are quite expensive to drill, most families cover their costs for this through remittances. Access to markets is also limited, since the villages are not alongside the major road and the transport and road infrastructure has again continued to suffer from under-investment.

Although agriculture employs around 60 per cent of the labour force country-wide, it generates only a fifth of the country's GDP. The national economy relies heavily on services – mostly trade, especially imported goods – and of course remittances. The negative effects of this asymmetrical structure of the economy are further exacerbated by under-investment in the infrastructure of rural areas such as roads, fresh drinking water and electricity. In spite of the water system being put in place in recent years, Pojan families have only two hours of running water a day, and have to make do with individually-opened wells the rest of the time. The situation is much better in Zvezdë, since it is nearer the mountain and hence to natural water sources. The problem with power shortages is country-wide, but especially rural areas are 'punished' by longer cuts and less voltage running through the system. The roads have continually been full of pot-holes, and corruptive practices in public works ensure that they need major repairs after each winter, even when thousands of euros are poured in each time.

> The problem about these investments is that whereas in Korçë there are power shortages of only eight hours, in the village these are 12 hours or more; whereas in Korçë they have running water 24 hours a day, in our village only three hours a day. Road and transport infrastructure are in a miserable state. Why should I then invest in the village? Whatever we are spending there we are doing simply in our own house, simply for the sake of nostalgia [Urim, 51, migrant in Thessaloniki].

> We have had problems with the electricity. We have had much loss because of that. Often the loaves of bread we have prepared to bake we have thrown away because there hasn't been enough electricity to bake them, or they went bad waiting for electricity to come… We can't use small generators because the machinery we use has a three-phase conductor and needs a lot of energy [Kozeta, 33, working in the family business – bakery – set up from remittances from her husband].

Under such conditions, migrants who are used to a different standard of living find it difficult to contemplate return, whilst those living in the villages can hardly wait to escape the life made so miserable by lack of the most basic living conditions. Urban areas are considered better places because these amenities are better (but by no means fully satisfactory), and also because there is hope that in the not-so-distant future things will improve.

Conclusion

As Ramírez *et al.* (2005) note in their 'state-of-the-art' working paper on gender, remittances and development, the interest of governments and international organisations in the potential use of remittances as a developmental tool has been on the increase. Albania has been one of the top recipients of remittances in the world, in per capita terms and as a share of its GDP (World Bank 2011). However, policy has not kept up with the pace of change through which the country has passed, particularly in relation to the gendered impact of migration and remittances. Successive Albanian governments have taken a passive role on migration, considering it merely as a means to export unemployment and import wealth through remittances (Azzarri and Carletto 2009; Germenji and Milo 2009; King and Vullnetari 2009a). Even when they have been pro-active, their actions have been generally ad-hoc and incoherent, in order to remedy the present, but not looking very much into the future. Besides limited ability and effectiveness, as well as a lack of political willingness, these actions have generally reflected an unconditional acceptance of the terms set by external actors such as the EU and supported by IOM. According to Geiger (2007), the EC, together with its delegation in Tirana, are the most important external actors in shaping such migration-related policies and practices in Albania.

Especially the NSM and its accompanying NAP on Remittances have clearly set out to address two aims through a number of initiatives. Both these aims are essentially financial and economic, rather than social or gender-related. First, an improvement of the mechanisms for remittance transfers is planned through the lowering of transfer costs, and the channelling of a larger share of remittances through the formal financial system. These strategies and programmes generally lack a gendered approach. In addition, they seem to be limited by an embedded culture amongst various organisations and local NGOs of working parallel to, rather than together with, one another. Some steps in the right direction are observed, especially related to the coordination of UN-funded initiatives. But, as our experience whilst carrying out the research that informs this book showed, there is still a long way to go.

Second, the mobilisation of the diaspora is envisaged through the increased capacity of, and cooperation with, migrant organisations in order to implement co-development policies and projects. Once again, whilst some projects have organised meetings with various migrant organisations abroad, to our knowledge initiatives where such migrant organisations are involved as fully active rather than as 'token' partners, are very limited. Research has suggested that collective remittances may have a more significant impact than individual ones on the local development of origin areas (Goldring 2003; Ramírez *et al.* 2005: 45). In the Albanian case, however, such types of remittances are very limited. Certainly in our study area they were almost non-existent and co-development was not an issue on the table, at least for the time being and under present conditions. Considering that the fertile ground (i.e. the desire) for such collective initiatives exists, as we were able to find out through our research, strengthening the role of migrant organisations as agents of development and change remains an important future objective.

On the issue of co-development policies and initiatives between Albania and Greece, we conclude that the outcomes of even existing initiatives are questionable. True, there are a number of projects being carried out that link both countries, but where migration is included, they are considered to meet the development and immigration objectives of the host country, i.e. Greece. Certainly Albanian migrant organisations in Greece are not involved as partners in such projects and consultation with them is only token. Chaloff (2008) came to similar conclusions in his study of co-development policies and practices between Albania and its other migration neighbour, Italy.

The discrepancy of our findings through our mapping and literature review at national level, and actual programmes and action at local level shows that launching a strategy or action plan is not enough to bring about change. Active participation of citizens of urban and especially rural areas in the implementation of such strategies needs to be addressed by equipping local stakeholders with the necessary skills to improve their performance and take the lead role in projects that affect their own communities. Equally, there is a need for greater cooperation not only amongst stakeholders nationally, but also across the border. Albanian migrant associations or informal groups in Greece should be included as participants in such initiatives, so that the way can be opened for networking and linking with Albanian counterparts.

Finally, the role of women in these various initiatives is differentiated by education and background. Albanian women have a strong presence in the NGO sector, whether as staff of international organisations or running national NGOs. However, the vast majority of them is part of the highly educated urban elite. This presence is further reduced for lower-skilled women and especially in rural areas, including in our study villages, where the presence of men in decision-making positions is absolutely dominant. Participation of rural women in leading roles at local level should be encouraged through affirmative action. Women are not simply the 'cashiers' of the family, as many of our interlocutors put it, but they are also capable of managing, administering, conceptualising and leading initiatives if provided with the right opportunities, support and spaces.

8

CONCLUSIONS AND RECOMMENDATIONS

In this final chapter we draw together a number of conclusions and make recommendations for policy and further research. We first summarise our key findings and relate them to the guiding questions set out in Chapter 1 and to the theoretical frameworks reviewed in Chapter 2. We assert the originality and significance of our findings on gender and remittances within the wider academic and policy debate on migration and development. The rest of this concluding chapter is then organised around the three key questions which Ramírez *et al.* (2005) posed in their agenda-setting policy paper which was the guiding inspiration for the research presented in this book, namely:

- How does the growing feminisation of migration affect remittance flows?
- How can remittances contribute to achieving gender equality?
- How can remittances be mobilised in order to achieve sustainable development that includes women?

Throughout this last chapter we liberally use italics to stress the main results and recommendations we wish to make.

Key Findings

At the outset of our research, and at the start of this book, we specified a number of questions and objectives. Our overall aim has been to explore the hitherto unexplored relationship between remittances – one of the key axes of the migration–development nexus – and gender. Reflecting the recursive relationship between migration and development, which we unpacked in some detail in Chapter 2, the gender–remittance dynamic can also be framed as two overarching questions, as pointed out in Chapter 1:

- How do the prevailing gender relations in Albanian society shape the sending, receiving and utilisation of remittances?
- How do the earning, transmission and decision-taking over remittances reshape gender relations in Albanian transnational migrant households?

These rather general research questions were then disaggregated into a series of more pragmatic questions which could be further broken down into specific items built into the questionnaire and interview schedules. These more pragmatic questions were:

- Who sends remittances, how much, and how often; and what conditions are put by, or on, the sender as to their use?
- Who receives remittances, and what influence do they have over their amount, frequency, and utilisation?
- How does the economic transaction of earning income and sending remittances affect gender relations within the migrant household abroad?
- How does the same remittance transaction affect gender roles and relations in the part of the transnational unit that remains 'at home' in Albania?

These questions represent an attempt to move beyond what we saw as the rather limited and stylised debate over gendering remittances which appears in the literature so far, namely whether women are 'better' remitters, and users of remittances, than men (cf. King and Vullnetari 2010). The more policy-related questions that were set out in Chapter 1 concerning how remittances interface with local development plans, how public policies can provide better options for utilising remittances to create social capital and sustainable livelihoods, and the key aim of building gender equality into these policy fields, are dealt with in the later sections of this concluding chapter.

So, what have we achieved in this book? First, and at the risk of false immodesty, it bears repeating that this is the first book-length, in-depth study of gender and remittances. In the pre-existing literature, there have been quite a few references to the gender–remittance nexus, and a small number of empirical studies, which we reviewed in detail in Chapter 2; but none of these, we venture to argue, match the scale of empirical research carried out here; and nor do most of the previous studies move beyond the dichotomous male-versus-female framing of the key research questions in the way we have done in our analysis. The Albanian case demonstrates convincingly that to ask 'Are women better remitters than men?' or 'Do women utilise remittances more sensibly than men?' are not the relevant questions. Quite apart from the issue of meaning and measurement behind such phrases as 'better remitters' or 'more sensibly' etc., the starting-point should be an analysis of gender structures in the society where migrants originate from, and how these gender relations are played out in various household, family and kinship contexts, within and across generations. The generational dimension, which is enshrined in the very term 'patriarchy', thus needs to be brought into the analysis as an intersecting variable with gender to produce 'gendered and generational geographies of power' (cf. King and Vullnetari 2009b; Mahler and Pessar 2001). Hence our first key finding: *understanding Albanian remittance dynamics from a gendered perspective implies a close analysis not only of gendered relations in Albanian society, but also how these relations are articulated with generations.*

Although we have seen that Albania is one of Europe's most patriarchal societies, the way this is expressed varies between the more traditional North of the country and the historically more open and less traditional South (where our research was based), and between urban and rural areas (our research being in the latter). Our results therefore show some differences, particularly as regards the agency of women, from an earlier study which was based on migration originating from the rural North (King *et al.* 2006). Nevertheless, we did indeed find that *remittances were absolutely and fundamentally shaped by prevailing gender and generational structures*, to the extent that, in Albanian migrant households, women are hardly allowed to be 'official' remitters; *the official remittance process remains esconced in the hands of men.*

Despite the continuing male control of remittance transactions, we nevertheless uncovered *some female participation in sending remittances, albeit only as a result of the 'permission' of their husbands* who allowed them to send some resources to their own (as opposed to their husbands') parents. Such remittances were often in-kind, rather than in cash; but if the latter, they were cloaked in 'non-remittance' phraseology like 'just for a coffee'.

Regarding the *mechanics of the remittance process* – how much is sent, how frequently, for what purposes etc., and who decides about these elements of the process – we found that *these questions could only be answered by exploring the kinship dynamics of a variety of forms of transnational household.* These household typologies, and how they interacted with migration and remittances, were set out in detail in Chapter 4. The consequent family and remittance arrangements were shown to be governed by several factors: first, whether the migrant was married or not; second, if married, whether the whole family had migrated or only the husband (almost never was it the wife on her own); third, the kind of migration status acquired in Greece (regularised, undocumented, 'ethnic-Greek' status etc.); fourth, and partly reflecting the previous factor, whether migrants were in Greece seasonally or longer-term; and finally a number of further family-demographic factors such as whether their parents were still alive, whether they were the youngest son, and the existence of other siblings who were migrants.

This stress on the *contextuality of the remittance process* also has implications for how we interpret remittance flows into Albania in terms of the Lucas and Stark (1985) typology of altruism vs. self-interest which we outlined in Chapter 2. We see evidence of both in our data; and also, therefore, of the intermediate type which Lucas and Stark labelled tempered altruism or enlightened self-interest. It is clear that the economic privations of so many Albanian families in the early post-communist years quickly led to the establishment of a pragmatic remittance culture where remittances, seen as the only means of salvation from poverty, became a 'moral duty' for younger men to support their residual family members. Narratives of remittance-senders, both in our study here and in other studies (King *et al.* 2003; 2006) revealed a strong sense of obligation and, in most cases, of satisfaction ('utility') gained from the improved standard of living that their foreign labour enabled their left-behind families to achieve. But as the migration process matured into the 2000s, we observe remittance priorities changing: settlement and integration abroad of nuclear families means that reduced amounts of remittances are sent, and money is invested in projects for the future – a house, a business, or better farming technology. This shift from altruism to self-interest is, however, exactly what the older generations, the erstwhile remittance-receivers, would want for their children and grandchildren. So the Albanian evidence shows that the divide between altruism and self-interest is to some extent a false dichotomy because of the strong family solidarity across the generations – but down the male line.

Lastly, in this highlighting of key general findings, we turn to the broader theoretical questions posed about the causal and reciprocal relations between migration and development in Chapter 2. The first causal link which we can clearly identify is that, in Albania, *mass-scale emigration has been largely the result of the underdevelopment of the country*. Migration – including internal relocation within the country – has been the population's response to an unheralded and unprecedented situation of 'new poverty' created by the uncertainties and socio-economic marginalisation effects of the neoliberal era, which removed the guarantees of the shared 'old poverty' which existed throughout the communist decades, yet which was felt to a lesser degree because of the people's isolation from the outside world and the regime's message that Albania was an earthly paradise. Although 'escape from poverty' has been the main driver of migration in Albania, other elements, characteristic of the immediate post-communist years throughout the Eastern bloc, also came into play and were noted in Chapter 3 – the desire to see and experience life in 'the West' after long decades of being denied passports and thus even the possibility of international mobility, and the emigration especially of academics, artists and scientists who saw a broader canvas for their intellectual endeavours abroad than in Albania.

If the Albanian case shows a clear exemplification of poverty and underdevelopment causing migration, what has been the nature of the relationship at the next stage of the migration–development nexus? What impact has migration had on the Albanian development process? How have migration and development interacted after the first bursts of migratory activity during the 1990s? Referring back to the notion of the 'migration hump' introduced in Chapter 2, is Albania approaching the top of the hump (the curve of increasing migration through time as development progresses); and if not, how much longer will migration continue before, in a certain way, it *has* to come to a halt simply because the reservoir of young aspirant migrants runs dry? These questions are more difficult to answer, for a whole series of reasons: the evidence is mixed; there are different effects in different parts of the country and for different social groups; the effects might be different at the micro-scale as opposed to the macro; we need to distinguish short-term effects from impacts over the longer term; and there are different ideological interpretations of what is going on.

Our research evidence collected for this book is far from enabling us to achieve a complete set of answers, for which recourse to other literature is necessary. We have reviewed much of this literature in two papers (King and Vullnetari 2003; 2009a) where we deal not only with the effects of remittances but also of return and diaspora engagement. Blending our own research findings with those of others, we arrive at the following conclusions, some clear-cut, others only tentative. The most clearly evident is the finding that *migration and the ensuing remittances have lifted tens if not hundreds of thousands of families and households out of poverty*. Of this there seems no doubt: it is a fact confirmed by our interviewees, both migrants and stakeholders, as well as by several teams of other researchers (De Soto *et al.* 2002; de Zwager *et al.* 2005; Gedeshi *et al.* 2003a; Kule *et al.* 2002). And this finding holds both for migrant households in Greece and for 'residual' remittance-receiving households in Albania.

Equally evident is the macro-economic impact of migration and remittances: *migration enabled Albania to export its unemployment problem* deriving from the neoliberal revolution in the country's economic structure – closure of factories, mines, state farms etc. – and to *boost its national economic accounts by remittances playing a major part in plugging the balance of payment deficit.* Indeed, without migration and remittances, it is difficult to envisage what shape the new, post-communist economy and society might have taken – with consequences too for political stability.

Yet this is far from the whole story. The longer-term effects of what has just been noted above may be less favourable, but to some extent here we are in the realms of speculation given the recency of Albania's migratory exodus. It seems to us that the analysis of future trends turns on the balance of outcome between two scenarios. On the one hand it may prove to be the case that migration, and its pay-off of remittances, fulfil a crucial staging post on the path to longer-term sustainable development. In this scenario, the function of remittances at an aggregate level will have been to secure some economic stability whilst other macro-economic variables, such as endogenous growth of production – either for exports or for import substitution – gather pace. In our research, we noted initiatives in intensive agricultural development in the plain surrounding the study villages, and the growth of garment factories in Korçë, partly sustained by foreign (amongst which, Greek) investment. At the individual or household level, remittances may likewise function to 'bridge the gap' between poverty alleviation and survival in the initial stages of migration to investment and sustainable livelihoods later on.

On the other hand, there are potential negative scenarios at both scales. Both individual households and the national economy may become so structurally dependent on remittances, and hence on continued migration, that other initiatives are choked off. In this scenario, the residual household continues to subsist on remittances and to disinvest in agriculture, leading to land abandonment, whilst at the national level remittances become permanently established as the structural plank upholding the economy whose main export thus becomes labour. Reliance on remittances carries other socio-economic dangers, which we have alluded to in various parts of the foregoing account. Remittance-driven 'development' has involved a construction boom both in the villages of origin of migrants and in the major Albanian towns and cities, above all Tirana, fed also by powerful flows of internal migrants. This has led to a considerable socio-economic spatial polarisation within the country. Meanwhile, the memory of the pyramid crisis fades only slowly: this was a remittance-fuelled financial collapse caused by a combination of 'excess' remittance income and insufficient productive outlets for it, together with, at that stage, a naïve understanding of the capitalist economy. Another negative effect of mass migration has been the brain drain, depriving Albania of half of its academics, researchers and scientists within the first post-communist decade (Gedeshi and Black 2006). The trick now is how to turn the 'drain' into a 'gain' by stimulating the return of the educated elite.

Returning once again to the 'migration hump' question, this has become difficult to answer because it is predicated on a notion of freedom to move abroad and, as we have seen, this is far from the case. Twenty years after the embassy siege in Tirana and the mass crossings of the mountains to Greece and of the Otranto Strait to Italy, Albanians have had less freedom to leave their country to seek work than they did then, in the ambiguous euphoria of the first post-communist years. So it is difficult to judge whether, and how much, more migration *would* take place if it was freely allowed. As we give the final touches to this book – December 2010 – the EU ruling on visa liberalisation with the Western Balkans has finally included the last two countries of Bosnia-Herzegovina and Albania (the other Western Balkan countries having been given this 'priviledge' gradually in the past two years or so; Kosovo is still some way away). As such, from 15 December 2010 Albanians who are in possession of a biometric passport are in principle free to visit the Schengen area (excluding the UK and Ireland) for a total of three months in a year. The group who will benefit the most are older parents of migrants settled abroad. Some young people may use the opportunity to work, although employment is not permitted under this type of entry. Yet again, with the labour markets severely contracting in most EU countries, especially in Greece and Italy, it remains to be seen to what degree this will be widespread.

Against this scenario that there is still a pent-up pressure for further migration which has been blocked until now, we point out three counter-variables, one economic, one demographic, and the other psychological. The economic one is the simple fact that Albania *has* developed, and done so with quite a fast rhythm, despite some setbacks. The economic imperative to migrate is no longer so desperately urgent as it was in the 1990s, and for the vast majority of the population whether rural or urban. Demographically, the country has a rapidly falling birth-rate; in fact it was already on a downward trajectory before 1990, but the decline has accelerated since then, partly because of changing norms about ideal family size (an indication of gender empowerment?), but partly too because of the fact that so many reproductively-active young adults have emigrated. And thirdly, there is nowadays a different social and psychological attitude towards emigration – no longer regarded as the *only* way forward by a cohort of young adults who see migration as an act of desperation and something almost to be despised and pitied.

These various findings and scenarios allow us only to conclude that *it is too early yet to say whether migration will on balance have long-term positive effects on Albania's economy and society*. This is where the policy environment becomes relevant, and this is dealt with in the subsequent parts of the chapter.

Remittances and the Feminisation of Migration

Post-communist migration in Albania started off as an overwhelmingly male event; generally it was men who migrated first whilst women stayed behind. This was especially the case in rural areas, including our study villages. This *gendered pattern of migration* was conditioned by existing *gender norms* in the (rural) origin society according to which women's mobility is very much structured within patriarchal power relations, and therefore limited. In addition, the physically challenging journey over the mountains to Greece, the potential risk of physical, verbal and sexual abuse by the Greek army as well as Albanian gangs, the difficult living conditions of migrant workers in Greece – sleeping crammed in sheds and barns in the fields – made such journeys to be constructed as sites of masculinity and masculine resistance. If any woman took such journeys, they did so accompanied by their spouse or other male relatives (Vullnetari 2009). Other options for regular emigration were extremely limited, especially for women and particularly for those living in rural areas. This *male-led typology of Albanian migration* was reflected strongly when females increasingly emigrated as 'dependents' to join their husbands in Greece after the first Greek regularisation programme of 1998 (see also King and Vullnetari 2009b). As we saw through the analysis of our survey data and in-depth interviews in Chapter 4, this was the typical migration typology followed in our study area as well.

However, the *participation of women in the migration project has been intensive whether as migrants, or when remaining behind in the villages*. Although women did not migrate independently, a large share of them contributed economically to the transnational household through their productive and reproductive work. Most migrant women work in domestic care and cleaning services, and a few in garment factories, hotels and restaurants, whereas some stayed at home in Thessaloniki to look after young children and the household. Some who lived in rural areas of Greece worked also in agriculture. Men were overwhelmingly employed in construction, agriculture, manufacturing and services. However, job improvement and diversification was much slower for women, partly because their jobs – especially in the domestic services sector – are more stable, and partly because a significant number of them work 'off the books', without social security. Employment for migrant women (and not only migrant women) *is sharply gendered*, confining female migrants to the largely 'domestic' cleaning and caring roles. This reflects the hegemonic gendered norms of Greek society,[1] which in many respects shares the wider historical experience of Balkan and Mediterranean patriarchy seen in perhaps its most extreme form in rural highland Albania. So women have had fewer opportunities to build migrant work careers in a trajectory of upward occupational mobility compared to men, some of whom have gone on to found their own small businesses, albeit mainly within their original sectors of employment, especially construction, house maintenance and allied trades.[2]

Nevertheless, the regular income that Albanian migrant women are able to bring to the migrant household has given them a certain degree of empowerment in intra-household negotiations of money and tasks. Regarding the latter, this is also affected by the exigencies of life in migration where both spouses work and thus both need to share their household chores and care for the children. Of influence too has been the surrounding mentality which is slightly more accepting of men who perform household chores, often regarded as 'female tasks': we say 'slightly' because Greece too remains an essentially patriarchal society.

Our in-depth interviews also revealed that *some women were empowered to some extent by migration* as they actively participated in decision-making about remittance-sending, although they were rarely remittance-senders themselves, at least in a formally-recognised sense. Albanian tradition requires that once a woman is married, her care responsibilities are transferred from her own parents and siblings to those of her husband. In our research this was not a universal condition and we were able to identify more nuanced situations. For instance, daughters sent remittances to their mothers and fathers in cash or in-kind – often labelled as 'presents' – but some sent these in the same amounts as to their in-laws; sisters helped their siblings in the villages, etc. However, often *migrant women were disempowered by the Greek immigration policy of the last decade and a half, which perpetuates patriarchal patterns of dependency and potential gender discrimination.*

Clearly, an increasing feminisation of migration flows – i.e. increased shares of migrant women participating, as has been the case for Albania since the late 1990s – has meant a certain decrease of remittances in sums and frequencies. As we discussed in Chapter 5, the process of settlement in Greece after the husband's reunification with his wife and children was accompanied by a refocusing of energies and resources on sustaining life in the host country. Remittances sent to elderly – most often *his* – parents, were consequently reduced to token amounts – usually no more than 'just for a coffee' and not more often than twice or three times a year. However, this was not the entire story, as other types of remittances might be on the increase. As the duration of migration extends, and provided that both spouses have worked for some years in Greece, some remittances are sent to Albania to be invested in property, often in the capital Tirana. A combination of ensuring a form of future social security for themselves and their children and the limited information on, and other types of, investment opportunities, seems to be behind such initiatives. Such properties also have powerful symbolic value – literally cementing the migrant's ties with the 'homeland' and acting as a visible demonstration of 'success' in the migration project (Dalakoglou 2009). In the case of immigrants in Greece this is reinforced by their perpetual insecurity of immigration status there.

Remittances and Gender Equality

When discussing the ways in which gender roles influence and are influenced by remittances, we also consider the position of women who are, inevitably, part of a migrant family, but who remain behind in the area of origin. Especially in *wife-headed households, women had more opportunities for decision-making not only about everyday activities, but also on managing remittances.* However, this was *not a straightforward process* and we found that even when they were the primary remittance receivers, they were not always the primary decision-makers. Male relatives – especially spouses – continued to play a significant role, albeit at a distance. A certain degree of change had taken place as men had come to rely – even more strongly than before – on women to manage the household and the children, by reason of their long physical absence. This was clearly shown by the share of households where decision-making was taken jointly by senders and receivers of remittances. Yet, *women also experienced being overburdened* with the tasks of single-handedly looking after their children, their home, and often being involved in income-generating activities such as agriculture or factory work.

Given that *the overwhelming majority of our respondents during the survey reported a male as the primary remittance sender*, it is not very easy to make comparisons between sending patterns based on sex. Our qualitative material brought more insights into this discussion, specifically for married women sending money to their parents and less so to their siblings. Remittances sent by these groups of migrants are not considered as the primary support for the family, and the wife's parents acknowledge that often it is up to their son-in-law whether any money is sent to them or not. However, our interviews with migrant men and women revealed that more complex negotiations took place, where women had some negotiating power. In some cases, following Smith's research (2009), intra-female remittances were passed on in a secretive mode, which a questionnaire survey, or even in-depth interviews, could not record. Certainly, then, the migration and remittance process creates new situations in which gender relations might be expressed differently. In some families husbands brought back symbolic presents for their wives, such as for their birthday or St Valentine's day, showing thus appreciation for them and being more open about their feelings of longing and affection, as influenced also by the distance and time apart.

Overall, the pace of change in gender relations was relatively faster in migratory situations, but much slower in the rural areas of origin. For instance, the continuing gender inequality in migrant communities of origin was reflected in the ways that parents of migrant men and women would usually only talk about their *sons* sending remittances, but would reveal if their daughters-in-law were co-senders only when probed further. This 'omission' was telling, particularly when daughters-in-law stayed at home because they had young children to look after. *The reproductive tasks that women do thus remain unacknowledged in the crucial role they have for the household economy.* Equally, remittances from married daughters were not usually reported as such, but labelled as 'presents'.

Because of these perceptions and also due to the male-led typology of migration from this area, *not much change appears to have taken place as a result of remittances in terms of gender roles in the origin community.* If anything, remittances have reinforced the perception of the role of men as principal income-providers in the household, with some exceptions. Equally, the independent migration of young single women for work continues to be an awkward issue and is not easily accepted. Even when women get opportunities for such emigration, for instance through the USA Diversity Lottery Visa, they are expected to be at least engaged before they leave. In the rare cases when they do migrate as singles, they live with relatives in the host countries, where once again a certain degree of surveillance of their behaviour is ensured. On the other hand, the absence of male partners and male family members has thrust women into the public eye because of the responsibilities they have had to take by working on their own, out in the fields and so on. Once again, *gender is combined with age and marital status in the ways in which it is shaped by migration and remittances.* For younger women, for instance, opportunities for power negotiations in the public sphere are much more limited. In other words, it depends on the social location, to use Mahler and Pessar's (2001) term.

When we consider the impact of remittance-receiving households on communities of origin, we conclude that *the status of most of these households has certainly improved, not only economically but also socially.* It is not only the money, but also the skills that migrants bring back which make such households more respected and highly-regarded than before, especially when prior to emigration they constituted some of the poorest in the villages. In addition, young single migrant men from such families have higher chances of contracting marriages with more affluent or highly educated women. Furthermore, socio-economic upward mobility resulting from remittances has acted as an incentive for other households to send their family members abroad.

Generally the *rural communities of origin have benefited enormously from the combination of financial and social remittances that have streamed from migration to Greece*: money, skills, knowledge, ideas, and gender norms, to name but a few. The challenges faced here are the mobilisation of what appears to be an untapped pool of energies and wishes to put some of these skills to the benefit of the local community. We discuss some policy implications related to this in the following section.

Mobilising Remittances to Achieve Sustainable Development that Includes Women

The selected study area in the district of Korçë is a *place with significant development potential*, because of its geographical location, favourable geomorphological, soil and climatic conditions for farming, relatively educated workforce, and a significant share of incoming capital through remittances. In addition, the agricultural sector – especially large-scale farming of vegetables, planting of apple orchards and breeding of livestock – has developed particularly well in recent years. The combination of these factors makes this area relatively prosperous when compared to other more mountainous villages in the hinterland, or in the north of Albania. For the majority of the population the issue is not one of survival, but one of development beyond that. This development has so far taken place almost entirely through private initiatives of migrants, as well as non-migrant households. The impact of policies on rural, regional and national development, as well as those on migration and gender, appears to be limited.

As discussed in Chapter 7, Albania has adopted a number of macro-strategies covering these issues, and rightly so since *macro-policies are important in shaping the gendered effects that both internal and international migration can have for a country*. However, a number of obstacles seem to stand in the way of expected positive results. First, the various strategies are rarely linked together; they and the institutions implementing them seem to be working alongside, rather than in cooperation with, one another. Our key stakeholders in Korçë who had participated as advisors on a number of regional strategies emphasised that this was one of the reasons for the poor record of outcomes. Second, monitoring the implementation of these strategies remains weak. In the few areas that this has been carried out by independent organisations, the level of implementation has been found to be very low, as we saw in the case of the NSM and its accompanying NAP on Migration (Onorato *et al.* 2007). Third, policy outcomes have been particularly influenced by the conflictual character of Albanian politics, as well as the lack of continuity and stability amongst civil servants at most levels (Chaloff 2008; Tahiraj 2007). Finally, and what is more relevant to the aims of our research, most policies do not employ gender as an integrative conceptual and analytical tool.

Previous research on harnessing the potential of remittances for development has emphasised *the importance of policies to provide the necessary physical, legislative and administrative infrastructure in order to promote a viable and sustainable business environment, and higher quality of human development.* If the Albanian central and local governments are serious about harnessing remittances and attracting FDI for local and national development, the infrastructure needs to take priority. Migrants, rural residents, returnees and key stakeholders who participated in our study repeatedly told us that reliable water and electricity supplies, adequate transport networks (especially in rural areas), strengthening of the rule of law, settling the issue of land ownership and reducing bureaucracy for businesses are the most basic requirements to achieve such goals. In turn, this development needs to address the priorities of various groups in society across gender, ethnicity and generation, but especially those of women.

In the previous chapter we discussed the key policies on migration, remittances, gender and development in Albania and those bilateral with Greece. We concluded that the agenda of such policies and programmes implemented within these frameworks appears to be influenced by the migration priorities of host countries. In this context, local development is used as a tool to stem further 'irregular' emigration, rather than being an end in itself. Such programmes appear to perpetuate the stereotype of men as the potential migrants; therefore the aim is to provide (male) employment opportunities in order to stem their 'irregular' emigration. On the other hand, generally less-educated and rural women are perceived as potential trafficking victims; therefore the aim is to reduce their unemployment, in order to avoid them being 'lured' away by 'traffickers' (men). Such agendas do not contribute to sustainable development, unless all aspects of human development are addressed, i.e. conditions where men and women can exercise freedom, equality and social empowerment, including – but not only – through emigration.

The migration agendas of host countries such as Greece, reflected especially in their immigration policies, affect development also in the ways they perceive and subsequently deal with migrants. Our research findings suggest that the significant benefits emigration to Greece has brought for individual migrants and their families, especially the poor, have come at a *high human and emotional cost for them.* Migrants and their family members, as well as representatives of migrant organisations and some key stakeholders, reported the continued shameful record of the Greek government, institutions, media and certain sections of Greek society regarding the discrimination, exploitation and exclusion of – especially Albanian –

migrant men, women and children. In recent years things are changing, partly due to pressure from EU institutions and the more mature and human-rights-oriented sections of Greek society. Recognising Albanian migrants as an integral part of Greek society would show not only empathy with the plight of migrants, but also recognise the significant contribution that migrants make to Greece and its economy.

Indeed, the scale and depth of the impact of Albanian migants on Greece's economy, and hence on the way its society has come to be serviced and supported, can hardly be over-stressed. Especially Albanians (but also Bulgarians, Poles, Georgians, Egyptians, Pakistanis etc.) have driven the expansion of the Greek economy at times of vital labour need – for instance during the frenetic period of construction of facilities for the 2004 Olympic Games in Athens. This *vital structural role that migrant workers play in the Greek economy* – to such an extent that it could not survive without them – is repeatedly acknowledged by informed economic commentators such as Baldwin-Edwards (2004b), Cavounidis (2006) and Fakiolas (2000), but is not widely grasped by most members of the Greek population. Such a *fundamental economic – but also demographic, social and cultural – contribution* needs to be appreciated and capitalised upon, by making migrants meaningful stakeholders in the country's development.

First, they should be given the right and adequate access to *permanent residence and citizenship* after so many years of living in Greece. Especially for those born in Greece, or who arrived there at a very young age, this is essentially their homeland (Gogonas 2007). Granting migrants such citizenship rights not only mitigates against the negative consequences mentioned earlier, but shows the democratic maturity of a government that does not feel threatened by a multicultural citizenry. Given that the legal status of most Albanian migrant women is attached to that of their husbands, migration perpetuates the dependency of women on their male relatives, rather than acting as a tool for emancipation. As a result, immigrant women may not be able to separate when they are the targets of violent partners. So, secondly, immigration policy in Greece should address the specific right of *migrant women living there to obtain residence permits on their own accord.* Third, *family members of migrants* such as spouses or parents should be able to visit and live with migrants in Greece, a process which should be accessible, less costly and less bureaucratic.

Migrants' secure status would in turn positively affect development in Albania, since they can focus on capitalising their earnings and developing their skills, rather than perpetually trying to stay legal in the host country. In particular, certain segments of (semi-)skilled migrants present significant potential as bridges between the two countries, by acting as guides and advisors for Greek companies that want to invest in Albania. Such examples have been confirmed by other research in the Albanian–Greek migration context (Labrianidis *et al.* 2004).

On the Albanian side, *the Albanian government should firmly advocate on behalf of migrants' rights in destination countries, as well as negotiate secure and accessible channels of regular migration for men and for women.* In trying to perform the role of the 'obedient student' for eligibility to be accepted as an EU member, the Albanian government has succumbed to the pressures of the EU and subdued the interests of its own citizens to those of host-country governments. Thus, various bi- and multi-lateral agreements have addressed primarily the fears of Greece and other EU countries of irregular migration (for one example see the negotiations of Readmission Agreements with the EU: IOM 2006a; 2006b). It is important that during such future agreements, the positive contribution of migrants – grounded on research – is made clear to destination-country governments such as Greece. As we have shown throughout this book, the complex and multiple pathways that migrant families employ as part of their livelihood strategy demonstrate agency and resilience, which, if supported by policy, could be rewarding for both countries at various levels. However, *Albania should simultaneously also pursue an integrated policy whereby development is not predicated on labour export and migrants' remittances, but on the provision of sound and long-term socio-economic opportunities back home.* Elements of such a development strategy were outlined earlier.

If further demographic, economic and socio-cultural polarisation of the country is to be avoided, especially between rural and urban areas, such policies, *which include transnationalism and return*, should consider that both of these may be selective processes. Rural areas, including the study villages, are already under pressure from the flight of the young and an increasing level of ageing of residents, especially farm owners. This situation will be compounded in the future as the type of return to these areas will most likely be of *retirement* (cf. Cerase 1974). This is not yet happening, but will do so in the next decades, as those who first migrated in the 1990s when they were young and early-middle-aged (some of the early migrants were in their 30s and 40s) reach retirement age. Time will tell what proportion of these eventual retirees will stay on in Greece where their children and future grandchildren are likely to be, and how many will return to Albania. Return may be an attractive option, for reasons of nostalgia, wider kinship connections, lower living costs, and the ease, as 'regularised' migrants (but time will also tell whether the regularised status extends beyond the working age), of moving across the transnational border space between southern Albania and northern Greece. The story will likely be different for younger returnees (see Illustration 7).

Illustration 7 Will they return? Mother of migrant son gazing across the mountains to Greece, waiting for her son's return, south-east Albania, 2008

Our findings and previous research confirm that the young, the more entrepreneurial and those with most financial and social capital will target urban areas in the case of an eventual return. For reasons of the slow pace of change regarding the patriarchal and conservative attitudes that we have frequently alluded to in this book, women will also most likely intend to return to urban areas, where they can expect to find more freedom and opportunities for work and socio-cultural life. Our results also suggest that those who are becoming bridges of transnational entrepreneurial activities are also in the majority men, whilst women's position is not prominent in these public arenas of power-negotiations and opportunities. The situation is similar in migrant organisations, where decision-making is strongly concentrated in the hands of men, whilst women perform secondary supportive roles. Although some of the local migrant organisations which participated in our group discussions in Greece are headed by women, these are minority examples. Equally, most associations in our rural areas of origin were comprised of men, a position which was taken as a given, considering their firm role as heads of households.

Any future project that includes women and local development needs to consider these gendered power dynamics as they manifest themselves in private and public spaces. Such a gendered approach would thus first and foremost need to address the very limited level of women's participation in public spaces of political power and decision-making. Second, it would avoid the potential 'instrumentalisation' of women, which can lead to increasing their burden of tasks, unless wider spaces are provided for their political participation and for their voices to be heard. Third, it could avoid the risk of reinforcing gender stereotypes. For instance, some of the existing development projects in the area targeted women as carers and cleaners without attempting to encourage the gendered sharing of various activities. Although no local development initiative in our particular research location is presently including collective remittances, we found that *there is potential for tapping into a powerful pool of financial and social capital to mobilise for local development.* However, this pool again mostly involved men.

Unfortunately, however, the task of generating social capital and a developed civil-society mentality in Albania comes up against the discredited and rejected past of forced cooperation, against which the countervailing trend towards individualisation seems to be all-conquering in Albania's neoliberal era – a case, if you will, of 'every man for himself', to which we would cynically add 'and forget about the women'. A further problem here is that Albanians have mainly migrated to countries (Greece and Italy) where social capital and trust in authority are not well-established. Except for certain parts of north-central Italy where, following Putnam's pioneering study (1993), trust in one's fellows and in local cooperative and business organisations is historically well-entrenched, both Greece and Italy are 'low-trust' societies where faith in the authorities and in local and national governments is not at a high level. This makes it all the more difficult for the optimistic thesis of Maroukis (2005b) – that returnees can be instrumental in building trust, democracy, and civil society in Albania – will be realised.

Finally, a cautionary remark is in order. Gendered development through the inclusion of migrants' remittances is not a panacea for ailing rural societies. Migrants have done their best to ensure the survival and human development of their families through the remittances they send. They have substituted the problematic social, economic and fiscal policies and systems of origin countries by achieving a great deal: financing the education, health care and pensions of family members; providing capital for farming and small family-run businesses; and generally ensuring the survival of their families and communities. It is the task of the government to create the structural spaces and frameworks where these and other private initiatives can develop securely and in a sustainable way, and indeed prosper. Burdening migrants with more developmental expectations is not reasonable and should be considered only if governments are truly serious and willing to shoulder their own responsibilities for local and national economic and human development.

A Final Word

We appreciate that in many ways Albania is a unique case deriving from its history of profound isolation during communism, its enduring poverty and economic backwardness, its dramatic pendulum swing from extreme economic autarchy to a rampant neoliberalism, and its relatively massive scale of post-1990 emigration. If these features make it unique, they also in the same breath make it rather ideal as a laboratory or test-case in which the multiple interactions of migration, gender, remittances and development can be considered on a kind of *tabula rasa*. We also believe that our research approach and methods have wide potential relevance to the analysis of gender and remittances in other contexts. Whether the outcomes of research will be the same is left for other researchers to find out. What we have done in this book is to make what we believe is a pioneering case-study, create new knowledge, and point the way for others to follow in other migration and development contexts.

NOTES

Chapter One

1 For the latest data see the UNDP's Human Development Report 2009. To set Albania within a global context, here are some specific indicators. On the Human Development Index (a composite of per capita income, education and life expectancy), Albania scores 0.818 and ranks 70th in the world (out of 182). Adult literacy (99.0 per cent, 19th out of 151) performs better than per capita income standardised at purchasing power parity ($7041, 93rd out of 181). Albania's HDI improvement in recent years (up from 0.784 in 2000) places it on a similar level and profile to many countries of Latin America and the Caribbean (UNDP 2009).

2 According to a scoping study on migrant remittances in developing countries (Sander 2003: 15), Albania ranked fourth in the world for the importance of remittances in GDP in 2001 (17.0 per cent, following Tonga 37.3 per cent, Lesotho 26.5 per cent and Jordan 22.8 per cent). However, these figures can be quite volatile, and on the whole the share of remittances in GDP in Albania has edged downwards in recent years, to 12 per cent in 2007 and 9 per cent in 2009, as the absolute level of remittances has levelled off. It also needs to be acknowledged that source data on remittances are themselves highly variable, depending above all on how unrecorded transfers are estimated. More on this in Chapter 2; and for Albania in Chapter 3.

3 This more 'optimistic' interpretation of the contribution of migration to development, namely that it can be a 'route out of poverty' for millions of people worldwide, has been pioneered by a recent, large-scale programme of research sponsored by the UK Department for International Development (DFID) and hosted by the University of Sussex (see Black 2009).

4 Social capital is a concept that refers to relationships between people within networks and across them (for a useful review see Portes 1998). At one level, social capital can be an individual asset in the shape of networks that an individual can posses and which s/he uses in order to integrate her/himself in society (Bourdieu 1985). At another level, social capital is a feature of society 'collectivity' manifested in the shape and volume of clubs, associations etc. (Putnam 2000). Social capital is thus created through the interactions between

individuals and allows a person to access various goods in society. Social capital has become very important for policy-making, especially in the field of poverty alleviation and development, pushed forth by international organisations such as the World Bank. They argue that it provides a bottom-up approach to poverty alleviation and can even act as a necessary ingredient of long-term sustainable development. Where such social capital is lacking, or is at low levels, these actors' policies should attempt to build it (see critiques in Das 2004; Mohan and Mohan 2002). The ethos of the multi-country project which our study was part of, was constructed along these lines. Das (2004), however, challenges this construction by arguing that the economic and political conditions in which the poor live affect the production of social capital and, therefore, its effectiveness in poverty alleviation and sustainable development.

5 The district of Korçë is part of the administrative Prefecture of Korçë along with the adjacent districts of Pogradec, Kolonjë and Devoll. The district of Korçë itself comprises 15 communes (rural administrative units each containing several villages) and two towns (municipalities) – Korçë and Maliq. The three study villages are part of the Pojan commune – the largest in the district – along with nine other villages. The commune headquarters are also situated in the village with the same name.

6 Macedonia is a very important destination for migrants from the Macedonian ethnic minority living in the villages alongside Lake Prespa.

7 This may not necessarily mean a dramatic increase between 2001 and 2008. Note that the census recorded population present at the time of enumeration, whilst population registers record resident population at the commune and municipality level, by place of legal residence (Lerch and Wanner 2008). These registers are largely manual and difficult to update with the rapid changes in population movements (Korça Regional Council 2005: 15). Moreover, it is in the individual commune/municipality's interest not to quantify the extent of the population loss, for fear of losing resources and being downgraded (Arrehag *et al.* 2005).

8 For these and other local population statistics, we are grateful to Mr Vasillaq Çinoku, chief of Pojan commune; Mr Sami Meçollari, director of statistics at the Korçë Regional Council; Mrs Klara Çelo, director of the NGO 'Korçë women'; and Mr Mehmetali Xhambazi, head of the Roma and Evgjit community in Pojan village.

9 The second of these three ethnic categories poses a problem of nomenclature. In simple terms, Evgjit are a Roma-like group which are either regarded as part of the broader Roma population or distinct from it. Various theories, none of them supported by solid historical evicence, exist as to their origin: one being that they originated from Egypt, whereas the Roma trace their origin to India (De Soto *et al.* 2005: 7–8). To call them Egyptians (Egjiptianë), as many authors do, is confusing as this conflates them with modern-day Egyptians who, though largely absent from Albania, are numerous as migrants in neighbouring Greece and Italy. Hence we opt for the more distinctive term Evgjit, though we do recognise that this word can have slightly derogatory tones in certain circles.

10 A map of Thessaloniki and its conurbation can be found online at: <http://www.nath.gr/Photos/thessaloniki_poleodomiko.jpg> [last accessed: December 2010].

11 Subsequently this has changed due above all to the publication in book form of Hatziprokopiou's Sussex DPhil thesis (Hatziprokopiou 2006). See also Kokkali (2010); Labrianidis et al. (2004); Pratsinakis (2005); Vullnetari (2008). For one of the pioneering works in Greek, see Labrianidis and Lyberaki (2001).

12 We have advanced this argument more explicitly in a recent working paper (King and Vullnetari 2010) which also contains a preliminary analysis of some of the data explored in more depth in this book.

Chapter Two

1 More than ten years ago Skeldon (1997: 14) remarked that it had become impossible to keep track of all the publications emerging on the topic of migration and development. Surely this is even more true today. We certainly do not attempt a complete review here, but instead draw attention to some key readings. In addition to Skeldon's fundamental text on the subject, see Ammassari and Black (2001), Appleyard (1989), Castles and Delgado Wise (2008), de Haas (2010), Deshingkar and Grimm (2005), Hammar *et al.* (1997), Papademetriou and Martin (1991), Van Hear and Nyberg Sørensen (2003). Finally, useful overviews of evolving international policy stances on migration and development are found in the International Organization for Migration's recent 'World Migration' reports (IOM 2005a; 2008), and the latest UNDP Human Development Report, which focuses specifically on migration and development (2009).

2 This is true of the report in general, with only the barest mention of gender empowerment (UNDP 2009: 60).

3 The 'migration interests' of the wealthy, former colonial countries seem to revolve around three priorities, supported by different policies. The first is to block unwanted migration, mainly large-scale, low-skilled migration from poor countries, including former colonies. For this, strict visa qualifications and border controls are implemented. The second is to attract the cleverest brains and most highly-skilled migrants from anywhere in the world, with scant regard for brain-drain impacts. Special admission procedures, financial thresholds and points systems are the regulatory and incentive mechanisms to encourage this kind of elite migrant recruitment. And the third is to allow in carefully monitored quotas of short-term contract migrants for labour-shortage sectors such as seasonal agricultural work or domestic service and care.

4 As Samers notes in his recent book on the geography, sociology and political economy of migration (2010: 104–6), there have been surprisingly few attempts to apply Giddens' structuration theory (which incorporates both structure and agency in a recursive model) to the migration setting, at least in an explicit sense. See Goss and Lindquist (1995) for a preliminary attempt; Bakewell (2010) for a recent overview.

5 Just as the literature on migration and development has escalated (see note 1 above), so too has that on remittances. Carling (2008a: 45) has deftly shown that, whilst the volume of global remittances has increased fivefold between the early 1980s and 2005, the number of journal articles on remittances has increased 30-fold, driven largely by interest from outside academia – i.e. from governments, development planners, NGOs etc. For key overview studies see Carling (2008a; 2008b), de Haas (2005), Ghosh (2006), Kapur (2004), Nyberg Sørensen (2005), Orozco (2007), Ratha (2003), Russell (1986; 1993), Taylor (1999), World Bank (2006a).

6 Samuel Munzele Maimbo, World Bank Africa specialist, quoted in Kunz (2008: 1389, 1406).

7 However, this trend towards inequality is not upheld by other studies, and much also depends on how inequality is measured (amongst the population, or regionally etc.) and what scales and thresholds are used. This is evident from other studies on Albania by Arrehag *et al.* (2005), Azzarri and Carletto (2009), De Soto *et al.* (2002) and Zezza *et al.* (2005). Time may also be a factor. It might be logical to expect that remittances have an intitial effect on enhancing inequality due to the selectivity of migration at the early stages of the migration process, but then, as more people have access to migration as the migration flow 'matures' and extends to other groups and areas of the country which were initially excluded, the effect becomes the opposite, and inequality is reduced (see Azzarri and Carletto 2009). Yet the reverse sequence may also occur, as Jones (1998) found in his study in rural Zacatecas in Mexico. At first interfamily inequality decreased at the level of the individual community, but later the opposite trend was observed. However, on a wider spatial scale, Jones found that rural areas improved relative to urban areas, since most migrants are drawn from rural areas. The effects of remittances on poverty reduction in Albania are reviewed in more detail in Chapter 3.

8 It might however be difficult to separate the data and isolate the impacts of remittances from internal and international migration within a household, since a considerable number of families use both types as part of household survival strategies (Afsar 2003; 2005: 12). This may have implications for the design of policy intervention tools.

9 Much of what is said in this paragraph refers to international rather than internal migration. In actual fact, females have traditionally been more numerically dominant in internal migration flows – an observation made by Ravenstein (1889: 288) in one of his famous 'laws of migration' ('woman is more migrant than man') 120 years ago.

10 Ghosh's review paper on migration and gender empowerment disaggregates gender-differentiated processes of female migration into marriage migration, family migration, forced migration and work migration; these are further divided into legal and irregular migration (2009). We concentrate here on work and family migration since these are the dominant types for Albanian migration.

11 Like Sri Lanka and Indonesia, the other two major 'exporters' of female migrants in Asia, women's migration in the Philippines is enabled by laws that

do not discriminate by gender and do not require adult women to get the permission of male relatives (Ghosh 2009: 9).

12 Oishi (2005) found that Filipina domestic workers received higher wages than those of other nationalities, such as Sri Lankans or Indonesians, because of their better education, ability to speak English, better reputation as 'clean' and 'good' workers, and greater knowledge of local laws and hence awareness of their rights.

13 One indicator for the 'maturing' of the gender–development nexus is the fact that it has its own dedicated journal, *Gender and Development*, published by Routledge for Oxfam since 1993. An upcoming issue – 18(3), 2011 – will be on migration.

14 Most, if not all, of these NGO reports draw conclusions from poorly designed and poorly researched studies, using particular concepts such as 'kidnapping' out of local context (for example in Albanian, besides its meaning as we understand it in English, the word also means to elope without the consent of the father), and most often interviewing women in rescue shelters or police stations. However, these women represent only a particular sub-group of those who are engaged in sex work, often the most vulnerable. While we absolutely agree that they should be part of research and given appropriate protection and assistance, we also believe that women working in the sex industry are not a homogenous group. As such, results from these particular studies cannot be generalised across the entire spectrum of these migrant women, which in fact include a complex continuum of age, education, social class, geographical background, consent for migration and participation in sex work, and so forth. The problematic portrayal in most reports of the 'innocent, naïve, young, uneducated village girl, often of Roma ethnicity' is far from the complex reality. Furthermore, even though most authorities in the field accept the lack of reliable statistics and that multiplier effects are often used in calculations (UNDP-Albania 2005: 82), many commentators and organisations feed the 'moral panic' around sex work and trafficking with their 'guesstimates'. Amongst these one reads that the number of 'trafficking slaves' by 1999 had reached 30,000 – which means more than 10 per cent of all Albanian female migrants around that time – and that 'entire villages and towns in Albania' had been 'robbed' of their young women (Van Hook *et al.* 2006: 30). For more balanced analyses see Campani (2000) and Mai (2001), and especially the detailed ethnographic study of Albanian sex work migrants in France by Davies (2009).

15 The difference in the two studies may lie in the methodology used – Semyonov and Gorodzeisky took a country-of-origin approach and drew their sample from major urban areas such as Manila, from migrants who were married and had children left in the Philippines, and who had emigrated primarily to the Middle East and East Asia; while Tacoli's was a host-country approach whose sample was purposively selected, concentrated only in Rome which has a high concentration of Filipina migrants in the care sector, and was more heterogeneous in terms of marital status.

Chapter Three

1 All photo illustrations by Julie Vullnetari, unless otherwise cited.

2 For more details see our reviews of the various statistical sources on Albanian migration: Barjaba and King (2005); King and Mai (2008); Vullnetari (2007).

3 The BoA registers only remittances transferred through the formal channels, i.e. banks and Money Transfer Operators (MTOs). It does this by calculating the difference between incoming and outgoing foreign currency, which does not exclude income from activities such as smuggling or drugs. Informal remittances – those brought in cash by migrants during visits or sent through friends, family and paid couriers – are estimated on the basis of household surveys carried out by the BoA. However, the BoA data may be overestimates; the IMF indicates that in reality remittances are much closer to estimates from surveys – between 43 and 60 per cent of the figures provided by the BoA. See IMF (2006: 45–7).

4 Based on a survey of 1,315 households in the south-eastern district of Korçë and using an asset-based measure of well-being, Arrehag *et al.* (2005) found that there was no significant difference between remittance-receiving and non-receiving households. This study is, however, geographically specific and focuses on one particular aspect of household well-being. These findings are contradicted by Castaldo and Reilly (2007), who, based on the 2002 ALSMS data and using a model based on household expenditure, argue that remittance-recipient households spend significantly more on durable goods and utilities than do those who do not receive remittances.

5 One way out of this subordination was for women to 'become' men, i.e. take on the social roles of men (without changing their sex). Becoming a 'sworn virgin' usually took place in order to retain property within the household unit when the family had no sons, or when the woman wanted to break her arranged betrothal. For an in-depth ethnography of the phenomenon, which is slowly dying out, see Young (2000); also Littlewood (2002) and Pritchett-Post (1998).

6 In addition, amongst some Muslim populations of the south a localised version of the Islamic law existed (Hall 1994: 82; Nicholson 2006).

7 This is not to say that observance of the *Kanun* has remained static since the fifteenth century. One of the reasons why the Franciscan monk Shtjefën Gjeçovi is said to have codified the *Kanun* in 1913 was to bring it more in line with the changes Albanian society was going through at the time. A number of scholars have analysed how the code underwent changes during the communist period, or has been adapted to fit post-1990 Albanian reality (and is sometimes distorted), including to be used in migratory situations. See for instance Mai (2001), Nixon (2009), Schwandner-Sievers (1999; 2001) and Tarifa (2008).

8 Some researchers suggest that this withdrawal of women from the labour market may have been related to increased levels of remittances coming into the relevant households (Konica and Filer 2005). This could in turn reflect the difficult labour market for women, but also the change in mentality as mentioned earlier. The survey does not indicate that increased remittances

make men participate less in the labour market. Such a finding would support the hypothesis that migration and subsequent remittances reinforce traditional patriarchal 'breadwinner' models.

Chapter Four

1 The education system in Albania comprises pre-school groups (ages 0–6); compulsory school years (ages 6–10 for primary education and ages 11–14 for lower secondary education); upper secondary education (ages 15–18) which can be general (similar to comprehensive schools in the UK) or vocational/professional; higher education at universities or higher education institutes (generally ages 19–23 for a four year degree, although some degrees last five to six years); and postgraduate studies at masters and doctoral level. Adults participating in our research had experienced this set-up. However, a number of changes have taken place recently: in 2004–05 compulsory education was extended by one year (to a total of nine years), and in 2009–10 upper secondary level was reduced by one year (to a total of three years).

2 For a detailed study of the progress of Albanian children in the Greek education system, including especially linguistic aspects, see Gogonas (2007).

3 Note, however, that the systematic collection of employment data through the questionnaire to remittance-recipients was only carried out for the principal remitter.

4 For similar findings on unrecognised qualifications and blocked access to higher-status employment amongst Albanian immigrants in Italy see King and Mai (2008: 130–42).

5 These findings are corroborated from interviews and focus-group discussions we held with stakeholders in Greece (group discussions of 26 and 28 March 2008 in Thessaloniki; in-depth interviews with Dr Maria Stratigaki at the Gender Studies Centre of Pantheion University in Athens, 28 December 2007; and Ms Dhimitra Malo, president of the Pan-Hellenic Network of Migrant Women based in Athens, 22 December 2007).

6 We did not proceed to interview this female-headed household as the sisters' father, back in Albania, was opposed to this idea: a clear example of the transnational expression of the 'gendered geography of power' (cf. Mahler and Pessar 2001).

7 Although Greece remains one of the EU's more xenophobic societies, there are signs that a more positive attitude towards the presence of immigrants has taken root in recent years. During the 1990s, Albanians were victims of a particularly virulent stigmatisation (see, for instance, Lazaridis 1996; 1999; Lazaridis and Koumandraki 2001).

8 For those migrants in Thessaloniki who do not have their own car, there are regular bus and shared taxi services across the border. Assuming no delays at the frontier posts, the road journey can take as little as three to four hours.

9 A conclusion stressed in many interviews and discussions with key informants.

Chapter Five

1 Albanian migration to Greece has unfolded with a clear spatio-temporal pattern. In the early years the dominant areas involved were the southern Albanian districts close to the Greek border – including the district of Korçë, where our study-villages are located. Hence southern Albanians are longest established in Greece and therefore more likely to be regularised. Would-be migrants from the remoter mountain regions of northern and north-east Albania were considered too poor to migrate externally and so made up the bulk of internal migrants to Tirana and Durrës (Zezza *et al.* 2005). With time, however, migrants from these northern districts have also switched to Greece, where they mainly work as seasonal migrants, with lower propensity to obtain a regularised status (Azzarri and Carletto 2009; Stampini *et al.* 2008).

2 Our survey question on this point offered a multiple answer option, whereas the BoA's shares totalled 100 per cent. It is also important to bear in mind that: we only focus on migrants in Greece; the villages where our research took place are very close to the Greek border; and our respondents' migrant relatives probably have higher levels of regularisation, thus enabling more frequent visits home.

3 PBI is a UK-based organisation which provides services for the remittance market such as possibilities to compare transfer costs and prices online for a number of countries, including Albania. Some of its early activities were funded by DFID. The information presented here was gathered through its interactive web-service, updated as of 18 December 2007 and available online at <http://www.sendmoneyhome.org/Search%20results.php?sending_to=Albania&sending_from=Greece> [last accessed: 24 December 2007]. See also pages 10–11 of its 'Sending Money Home: Albania' brochure for a detailed list of remittance transfer costs between Greece and Albania, available online at: <http://www.iomtirana.org.al/Remitance/al/Sending%20money%20home-al.pdf> [last accessed: 19 December 2007]. However, this information may well be outdated by now.

4 The fact that these surveys were sponsored by the Bank of Albania might help to explain the lower rates of use of 'competition' MTO channels.

5 In one case, the father of a migrant son held a debit card on his son's account with a bank in Korçë. The father went to Korçë and withdrew cash from the account each time the family needed it, by using the ATM machine outside the bank. The service was rated as particularly easy to use and very convenient, since the transaction could take place at any time of the day.

6 Based on some of our earlier research, we have made the case elsewhere for the importance of combining gender and generation as intersectional variables in the analysis of Albanian migration, remittances and transnational care (King and Vullnetari 2009b).

Chapter Six

1 In this we follow the UNDP thinking, now established over many years in their Human Development Reports, the latest of which breaks new ground by explicitly linking migration and development in a positive way – i.e. by advancing the thesis that human mobility can enhance development (UNDP 2009: v, 1). UNDP has also carried out pioneering conceptual thinking on the gender dimensions of human development, building gender into many of its quantitative human development indices (HDIs). Gender and 'pro-women policies' were also the focus of a recent UNDP National Human Development Report on Albania although, disappointingly, this latter report said very little about migration, except to draw attention to the issue of the trafficking of young women (UNDP-Albania 2005: 76, 79).

2 Many Albanians still keep notebooks in which they note the value and type of presents friends and relatives brought to someone's wedding, or the sum of money they gave the bereaved family following someone's death. The money or the present is considered as 'a social debt' which needs to be paid back at equivalent value during similar events.

3 Besides the official payment for various types of medical treatment and most medicines, there are also under-the-table payments to GPs, doctors, nurses, surgeons and midwives. These have soared in recent years, reflecting on the one hand the low salaries of the medical personnel, but also the inability of the public sector to rid itself of corrupt and nepotistic practices.

4 For a discussion of the use of remittances in housing from Ghanaian migrants residing in the Netherlands, see Smith and Mazzucato (2009).

5 Our work on the Greek–Albanian remittance corridor, and especially that filament of the corridor linking the Korçë district with Thessaloniki, exists alongside the Italy–Albania remittance corridor which connects the two countries especially across the southern Adriatic Sea route linking Vlorë and Durrës on the one hand with the south-east Italian region of Apulia on the other (see Hernández-Coss *et al.* 2006).

6 We would like to acknowledge the influence that two of our MA students – Rodolfo Cordova Alçaraz and Christina Lord – had on our thinking on this, through the work they undertook for their own MA papers on this theme as part of the 2010 spring term course on Migration, Inequality and Social Change at the University of Sussex.

7 Corroborated also from interviews with key informants: Dr Irena Nikaj of Korçë University, November 2007 and Mr Vasillaq Çinoku, head of Pojan commune, March 2008.

8 Dalakoglou's study of a 'Greek house' built by a long-term migrant settled in Athens in his home village in northern Albania is a detailed evocation of the combination of technological remittances with a material culture perspective. The migrant (Fatos) is a construction worker in Athens and he has painstakingly transported the materials for his new 'home' in Albania (which he calls his 'Greek house') over several ten-hour trips with his building lorry: 'the entire house is flowing from Greece, part by part' (2009: 56). Yet the house

comprises 'multiple, diverse and contradictory elements', being Greek in style and most of the building materials, yet faced with local Albanian stone; it has a 'Greek' swimming pool adjacent to an 'Albanian' vegetable plot; it is (for Albania) the height of technological and stylistic sophistication, yet it is uninhabited for most of the year, since Fatos and his family (wife and two children) are highly unlikely to return to live there. In a clever juxtaposition of mirrored processes, Dalakoglou also describes the 'Albanian' elements of the family's apartment in Athens, with its low coffee-table and Albanian-style low benches covered with Albanian fabric – a kind of reverse technological/material remittance flow.

9 McCarthy *et al.* (2006), using data from the 2002 and 2003 ALSMS, similarly conclude that migration in rural Albania has affected land reallocation towards less labour-intensive production, although their findings suggest that most of this diversion is towards the livestock sector.

Chapter Seven

1 Transparency International Corruption Perceptions Indices of 2008 and 2009, available online at: <http://www.transparency.org/news_room/in_focus/2008/cpi2008/cpi_2008_table> and <http://www.transparency.org/policy_research/surveys_indices/cpi/2009/cpi_2009_table> [last accessed: 27 May 2010].

2 A similar bilateral relationship has evolved between Albania and Italy, based on migration, investment, cultural cooperation, humanitarian missions (often with a quasi-military character), and built to some extent on an earlier historical layer of colonialism. For details see Mai (2003).

3 Co-development in this context is the combination by a migrant host country of immigration policies with policies for development cooperation where priority is given to the development of migrants' origin country, and which is accompanied by an active policy of involving migrants in development programmes, aimed at their country of origin. This formulation follows the discussion in Ramírez *et al.* (2005: 31).

4 Note how women are always grouped together with children in such programmes and policies. This infantilisation and patronising attitude towards women's bodies is further reflected in the awareness-raising campaigns most of which warn women not to emigrate, lest they fall prey to abusive and criminal men. In fact, many Albanian women emigrate precisely in order to get away from these abusive men – their husbands and at times fathers and brothers. The female body thus becomes the socio-spatial scale where the power dynamics for 'ownership' of the body, and the morals it represents, are played out between national and global actors.

5 From an interview with representatives of the Development Cooperation department within the Hellenic Aid, January 2008.

6 Reports on deported Albanians or those caught by Albanian guards before even crossing to Greece appear regularly in the Albanian independent dailies. As we write the final pages of this book, the media is reporting deportations of significant numbers of undocumented Albanians. In earlier years these migrants were generally tolerated, as their cheap and exploitable labour was needed for Greek employment sectors such as agriculture and construction. But as the Greek economy contracts, their expendability becomes clear. Their deportation, however, sends chilling signals to their longer-term and settled compatriots, who although legal, may not have their two-year staying permits renewed if their labour is no longer needed. As the majority of Albanian migrants in Greece have never been legally given an opportunity for longer-term settlement, even after contributing to the country for more than a decade, we hope that the economic crisis will not become a human rights crisis.

7 From an interview with representatives of the Greek Ministry of Interior, 11 January 2008.

8 The mapping involved consulting the UNDP 2006 study of the NGO sector in Albania (Misha 2006), the online NGO directory run by Partners Albania, the online directory of the Regional Development Agency in Korçë, as well as information collected at the Civil Society Development Center in Korçë, through survey questionnaires administered via e-mail to a selection of NGOs and from the Donor Dialogue monthly e-briefings.

9 From in-depth interview with Mr Vasillaq Çinoku, chief of Pojan commune and relevant material provided by his staff; 29 February and 5 March 2008.

Chapter Eight

1 Greek society, like the other more 'advanced' societies of Southern Europe – Italy and Spain especially, also Portugal, Cyprus, Lebanon etc. – has seen a rapid evolution of native women's employment and lifestyle – shifting from 'homemaker' roles to full- or part-time employment – which can only be sustained, within the continuing masculinist culture of males not sharing household and child-rearing responsibilities, by employing migrant women as 'substitute' homemakers and carers of children and elderly or frail relatives. See King and Zontini (2000) for an exposition of the 'South European model' of gender, migration and employment.

2 We do not mean to automatically imply that only Albanian men are able to set up businesses in Greece: this avenue is theoretically open to women too, but is probably more difficult for them given their 'double' marginalisation within both Greek and Albanian society. See Lazaridis (2003) for a small-scale study of immigrant women as entrepreneurs in Greece.

BIBLIOGRAPHY

Abazi, E. and Mema, M. (2007) *The Potentials of Remittances for Income Generating Activities Leading to Local Economic Development in Albania. The Case of Durrës.* Tirana: IOM and ILO.

Abdi, C.M. (2006) *Diasporic Lives and Threatened Identities: Gender Struggles of Somalis in America.* Brighton: University of Sussex, DPhil thesis in Sociology.

Acosta, P. (2007) Entrepreneurship, labor markets and international remittances: evidence from El Salvador, in Koc, O. and Schiff, M. (eds) *International Migration Policy and Economic Development: Studies across the Globe.* Washington DC: World Bank, 141–59.

ACPS (2002) *An Annotated Compendium Relating to the Albanian Legislation, State Structure, and Policy on Emigration Since 1990.* Tirana: Albanian Centre for Parliamentary Studies.

Adams, R. (2006) *Remittances and Poverty in Ghana.* Washington DC: World Bank Policy Research Working Paper 3838.

Adams, R. and Page, J. (2003) *International Migration, Remittances and Poverty in Developing Countries.* Washington DC: World Bank Policy Research Working Paper 3179.

Afsar, R. (2005) Bangladesh: internal migration and pro-poor policy. Paper presented to the Regional Conference on Migration and Development in Asia, Lanzhou, China, 14–16 March 2005.

Afsar, R. (2003) Internal migration and the development nexus: the case of Bangladesh. Paper presented to the Regional Conference on Migration, Development and Pro-Poor Policy Choices in Asia, Dhaka, Bangladesh, 22–24 June 2003.

Agarwal, R. and Horowitz, A.W. (2002) Are international remittances altruism or insurance? Evidence from Guyana using multiple-migrant households, *World Development*, 30(11): 2033–44.

Ammassari, S. and Black, R. (2001) *Harnessing the Potential of Migration and Return to Promote Development. Applying Concepts to West Africa.* Geneva: IOM Migration Research Series Paper 5.

Amnesty International (2006) *Albania: Violence Against Women in the Family, 'It's Not Her Shame'.* London: Amnesty International.

Amuedo-Dorantes, C. and Pozo, S. (2006) Migration, remittances, and male and female employment patterns, *American Economic Review*, 96(2): 222–26.

Anderson, B. (2000) *Doing the Dirty Work? The Global Politics of Domestic Labour.* London: Zed Books.

Anderson, B., Ruhs, M., Rogaly, B. and Spencer, S. (2006) *Fair Enough? Central and East European Migrants in Low-Wage Employment in the UK.* Oxford: University of Oxford, COMPAS.

Appleyard, R. (1992) International migration and development: an unresolved relationship, *International Migration*, 30(3–4): 251–66.

Appleyard, R. (1989) Migration and development: myths and realities, *International Migration Review*, 23(3): 486–99.

Arrehag, L., Sjöberg, Ö. and Sjöblom, M. (2005) Cross-border migration and remittances in a post-communist society: return flows of money and goods in Korçë district, Albania, *South Eastern Europe Journal of Economics*, 3(1): 9–40.

Azzarri, C. and Carletto, C. (2009) Modelling migration dynamics in Albania: a hazard function approach, *Southeast European and Black Sea Studies*, 9(4): 407–33.

Backer, B. (1983) Mother, sister, daughter, wife: the pillars of traditional Albanian patriarchal society, in Utas, B. (ed.) *Women in Islamic Societies: Social Attitudes and Historical Perspectives.* London: Curzon, 48–65.

Baily, S. (1992) The village outward approach to the study of social networks: a case study of the Agnonesi diaspora abroad, *Studi Emigrazione*, 29(105): 43–67.

Bakewell, O. (2010) Some reflections on structure and agency in migration theory, *Journal of Ethnic and Migration Studies*, 36(10): 1689–1708.

Baldassar, L. (2007) Transnational families and aged care: the mobility of care and the migrancy of ageing, *Journal of Ethnic and Migration Studies*, 33(2): 275–97.

Baldassar, L., Wilding, R. and Baldock, C. (2007) Long-distance care-giving: transnational families and the provision of aged care, in Paoletti, I. (ed.) *Family Caregiving for Older Disabled People: Relational and Institutional Issues.* New York: Nova Science Publishers, 201–27.

Baldock, C. (2003) Long-distance migrants and family support: a Dutch case-study, *Health Sociology Review*, 12(1): 45–54.

Baldwin-Edwards, M. (2004a) *Statistical Data on Immigrants in Greece. An Analytic Study of Available Data and Recommendations for Conformity with European Union Standards.* Athens: Mediterranean Migration Observatory.

Baldwin-Edwards, M. (2004b) Albanian emigration and the Greek labour market: economic symbiosis and social ambiguity, *South-East Europe Review*, 7(1): 51–66.

Baldwin-Edwards, M. and Apostolatou, K. (2009) Greece, in Fassmann, H., Reeger, U. and Sievers, W. (eds) *Statistics and Reality: Concepts and Measurements of Migration in Europe.* Amsterdam: Amsterdam University Press, 233–62.

Baldwin-Edwards, M. and Kolios, N. (2008) *Immigrants in Greece: Characteristics and Issues of Regional Distribution.* Athens: ISTAME.

Balliu, Q. (2007) *Enhancing the Impact of Migrant Remittances in Albania by Creating an Integrated Migrant Remittances System. Study on Remittances for Potential Local Economic Development in Vlora Region.* Tirana: IOM and ILO

Barjaba, K. (2000) Contemporary patterns in Albanian emigration, *South-East Europe Review*, 3(2): 57–64.

Barjaba, K. and King, R. (2005) Introducing and theorising Albanian migration, in King, R., Mai, N. and Schwandner-Sievers, S. (eds) *The New Albanian Migration.* Brighton: Sussex Academic Press, 1–28.

Belba, A. (2005) Roli i pozitës gjeografike në zhvillimin ekonomik të rajonit të Korçës (The role of geographic location in the economic development of the Korçë region), *Studime Gjeografike*, 15: 86–94.

Bezhani, M. (2001) *Women Entrepreneurs in Albania.* Geneva: ILO, SEED [Small Enterprise Development] Working Paper 29.

Bitzenis, A. and Nito, E. (2006) Lack of financial intermediaries as a decisive barrier to entrepreneurship in Albania, *South Eastern Europe Journal of Economics*, 4(1): 95–114.

Bjerén, G. (1997) Gender and reproduction, in Hammar, T., Brochmann, G., Tamas, K. and Faist, T. (eds) *International Migration, Immobility and Development: Multidisciplinary Perspectives.* Oxford: Berg, 219–46.

Black, R. (2009) *Making Migration Work for Development.* Brighton: University of Sussex Development Research Centre on Migration, Globalisation and Poverty.

Black, R., Jones, L., Pantiru, M.C., Sabates-Wheeler, R., Skeldon, R. and Vathi, Z. (2007) *Understanding Migration as a Driver of Poverty Reduction in Europe and Central Asia.* Brighton: University of Sussex, Development Research Centre on Migration, Globalisation and Poverty, Working Paper C9.

BoA (2010a) *Balance of Payments Bulletin 2009.* Tirana: Bank of Albania.

BoA (2010b) *Annual Report 2009.* Tirana: Bank of Albania.

BoA (2009) *Annual Report 2008.* Tirana: Bank of Albania.

BoA (2008) *Annual Report 2007.* Tirana: Bank of Albania.

Bonifazi, C. (2007) *L'Immigrazione Straniera in Italia.* Bologna: il Mulino.

Bonifazi, C. and Sabatino, D. (2003) Albanian migration to Italy: what official data and survey results can reveal, *Journal of Ethnic and Migration Studies*, 29(6): 967–95.

Boserup, E. (1970) *Woman's Role in Economic Development.* New York: St. Martin's Press.

Bourdieu, P. (1985) The forms of capital, in Richardson, J. (ed.) *Handbook of Theory and Research for the Sociology of Education.* New York: Greenwood, 241–58.

Brunnbauer, U. (2000) From equality without democracy to democracy without equality? Women and transition in South-East Europe, *South-East Europe Review*, 3(3): 151–68.

Cai, Q. (2003) Migrant remittances and family ties: a case study in China, *International Journal of Population Geography*, 9(6): 471–83.

Campani, G. (2000) Immigrant women in southern Europe: social exclusion, domestic work and prostitution in Italy, in King, R., Lazaridis, G. and Tsardanidis, C. (eds) *Eldorado or Fortress? Migration in Southern Europe*. London: Macmillan, 145–69.

Campani, G. (1995) Women migrants: from marginal subjects to social actors, in Cohen, R. (ed.) *The Cambridge Survey of World Migration*. Cambridge: Cambridge University Press, 546–50.

Caritas/Migrantes (2009) *Immigrazione Dossier Statistico 2009*. Rome: Edizioni Idos.

Carletto, G., Davis, B., Stampini, M. and Zezza, A. (2006) A country on the move: international migration in post-communist Albania, *International Migration Review*, 40(4): 767–85.

Carletto, G., Davis, B., Stampini, M., Trento, S. and Zezza, A. (2004) *Internal Mobility and International Migration in Albania*. Rome: FAO, ESA Working Paper 13.

Carling, J. (2008a) Integrating remittances: more questions for deeper insight and better policies, in Castles, S. and Delgado Wise, R. (eds) *Migration and Development: Perspectives from the South*. Geneva: IOM, 43–64.

Carling, J. (2008b) The determinants of migrant remittances, *Oxford Review of Economic Policy*, 24(3): 582–99.

Carver, R. (1999) *The Accursed Mountains. Journeys in Albania*. London: Flamingo.

Cassarino, J.P. (2004) Theorising return migration: the conceptual approach to return migration revisited, *International Journal of Multicultural Societies*, 6(2): 253–79.

Castaldo, A. and Reilly, B. (2007) Do migrant remittances affect the consumption patterns of Albanian households?, *South Eastern Europe Journal of Economics*, 1(1): 25–54.

Castles, S. (2010) Theories of migration and societal change, *Journal of Ethnic and Migration Studies*, 36(10): 1565–86.

Castles, S. and Delgado Wise, R. (eds) (2008) *Migration and Development: Perspectives from the South*. Geneva: IOM.

Castles, S. and Miller, M. (2003) *The Age of Migration*. Basingstoke: Palgrave-Macmillan (3rd edition).

Cavounidis, J. (2006) Labour market impact of migration: employment structures and the case of Greece, *International Migration Review*, 40(3): 635–60.

Cavounidis, J. (2004) Migration to Greece from the Balkans, *South Eastern Europe Journal of Economics*, 2(1): 35–59.

Cerase, F. (1974) Expectations and reality: a case study of return migration from the United States to Southern Italy, *International Migration Review*, 8(2): 245–62.

Chaloff, J. (2008) *Albania and Italy Migration Policies and their Development Relevance. A Survey of Innovative and 'Development-Friendly' Practices in Albania and Italy*. Rome: CeSPI Working Paper 51.

Chant, S. (ed.) (1992) *Gender and Migration in Developing Countries*. London: Belhaven Press.

Chiodi, L. and Devole, R. (2005) Albanian migrants in Italy and the struggle for recognition in the transnational public sphere, in Chiodi, L. (ed.) *The Borders of the Polity. Migration and Security Across the EU and the Balkans*. Ravenna: Longo Editore, 169–208.

Cohen, J. (2010) Oaxacan migration and remittances as they relate to Mexican migration patterns, *Journal of Ethnic and Migration Studies*, 36(1): 149–61.

Cohen, R. (ed.) (1995) *The Cambridge Survey of World Migration*. Cambridge: Cambridge University Press.

Colleo, A.L. and Perrelli Branca, M.C. (2008) *Fostering the social dimension of the migration-development nexus in Albania: concrete orientations*. Bologna: NOMISMA - Association for Economic Studies S.P.A. Report for the MIGRAVALUE EC-funded project.

Conway, D. and Cohen, J. (1998) Consequences of migration and remittances for Mexican transnational communities, *Economic Geography*, 74(1): 26–44.

Curran, S. and Saguy, A.C. (2001) Migration and cultural change: a role for gender and social networks, *Journal of International Women's Studies*, 2(3): 54–77.

Dabalen, A. and Miluka, J. (2010) Who is bearing the burden? Exploring the role of Albanian international migration on education, *East European Economics*, 48(6): 37–58.

Dalakoglou, D. (2010) The road. An ethnography of the Albanian–Greek cross-border motorway, *American Ethnologist*, 37(1): 132–49.

Dalakoglou, D. (2009) Building and ordering transnationalism: the 'Greek house' in Albania as a material process, in Miller, D. (ed.) *Anthropology and the Individual: A Material Culture Perspective*. Oxford: Berg, 51–68.

Das, R.J. (2004) Social capital and poverty of the wage-labour class: problems with the social capital theory, *Transactions of the Institute of British Geographers*, 29(1): 27–45.

Davies, J. (2009) *My Name is not Natasha. How Albanian Women in France use Trafficking to overcome Social Exclusion (1998–2001)*. Amsterdam: Amsterdam University Press.

de Haas, H. (2010) Migration and development: a theoretical perspective, *International Migration Review*, 44(1): 227–64.

de Haas, H. (2007a) *Remittances, Migration and Social Development*. Geneva: United Nations Research Institute for Social Development, Social Policy and Development Programme Paper 37.

de Haas, H. (2007b) *The Impact of International Migration on Social and Economic Development in Moroccan Sending Regions: A Review of the Empirical Literature*. Oxford: University of Oxford, James Martin 21st Century School, International Migration Institute Working Paper 3.

de Haas, H. (2005) International migration, remittances and development: myths and facts, *Third World Quarterly*, 26(8): 1269–84.

de la Brière, B., de Janvry, A., Sadoulet, E. and Lambert, S. (2002) The roles of destination, gender, and household composition in explaining remittances: an analysis for the Dominican Sierra, *Journal of Development Economics*, 68(2): 309–28.

de la Cruz, B.E. (1995) The socio-economic dimensions of remittances: a case study of five Mexican families, *Berkeley McNair Journal*, 3: 1–10.

De, P. and Ratha, D. (2005) *Remittance Income and Household Welfare: Evidence from Sri Lanka Integrated Household Survey*. Washington DC: World Bank unpublished report.

de Rapper, G. (2005) Better than Muslims, not as good as Greeks: emigration as experienced and imagined by the Albanian Christians of Lunxhëri, in King, R., Mai, N. and Schwandner-Sievers, S. (eds) *The New Albanian Migration*. Brighton: Sussex Academic Press, 173–94.

De Soto, H., Beddies, S. and Gedeshi, I. (2005) *Roma and Egyptians in Albania*. Washington DC: World Bank.

De Soto, H., Gordon, P., Gedeshi, I. and Sinoimeri, Z. (2002) *Poverty in Albania. A Qualitative Assessment*. Washington DC: World Bank Technical Paper 520.

de Waal, C. (2005) *Albania Today: A Portrait of Post-Communist Turbulence*. London: I.B.Tauris.

de Zwager, N., Gedeshi, I., Germenji, E. and Nikas, C. (2005) *Competing for Remittances*. Tirana: IOM Tirana.

Deere, C.D. (1976) Rural women's subsistence production in the capitalist periphery, *Review of Radical Political Economy*, 8(1): 9–17.

Deshingkar, P. (2006) *Internal Migration, Poverty and Development in Asia*. Brighton: Institute of Development Studies and Overseas Development Institute.

Deshingkar, P. and Grimm, S. (2005) *Internal Migration and Development: a Global Perspective*. Geneva: IOM.

Durham, M.E. (2000) *High Albania. A Victorian Traveller's Balkan Odyssey (1909)*. London: Phoenix.

Duval, L. and Wolff, F.C. (2010) Remittances matter: longitudinal evidence from Albania, *Post-Communist Economies*, 22(1): 73–97.

EBRD (2009) *Strategy for Albania 2009–2012*. London: European Bank for Reconstruction and Development.

Ehrenreich, B. and Hochschild, A.R. (2003) Introduction, in Ehrenreich, B. and Hochschild, A. R. (eds) *Global Woman: Nannies, Maids and Sex Workers in the New Economy*. New York: Metropolitan Books, 1–14.

Ekonomi, M., Gjermeni, E., Danaj, E., Lula, E. and Beci, L. (2006a) *Krijimi i Mundësive Ekonomike për Gratë dhe Vajzat në Shqipëri: një Strategji për Parandalimin e Trafikimit* [*The Creation of Economic Opportunities for Women and Girls in Albania. A Strategy for the Prevention of Trafficking*]. Tirana: Aleanca Gjinore për Zhvillim.

Ekonomi, M., Sokoli, L., Danaj, S. and Picari, B. (2006b) *Representation and the Quality of Democracy in Albania. A Gender Perspective*. Tirana: Gender Alliance for Development.

Enloe, C. (1988) *Bananas, Beaches and Bases*. Berkeley: University of California Press.

ERRC (1997) *No Record of the Case. Roma in Albania*. Budapest: European Roma Rights Centre.

European Commission (2008) *Albania 2008 Progress Report*. Brussels: European Commission.

Faist, T. (2008) Migrants as transnational development agents: an inquiry into the newest round of the migration–development nexus, *Population, Space and Place*, 14(1): 21–42.

Fakiolas, R. (2003) Regularising the undocumented migrants in Greece: procedures and effects, *Journal of Ethnic and Migration Studies*, 29(3): 535–61.

Fakiolas, R. (2000) Migration and unregistered labour in the Greek economy, in King, R., Lazaridis, G. and Tsardanidis, C. (eds) *Eldorado or Fortres? Migration in Southern Europe*. London: Macmillan, 57–78.

Fakiolas, R. and Maratou-Alipranti, L. (2000) Foreign female immigrants in Greece, *Papers: Revista de Sociología*, 60: 101–17.

Fergany, N. (1982) The impact of migration on national development in the Arab region: the case of the Yemen Arab Republic, *International Migration Review*, 16(4): 757–80.

Finch, J. and Mason, J. (1993) *Negotiating Family Responsibilities*. London: Routledge.

Fischer, P., Martin, R. and Straubhaar, T. (1997) Interdependencies between development and migration, in Hammar, T., Brochmann, G., Tamas, K. and Faist, T. (eds) *International Migration, Immobility and Development*. Oxford: Berg, 91–132.

Frank, A.G. (1969) *Capitalism and Underdevelopment in Latin America*. New York: Monthly Review Press.

Frashëri, A. (2007) Nationwide remittance beneficiaries survey, *Bank of Albania Economic Bulletin*, 10(3): 63–80.

Froebel, F., Heinrichs, J. and Kreye, O. (1980) *The New International Division of Labour*. Cambridge: Cambridge University Press.

Fuga, A. (2004) *Shoqëria Periferike. Sociologji e Ndryshimit në Shqipëri*. Tirana: Ora. [Updated publication of the French edition: Fuga, A. (2000) *Identités Péripheriques en Albanie*. Paris: L'Harmattan].

Fuga, A. and Dervishi, Z. (2002) *Ndërmjet Fshatit dhe Qytetërimit Global. Integrimi Shoqëror i të Rinjve të Zonave Fshatare në Dritëhijet e Arsimimit të Mesëm. Trajtesë Sociologjike [Between the Village and Global Cultures. Social Integration of Rural Youth Against the Backdrop of Secondary Education. A Sociological Analysis*]. Tirana: Jerusalem.

Gammeltoft, P. (2002) Remittances and other financial flows to developing countries, *International Migration*, 40(5): 181–211.

Gardner, K. and Grillo, R. (2002) Transnational households and ritual: an overview, *Global Networks*, 2(3): 179–90.

Gedeshi, I. (2000) Roli i remitancave të emigracionit shqiptar e ndikimi i tyre në ekonominë e vendit [The role of Albanian remittances and their impact on the country's economy], *Politika dhe Shoqëria*, 1(2): 55–68.

Gedeshi, I. and Black, R. (2006) *From Brain Drain to Brain Gain: Mobilising Albania's Skilled Diaspora.* Tirana: UNDP Albania.

Gedeshi, I., Mara, H. and Preni, X. (2003a) *The Encouragement of Social–Economic Development in Relation to the Growth of the Role of the Remittances.* Tirana: Centre for Economic and Social Studies.

Gedeshi, I., Mara, H. and Preni, X. (2003b) *Economic Activities and Employment Opportunities in Rural Areas Within the Pilot Communes of Korça Clean and Green Project.* Tirana: UNDP-Albania unpublished report.

Geiger, M. (2007) Migration management in Albania. Mapping and evaluating outside intervention, *Migration Letters*, 4(2): 119–33.

Germenji, E. (2010) The global crisis and its propogation in Albania, in Bartlett, W. and Monastiriotis, V. (eds) *South East Europe after the Economic Crisis: New Dawn or Back to Business as Usual?.* London: LSE Research on South Eastern Europe, 53–57.

Germenji, E. and Milo, L. (2009) Return and labour status at home: evidence from returnees in Albania, *Southeast European and Black Sea Studies*, 9(4): 497–517.

Germenji, E. and Swinnen, J. (2004) Effects of remittances on household-based farm production behaviour. Paper presented to the conference 'New Perspectives on Albanian Migration and Development', Korçë, Albania, 16–17 September 2004.

Ghosh, B. (2006) *Migrants' Remittances and Development: Myths, Rhetoric and Realities.* Geneva: IOM and the Hague Process on Refugees and Migration.

Ghosh, J. (2009) *Migration and Gender Empowerment: Recent Trends and Emerging Issues.* New York: UNDP Human Development Report Research Paper 4.

Giddens, A. (1984) *The Constitution of Society: Outline of the Theory of Structuration.* Cambridge: Polity.

Gjoça, J. (2010) Kryetar 'dikushi' në protestë [The anonymous migrants' association director at the protest]. *Tribuna.* 14 May 2010, 7(321): 4.

Gjonça, A., Aassve, A. and Mencarini, L. (2008) Albania: trends and patterns, proximate determinants and policies of fertility change, *Demographic Research*, 19(11): 261–92.

Glick Schiller, N. and Faist, T. (2009) Migration, development and social transformation, *Social Analysis*, 53(3): 1–13.

Glick Schiller, N., Basch, L. and Szanton Blanc, C. (1995) From immigrant to transmigrant: theorising transnational migration, *Anthropological Quarterly*, 68(1): 48–63.

GoA (2005a) *National Strategy on Migration.* Tirana: Government of Albania (GoA) and IOM.

GoA (2005b) *National Action Plan on Migration.* Tirana: Government of Albania (GoA) and IOM.

Gogonas, N. (2007) *Ethnolinguistic Vitality and Language Maintenance in Second-Generation Migrants: A Study of Albanian and Egyptian Pupils in Athens*. Brighton: University of Sussex, DPhil thesis in Linguistics.

Goldring, L. (2003) *Re-thinking remittances: social and political dimensions of individual and collective remittances*. Toronto: York University, CERLAC [Center for Research on Latin America and the Caribbean] Working Paper.

Goss, J. and Lindquist, B. (1995) Conceptualizing international labor migration: a structuration perspective, *International Migration Review*, 29(2): 317–51.

Grassmuck, S. and Pessar, P.R. (1991) *Between Two Islands: Dominican International Migration*. Los Angeles: University of California Press.

Griffin, K. (1976) On the emigration of the peasantry, *World Development*, 4(5): 353–61.

Gropas, R. and Triandafyllidou, A. (2005) *Overview of Country Reports prepared for the POLITIS project 'Building Europe with New Citizens? An Inquiry into the Civic Participation of Naturalised Citizens and Foreign Residents in 25 Countries'*. Athens: ELIAMEP.

Guarnizo, L.E. (2003) The economics of transnational living, *International Migration Review*, 37(3): 666–99.

Guiraudon, V. and Lahav, G. (2000) A reappraisal of the state's sovereignty debate: the case of migration control, *Comparative Political Studies*, 33(2): 163–95.

Hagen-Zanker, J. and Siegel, M. (2007) *The Determinants of Remittances: A Review of the Literature*. Maastricht: Maastricht Graduate School of Governance Working Paper 3.

Hahamovitch, C. (2003) Creating perfect immigrants: guestworkers of the world in historical perspective, *Labor History*, 44(1): 69–94.

Hall, D. (1994) *Albania and the Albanians*. London: Pinter.

Halpern, J., Kaser, K. and Wagner, R. (1996) Patriarchy in the Balkans: temporal and cross-cultural approaches, *The History of the Family*, 1(4): 425–42.

Hammar, T., Brochmann, G., Tamas, K. and Faist, T. (eds) (1997) *International Migration, Immobility and Development: Multidisciplinary Perspectives*. Oxford: Berg.

Hatziprokopiou, P. (2006) *Globalisation, Migration and Socio-Economic Change in Contemporary Greece: Processes of Social Incorporation of Balkan Immigrants in Thessaloniki*. Amsterdam: Amsterdam University Press.

Hatziprokopiou, P. (2004) Balkan immigrants in the Greek city of Thessaloniki: local processes of incorporation in an international perspective, *European Urban and Regional Studies*, 11(4): 321–38.

Hatziprokopiou, P. (2003) Albanian immigrants in Thessaloniki, Greece: processes of economic and social incorporation, *Journal of Ethnic and Migration Studies*, 29(6): 1033–57.

Hemming, A. (2009) Migrant identity on display: the *xhiro* in Rrëshen, *Southeast European and Black Sea Studies*, 9(4): 575–88.

Hennebry, J. and Preibisch, K. (2009) A model for managed migration? Re-examining best practices in Canada's Seasonal Agricultural Worker Program', *International Migration*, early online view.

Hermele, K. (1997) The discourse on migration and development, in Hammar, T., Brochmann, G., Tamas, K. and Faist, T. (eds) *International Migration, Immobility and Development: Multidisciplinary Perspectives*. Oxford: Berg, 133–59.

Hernández-Coss, R., De Luna Martinez, J., Amatuzio, A., Borowik, K. and Lagi, F. (2006) *The Italy-Albanian Remittance Corridor. Shifting from the Physical Transfer of Cash to a Formal Money Transfer System*. Washington DC: The World Bank and Convergence.

Hoddinott, J. (1994) A model of migration and remittances applied to Western Kenya, *Oxford Economic Papers*, 46(3): 459–76.

Hondagneu-Sotelo, P. (1994) *Gendered Transitions: Mexican Experiences of Immigration*. Berkeley: University of California Press.

Hugo, G. (2005) *Migrants in Society: Diversion and Cohesion*. Geneva: Global Commission on Migration.

Hugo, G. (2000) Migration and women's empowerment, in Presser, H.B. and Sen, G. (eds) *Women's Empowerment and Demographic Process*. Oxford: Oxford University Press, 287–317.

IMF (2006) *Albania Selected Issues*. Washington DC: IMF Country Report 06/285.

INSTAT (2007a) *Albania in Figures 2007*. Tirana: Instituti i Statistikës.

INSTAT (2007b) *Foreign Trade, 2002–2006*. Tirana: Instituti i Statistikës.

INSTAT (2004a) *The Population of Albania 2001, Korçë*. Tirana: Instituti i Statistikës.

INSTAT (2004b) *The Population of Albania 2001*. Tirana: Instituti i Statistikës.

INSTRAW (2006) *The Development Potential of Remittances. A Gender Perspective. Qualitative Research Methodology*. Santo Domingo: INSTRAW Working Paper.

IOM (2008) *World Migration 2008: Managing Labour Mobility in the Evolving Global Economy*. Geneva: IOM.

IOM (2006a) *Return and Readmission to Albania. The Experiences of Selected EU Member States*. Tirana: IOM.

IOM (2006b) *Return and Readmission. The Case of Albania*. Tirana: IOM.

IOM (2005a) *World Migration 2005: Costs and Benefits of International Migration*. Geneva: IOM.

IOM (2005b) *Migration and Remittances in Moldova*. Chisinau: IOM.

Iosifides, T. and King, R. (1998) Socio-spatial dynamics and exclusion of three immigrant groups in the Athens conurbation, *South European Society and Politics*, 3(3): 205–29.

ISB (2008) *Social Inclusion and Social Protection in Albania*. Brussels: European Commission. Prepared by the Institute of Contemporary Studies [Instituti i Studimeve Bashkëkohore] Tirana for the EC DG for Employment, Social Affairs and Equal Opportunities.

Jarvis, C. (2000) The rise and fall of Albania's pyramid schemes, *Finance and Development*, 37(1): 1–29.

Jazayery, L. (2002) The migration-development nexus: Afghanistan case study, *International Migration*, 40(5): 231–54.

Jones, R.C. (1998) Remittances and inequality: a question of migration stage and geographic scale, *Economic Geography*, 74(1): 8–25.

Kabeer, N. (2000) *The Power to Choose: Bangladeshi Women and Labour Market Decisions in London and Dhaka*. London: Verso.

Kanellopoulos, K. and Gregou, M. (2006) *Policy Report on Migration, Asylum and Return in Greece*. Athens: Centre of Planning and Economic Research (KEPE).

Kapllani, G. (2009) *A Short Border Handbook*. London: Portobello.

Kapur, D. (2004) *Remittances: The New Development Mantra?* Geneva: United Nations Conference on Trade and Development and the Intergovernmental Group of Twenty-Four on International Monetary Affairs. G-24 Discussion Paper Series, 29.

Karafolas, S. and Konteos, G. (2010) Choice of money transfer methods in the case of Albanian immigrants in Greece, *Transition Studies Review*, 16(6): 962–78.

Karafolas, S. and Sariannidis, N. (2009) The banking network as a transmission channel of migrant remittances: the case of Greek and Italian banks in Albania *Transition Studies Review*, 15(4): 674–84.

Kaser, K. (1996) Introduction: household and family contexts in the Balkans, *The History of the Family*, 1(4): 375–86.

Kasimis, C. and Papadopoulos, A.G. (2005) The multifunctional role of migrants in the Greek countryside: implications for the rural economy and society, *Journal of Ethnic and Migration Studies*, 31(1): 99–127.

Kilic, T., Carletto, G., Davis, B. and Zezza, A. (2007) *Investing Back Home: Return Migration and Business Ownership in Albania*. Washington DC: World Bank Policy Research Working Paper 4366.

Kindleberger, C.P. (1965) *Europe's Postwar Growth: The Role of Labour Supply*. New York: Oxford University Press.

King, R. (2005) Albania as a laboratory for the study of migration and development, *Journal of Southern Europe and the Balkans*, 7(2): 133–56.

King, R. (2002) Towards a new map of European migration, *International Journal of Population Geography*, 8(2): 89–103.

King, R. (2000a) Generalizations from the history of return migration, in Ghosh, B. (ed.) *Return Migration: Journey of Hope or Dispair?* Geneva: UN and IOM, 7–55.

King, R. (2000b) Southern Europe in the changing global map of migration, in King, R., Lazaridis, G. and Tsardanidis, C. (eds) *Eldorado or Fortress? Migration in Southern Europe*. Basingstoke: Macmillan, 1–26.

King, R. (ed.) (1986) *Return Migration and Regional Economic Problems*. London: Croom Helm.

King, R., Black, R., Collyer, M., Fielding, A. and Skeldon, R. (2010) *People on the Move: An Atlas of Migration*. Berkeley: University of California Press.

King, R., Dalipaj, M. and Mai, N. (2006) Gendering migration and remittances: evidence from London and Northern Albania, *Population, Space and Place*, 12(6): 409–34.

King, R. and Mai, N. (2008) *Out of Albania: From Crisis Migration to Social Inclusion in Italy*. Oxford: Berghahn.

King, R. and Mai, N. (2004) Albanian immigrants in Lecce and Modena: narratives of rejection, survival and integration, *Population, Space and Place*, 10(6): 455–77.

King, R. and Mai, N. (2002) Of myths and mirrors: interpretations of Albanian migration to Italy, *Studi Emigrazione*, 39(145): 161–99.

King, R., Mai, N. and Dalipaj, M. (2003) *Exploding the Migration Myths: Analysis and Recommendations for the European Union, the UK and Albania*. London: The Fabian Society and Oxfam.

King, R. and Vullnetari, J. (2010) *Gender and remittances in Albania: or why 'Are women better remitters than men?' is not the right question*. Brighton: Sussex Centre for Migration Research Working Paper 58.

King, R. and Vullnetari, J. (2009a) Remittances, return, diaspora: framing the debate in the context of Albania and Kosova, *Southeast European and Black Sea Studies*, 9(4): 385–406.

King, R. and Vullnetari, J. (2009b) The intersections of gender and generation in Albanian migration, remittances and transnational care, *Geografiska Annaler: Series B, Human Geography*, 91(1): 19–38.

King, R. and Vullnetari, J. (2006) Orphan pensioners and migrating grandparents: the impact of mass migration on older people in rural Albania, *Ageing and Society*, 26(5): 783–816.

King, R. and Vullnetari, J. (2003) *Migration and Development in Albania*. Brighton: University of Sussex, Development Research Centre on Migration, Globalisation and Poverty, Working Paper C5.

King, R. and Zontini, E. (2000) The role of gender in the South European immigration model, *Papers: Revista de Sociología*, 60: 35–52.

Koc, I. and Onan, I. (2004) International migrants' remittances and the welfare status of the left-behind families in Turkey, *International Migration Review*, 38(1): 78–112.

Kofman, E. (2004) Gendered global migrations, *International Feminist Journal of Politics*, 6(4): 643–65.

Kofman, E. (2000) The invisibility of skilled female migrants and gender relations in studies of skilled migration in Europe, *International Journal of Population Geography*, 6(1): 45–59.

Kokkali, I. (2010) *Migrants Albanais en Grèce: De la Dissimulation Identitaire à l'Invisibilité Territoriale*. Paris: Éditions Universitaires Européennes.

Konica, N. and Filer, R. (2005) *Albanian Emigration. Causes and Consequences*. Prague: Charles University, CERGE [Center for Economic Research and Graduate Education] Working Paper 181.

Konidaris, G. (2005) Examining policy responses to immigration in the light of interstate relations and foreign policy objectives: Greece and Albania, in King, R., Mai, N. and Schwandner-Sievers, S. (eds) *The New Albanian Migration*. Brighton: Sussex Academic Press, 64–92.

Korçë Municipality (2005) *Local Action Plan for the Environment*. Tirana: Regional Environmental Centre (REC) for Central and Eastern Europe.

Korça Regional Council (2005) *Regional Development Strategy, Millennium Development Goals. Korça Region*. Korça: Korça Regional Council.

Korovilas, J. (1999) The Albanian economy in transition: the role of remittances and pyramid investment schemes, *Post-Communist Economies*, 11(3): 399–415.

Kretsi, G. (2005) The uses of origin: migration, power-struggle and memory in southern Albania, in King, R., Mai, N. and Schwandner-Sievers, S. (eds) *The New Albanian Migration*. Brighton: Sussex Academic Press, 193–212.

Kring, T. (2007) *Enhancing the Impact of Migrant Remittances in Albania*. Geneva: ILO and IOM Working Paper.

Kule, D., Mançellari, A., Papapanagos, H., Qirici, S. and Sanfey, P. (2002) The causes and consequences of Albanian emigration during transition: evidence from micro-data, *International Migration Review*, 36(1): 229–39.

Kunz, R. (2008) 'Remittances are beautiful'? Gender implications of the new global remittances trend, *Third World Quarterly*, 29(7): 1389–409.

Labrianidis, L. and Hatziprokopiou, P. (2005) The Albanian migration cycle: migrants tend to return to their country of origin after all, in King, R., Mai, N. and Schwandner-Sievers, S. (eds) *The New Albanian Migration*. Brighton: Sussex Academic Press, 93–117.

Labrianidis, L. and Lyberaki, A. (2001) *Albanian Migrants in Thessaloniki*. Athens: Paratiritis [in Greek].

Labrianidis, L., Lyberaki, A., Tinios, P. and Hatziprokopiou, H. (2004) Inflow of migrants and outflow of investment: aspects of interdependence between Greece and the Balkans, *Journal of Ethnic and Migration Studies*, 30(6): 1183–208.

Labrianidis, L. and Sykas, T. (2009) Geographical proximity and immigrant labour in agriculture: Albanian immigrants in the Greek countryside, *Sociologia Ruralis*, 49(4): 394–414.

Lamani, M. (2003) *Gratë në Kuvend* [*Women in Parliament*]. Tirana: Kuvendi i Shqipërisë. Sektori i Kërkimit dhe Biblioteka.

Lazaridis, G. (2003) From maids to entrepreneurs: immigrant women in Greece, in Freedman, J. (ed.) *Gender and Insecurity*. Aldershot: Ashgate, 173–94.

Lazaridis, G. (1999) The helots of the new millennium: ethnic-Greek Albanians and 'other' Albanians in Greece, in Anthias, F. and Lazaridis, G. (eds) *Into the Margins: Migration and Exclusion in Southern Europe*. Aldershot: Ashgate, 105–21.

Lazaridis, G. (1996) Immigration to Greece: a critical evaluation of Greek policy, *New Community*, 22(2): 335–48.

Lazaridis, G. and Koumandraki, M. (2007) Albanian migration to Greece: patterns and processes of inclusion and exclusion in the labour market, *European Societies*, 9(1): 91–111.

Lazaridis, G. and Koumandraki, M. (2001) Deconstructing naturalism: the racialisation of ethnic minorities in Greece, in King, R. (ed.) *The Mediterranean Passage: Migration and New Cultural Encounters in Southern Europe*. Liverpool: Liverpool University Press, 279–301.

Lazaridis, G. and Wickens, E. (1999) 'Us' and the 'Others': ethnic minorities in Greece, *Annals of Tourism Research*, 26(3): 632–55.

Léon-Ledesma, M. and Piracha, M. (2004) International migration and the role of remittances in Eastern Europe, *International Migration*, 42(4): 65–83.

Lerch, M. and Wanner, P. (2008) *Demographic Data in Albania: Results of An Assessment*. Geneva: Geneva University.

Lerch, M. and Wanner, P. (2006) *Les Transfers des Fonds des Migrants Albanais. Facteurs Déterminant leur Réception*. Geneva: Swiss Forum for Migration and Population Studies Working Paper 45.

Levitt, P. (1998) Social remittances: migration driven local-level forms of cultural diffusion, *International Migration Review*, 32(4): 926–48.

Levitt, P. and Jaworsky, B.N. (2007) Transnational migration studies: past developments and future trends, *Annual Review of Sociology*, 33: 129–56.

Lewis, J.R. (1986) International labour migration and uneven regional development in labour exporting countries, *Tijdschrift voor Economische en Sociale Geografie*, 77(1): 27–41.

Lianos, T. (2007) Brain drain and brain loss: immigrants to Greece, *Journal of Ethnic and Migration Studies*, 33(1): 129–40.

Lindley, A. (2009) The early-morning phonecall: remittances from a refugee diaspora perspective, *Journal of Ethnic and Migration Studies*, 35(8): 1315–34.

Lipton, M. (1980) Migration from rural areas of poor countries: the impact on rural productivity and income distribution, *World Development*, 8(1): 1–24.

Littlewood, R. (2002) Three into two. The third sex in Northern Albania, *Anthropology and Medicine*, 9(1): 37–50.

Logoreci, A. (1977) *The Albanians. Europe's Forgotten Survivors*. London: Victor Gollancz.

Long, L. and Celebic, S. (2006) Perspectives on the EC/Albanian Readmission Agreement, in IOM (ed.) *Return and Readmission to Albania. The Experiences of Selected EU Member States*. Tirana: IOM, 11–40.

Lowell, L. (2002) *Some Developmental Effects of the International Migration of Highly Skilled Persons*. Geneva: ILO International Migration Papers, 46.

Lubonja, F. (2001) Privacy in a totalitarian regime, *Social Research*, 68(1): 236–53.

Lucas, R.E. and Stark, O. (1985) Motivations to remit: evidence from Botswana, *Journal of Political Economy*, 93(5): 901–18.

Lundström, S. and Ronnås, P. (2006) *Migration and Pro-Poor Growth in Albania. An Integrated Economic Analysis*. Stockholm: SIDA, Country Economic Report 2006/5.

Lyberaki, A. and Maroukis, T. (2005) Albanian immigrants in Athens. New survey evidence on employment and integration, *Southeast European and Black Sea Studies*, 5(1): 21–48.

Mahler, S.J. and Pessar, P. (2001) Gendered geographies of power: analyzing gender across transnational spaces, *Identities*, 7(4): 441–59.

Mai, N. (2005) The Albanian diaspora-in-the-making: media, migration and social exclusion, *Journal of Ethnic and Migration Studies*, 31(3): 543–61.

Mai, N. (2003) The cultural construction of Italy in Albania and vice versa: migration dynamics, strategies of resistance and politics of mutual self-definition across colonialism and post-colonialism, *Modern Italy*, 8(1): 77–94.

Mai, N. (2002) *Between Losing and Finding Oneself. The Role of Italian Television in the Albanian Migration to Italy*. Brighton: University of Sussex, DPhil thesis in Media and Cultural Studies.

Mai, N. (2001) Transforming traditions: a critical analysis of the trafficking and exploitation of young Albanian girls in Italy, in King, R. (ed.) *The Mediterranean Passage: Migration and New Cultural Encounters in Southern Europe*. Liverpool: Liverpool University Press, 258–78.

Marcus, G. (1995) Ethnography in/of the World System, the emergence of multi-sited ethnography, *Annual Review of Anthropology*, 24: 95–117.

Markova, E. and Reilly, B. (2006) *Bulgarian Migrant Remittances and Legal Status: Some Micro-Level Evidence from Madrid*. Brighton: Sussex Centre for Migration Research Working Paper 37.

Maroukis, T. (2008) *Undocumented Migration. Counting the Uncountable. Data and Trends across Europe. Country Report Greece*. Athens: Country report prepared for the 'Clandestino' research project, funded under the 6th Framework Programme of the Europian Union.

Maroukis, T. (2005a) Albanian migrants in Athens and the emergence of a transborder public sphere, in Chiodi, L. (ed.) *The Borders of the Polity. Migration and Security Across the EU and the Balkans*. Ravenna: Longo Editore, 189–207.

Maroukis, T. (2005b) Albanian migrants in Greece: transcending 'borders' in development, *Journal of Southern Europe and the Balkans*, 7(2): 213–33.

Martin, P. (2004) *Migration and Development: Toward Sustainable Solutions*. Geneva: ILO, International Institute for Labour Studies Discussion Paper 153.

Martin, P.L. and Taylor, J.E. (1996) The anatomy of a migration hump, in Taylor, J. E. (ed.) *Development Strategy, Employment and Migration: Insights from Models*. Paris: OECD, 43–62.

Massey, D. (1994) *Space, Place and Gender*. Minneapolis: University of Minnesota Press.

Massey, D. (1987) The ethnosurvey in theory and practice, *International Migration Review*, 21(4): 1498–522.

Massey, D., Arango, J., Hugo, G., Kouaouci, A., Pellegrino, A. and Taylor, J.E. (1993) Theories of international migration: a review and appraisal, *Population and Development Review*, 19(3): 431–66.

McCarthy, N., Carletto, G., Davis, B. and Maltsoglou, I. (2006) *Assessing the Impact of Massive Out-Migration on Agriculture*. Rome: FAO, ESA Working Paper 14.

McKay, D. (2005) Reading remittance landscapes: female migration and agricultural transition in the Philippines', *Geografisk Tidsskrift*, 105(1): 89–99.

McKay, S.C. (2007) Filipino sea men: constructing masculinities in an ethnic labour niche, *Journal of Ethnic and Migration Studies*, 33(4): 617–33.

Meka, E., Bendo, L. and Frashëri, A. (2007) *Remittances and Financial Products in Albania: Reality and the Future*. Tirana: IOM and ILO.

Meka, E., Dono, I. and Hasani, M. (2008) *Country Paper on Banking System and Remittances: Albania*. Tirana: Albanian Association of Banks and Hope for the Future. Country report for the project 'MIGRAVALUE – Steering Economic and Social Cohesion in the CADSES Space: Valuing Migration as a Development Tool' within the framework of the Community initiative programme Interreg IIIB CADSES.

Miluka, J., Carletto, G., Davis, B. and Zezza, A. (2007) *The Vanishing Farms? The Impact of International Migration on Albanian Farms*. Washington DC: World Bank Policy Research Working Paper 4367.

Minnesota Advocates for Human Rights (1996) *Domestic Violence in Albania*. Minneapolis: Minnesota Advocates for Human Rights.

Miracle, M.P. and Berry, S.S. (1970) Migrant labour and economic development, *Oxford Economic Papers*, 22(1): 86–108.

Misha, A. (2006) *Report on Civil Society Needs Assessment in Albania*. Tirana: UNDP and SNV.

Misja, V. (1998) *Emigracioni Ndërkombëtar në Shqipëri Gjatë Periudhës së Tranzicionit* [*Emigration in Albania during the Transition Period*]. Tirana: Marin Barleti.

Mohan, G. and Mohan, J. (2002) Placing social capital, *Progress in Human Geography*, 26(2): 191–210.

Moreno-Fontes Chammartin, G. and Cantú-Bazaldúa, F. (2003) *Identification of Potential for Increasing Employment and Productive Investment in Albania, Moldova and Ukraine Based on Remittances*. Geneva: ILO International Migration Papers 74.

Morokvasic, M. (1984) Birds of passage are also women, *International Migration Review*, 18(4): 886–907.

Murphy, R. (2005) Helping migration to improve livelihoods in China: vocational training, development of small businesses and agribusinesses and support for those left behind, in IOM (ed.) *Migration, Development and Poverty Reduction in Asia*. New York: United Nations, 223–41.

Murzaku, I.A. and Dervishi, Z. (2003) Albanians' first post-communist decade. Values in transition: traditional or liberal?, *East European Quarterly*, 37(2): 231–56.

Musaj, F. (2002) *Gruaja në Shqipëri, 1912–1939* [*Women in Albania, 1912–1939*]. Tirana: Akademia e Shkencave e Shqipërisë, Instituti i Historisë.

Myrdal, G. (1957) *Rich Lands and Poor*. New York: Harper and Row.

Nash, J. and Fernandez Kelly, M.P. (eds) (1983) *Women, Men, and the International Division of Labor.* Albany: State University of New York Press.

Nichols, S. (2002) Another kind of remittance: transfer of agricultural innovations by migrants to their communities of origin. Paper presented to the Second Colloquium on International Migration: Mexico-California, University of California, Berkeley, 29 March.

Nicholson, B. (2006) Women who shared a husband. Polygyny in southern Albania in the early 20th century, *The History of the Family*, 11(1): 45–57.

Nicholson, B. (2004a) Migrants as agents of development: Albanian return migrants and micro-enterprise, in Pop, D. (ed.) *New Patterns of Labour Migration in Central and Eastern Europe.* Cluj Napoca: Public Policy Center, 94–110.

Nicholson, B. (2004b) The tractor, the shop and the filling-station: work migration as self-help development in Albania, *Europe-Asia Studies*, 56(6): 877–90.

Nicholson, B. (2001) From migrant to micro-entrepreneur: do-it-yourself development in Albania, *South-East Europe Review*, 4(3): 39–42.

Nikas, C. and King, R. (2005) Economic growth through remittances: lessons from the Greek experience of the 1960s applicable to the Albanian case, *Journal of Southern Europe and the Balkans*, 7(2): 235–57.

Nixon, N. (2009) 'You can't eat shame with bread': gender and collective shame in Albanian society, *Southeast European and Black Sea Studies*, 9(1): 105–21.

Nixon, N. (2006) The absence of gender: Albania's National Strategy on Migration, *Albanian Journal of Politics*, 2(1): 44–61.

Nyberg Sørensen, N. (2005) *Migrant Remittances, Development and Gender.* Copenhagen: Danish Institute for International Studies.

Nyberg Sørensen, N. (2004) *Migrant Transfers as a Development Tool. The Case of Morocco.* Copenhagen: Danish Institute for International Studies Working Paper 17.

Nyberg Sørenson, N., van Hear, N. and Engberg-Pedersen, P. (2002) *The Migration–Development Nexus: Evidence and Policy Options.* Geneva: IOM.

Oberai, A.S. and Singh, H.K. (1980) Migration, remittances and rural development: findings of a study in Indian Punjab, *International Labour Review*, 119(2): 229–41.

Oishi, N. (2005) *Women in Motion: Globalization, State Policies and Labour Migration in Asia.* Stanford: Stanford University Press.

Onorato, M., Keta, M. and Totozani, I. (2007) *Raport mbi Zbatimin e Planit Kombëtar të Veprimit për Migracionit* [*Report on the Implementation of the National Action Plan on Migration*]. Tirana: Instituti Europian i Tiranës.

Orgocka, A. (2005) Albanian highly skilled women in the US, in King, R., Mai, N. and Schwandner-Sievers, S. (eds) *The New Albanian Migration.* Brighton: Sussex Academic Press, 139–53.

Orozco, M. (2007) *Making the Most of Family Remittances.* Washington DC: Inter-American Dialogue, Second Report of Task Force on Remittances.

Orozco, M., Lowell, L.B. and Schneider, J. (2006) *Gender-Specific Determinants of Remittances: Differences in Structure and Motivation*. Washington DC: Institute for the Study of International Migration, Georgetown University. Report to the World Bank Gender and Development Group, PREM.

Osaki, K. (1999) Economic interactions of migrants and their households of origin: are women more reliable supporters?, *Asian and Pacific Migration Journal*, 8(4): 447–71.

OSCE/ODIHR (2007) *Republic of Albania Local Elections 2007. OSCE/ODIHR Election Observation Mission Report*. Warsaw: OSCE and the Office for Democratic Institutions and Human Rights.

Papademetriou, D.G. (1991) Migration and development: the unsettled relationship, in Papademetriou, D. G. and Martin, P. L. (eds) *The Unsettled Relationship: Labor Migration and Economic Development*. Westport: Greenwood Press, 213–20.

Papademetriou, D.G. and Martin, P.L. (eds) (1991) *The Unsettled Relationship: Labor Migration and Economic Development*. Westport: Greenwood Press.

Papapanagos, H. and Sanfey, P. (2001) Intention to emigrate in transition countries: the case of Albania, *Journal of Population Economics*, 14(3): 491–504.

Parreñas, R.S. (2008) Transnational fathering: gendered conflicts, distant disciplining and emotional gaps, *Journal of Ethnic and Migration Studies*, 34(7): 1057–72.

Parreñas, R.S. (2005) *Children of Global Migration: Transnational Families and Gendered Woes*. Stanford: Stanford University Press.

Parreñas, R.S. (2003) The care crisis in the Philippines: children and transnational families in the new global economy, in Ehrenreich, B. and Hochschild, A. (eds) *Global Woman: Nannies, Maids and Sex Workers in the New Economy*. New York: Metropolitan Books, 39–54.

Parreñas, R.S. (2000) Migrant Filipina domestic workers and the international division of reproductive labour, *Gender and Society*, 14(4): 560–80.

PBI (2005) *Sending Money Home: Albania*. London: Profile Business Intelligence. <http://www.iomtirana.org.al/Remitance/al/Sending%20money%20home-al.pdf> [last accessed: 19 December 2007].

Pérez-Armendáriz, A. and Crow, D. (2010) Do migrants remit democracy? International migration, political beliefs, and behavior in Mexico, *Comparative Political Studies*, 43(1): 119–48.

Phizacklea, A. (ed.) (1983) *One Way Ticket: Migration and Female Labour*. London: Routledge and Kegan Paul.

Piotrowski, M. (2009) Sibling influences on migrant remittances. Evidence from Nang Rong, Thailand, *Journal of Population Ageing*, 1(2–4): 193–224.

Piper, N. (2005) *Gender and Migration*. Geneva: Global Commission on International Migration Paper 10.

Piperno, F. (2005) Albanian migrants' remittances: a development opportunity?, in King, R., Mai, N. and Schwandner-Sievers, S. (eds) *The New Albanian Migration*. Brighton: Sussex Academic Press, 118–38.

Poirine, B. (1997) A theory of remittances as an implicit family loan arrangement, *World Development*, 25(4): 589–611.

Portes, A. (1998) Social capital: its origins and applications in modern sociology, *Annual Review of Sociology*, 24: 1–24.

Pratsinakis, E. (2005) Aspirations and strategies of Albanian immigrants in Thessaloniki, *Journal of Southern Europe and the Balkans*, 7(2): 195–212.

Pritchett-Post, S.E. (1998) *Women in Modern Albania. Firsthand Accounts of Culture and Conditions from Over 200 Interviews*. Jefferson and London: McFarland and Co.

Puri, S. and Ritzema, T. (1999) *Migrant Worker Remittances, Micro-Finance and the Informal Economy: Prospects and Issues*. Geneva: ILO Working Paper 21.

Putnam, R. (2000) *Bowling Alone: The Collapse and Revival of American Community*. New York: Simon Schuster.

Putnam, R. (1993) *Making Democracy Work: Civic Traditions in Modern Italy*. Princeton: Princeton University Press.

Raghuram, P. (2004) The difference that skills make: gender, family migration strategies and regulated labour markets, *Journal of Ethnic and Migration Studies*, 30(2): 303–21.

Ramírez, C., Garcia Dominguez, M. and Míguez Morais, J. (2005) *Crossing Borders: Remittances, Gender and Development*. Santo Domingo: INSTRAW Working Paper.

Ratha, D. (2003) Workers' remittances: an important and stable source of external developmental finance, in *Global Development Finance*. Washington DC: World Bank, 157–74.

Ratha, R., Mohapatra, S. and Silwal, A. (2010) Outlook for remittance flows 2010–11. Remittance flows to developing countries remained resilient in 2009. 23 April 2010. Washington DC: World Bank Migration and Remittances Team, Development Prospects Group, Migration and Development brief 12, available online at: <http://siteresources.worldbank.org/INTPROSPECTS/Resources/334934_1110315015165/MigrationAndDevelopmentBrief12.pdf> [last accessed: June 2010].

Ravenstein, E.G. (1889) The laws of migration, *Journal of the Royal Statistical Society*, 52(2): 241–305.

Rempel, H. and Lobdell, R. (1978) The role of urban-to-rural remittances in rural development, *Journal of Development Studies*, 14(3): 324–41.

Reuters (2003) On Albanian border, taxis with four legs. *Reuters News Agency* [13 June 2003].

Rëmbeci, G. (2009) Nationwide remittance beneficiaries survey, *Bank of Albania Economic Bulletin*, 12(3): 107–24.

Rovolis, A. and Tragaki, A. (2006) Ethnic characteristics and geographical distribution of immigrants in Greece, *European Urban and Regional Studies*, 13(2): 99–111.

Russell, S. (1993) Migrant remittances and development, *International Migration*, 31(3–4): 267–87.

Russell, S. (1986) Remittances from international migration: a review in perspective, *World Development*, 14(6): 677–96.

Safa, H. (1995) *The Myth of the Male Breadwinner: Women and Industrialization in the Caribbean*. Boulder: Westview Press.

Salih, R. (2001) Moroccan migrant women: transnationalism and gender, *Journal of Ethnic and Migration Studies*, 27(4): 655–71.

Saltmarshe, D. (2001) *Identity in a Post-Communist Balkan State: An Albanian Village Study*. Aldershot: Ashgate.

Samers, M. (2010) *Migration*. London: Routledge.

Sampson, S. (1996) The social life of projects, importing civil society in Albania, in Hann, C. and Down, E. (eds) *Civil Society, Challenging Western Models*. London: Routledge, 121–42.

Sander, C. (2003) *Migrant Remittances to Developing Countries*. London: Bannock Consulting for DFID.

Sassen, S. (2000) Women's burden: counter-geographies of globalization and the feminization of survival, *Journal of International Affairs*, 53(2): 503–24.

Sassen, S. (1988) *The Mobility of Labor and Capital: A Study in International Investment and Labor Flow*. Cambridge: Cambridge University Press.

Schwandner-Sievers, S. (2006) 'Culture' in court: Albanian migrants and the anthropologist as expert witness, in Pink, S. (ed.) *Applications of Anthropology. Professional Anthropology in the Twenty-First Century*. Oxford: Berghahn, 209–32.

Schwandner-Sievers, S. (2001) The enactment of 'tradition': Albanian constructions of identity, violence and power in times of crisis, in Schmidt, B. E. and Schröder, I. W. (eds) *Anthropology of Violence and Conflict*. London: Routledge, 97–119.

Schwandner-Sievers, S. (1999) Humiliation and reconciliation in Northern Albania. The logics of feuding in symbolic and diachronic perspectives, in Elwert, G., Feuchtwang, S. and Neubert, D. (eds) *Dynamics of Violence. Processes of Escalation and De-Escalation in Violent Group Conflicts*. Berlin: Duncker and Humbolt, 133–52.

Semyonov, M. and Gorodzeisky, A. (2005) Labor, migration, remittances and household income: a comparison between Filipino and Filipina overseas workers, *International Migration Review*, 39(1): 45–68.

Sen, A. (1999) *Development as Freedom*. New York: Anchor Books.

Senturia, K. (1997) A woman's work is never done: women's work and pregnancy outcome in Albania, *Medical Anthropology Quarterly*, 11(3): 375–95.

Shryock, A.J. (1988) Autonomy, entanglement, and the feud: prestige structures and gender values in Highland Albania, *Anthropological Quarterly*, 61(3): 113–18.

Sjöberg, Ö. (1994) Rural retention in Albania: administrative restrictions on urban-bound migration, *East European Quarterly*, 28(2): 205–33.

Sjöberg, Ö. (1991) *Rural Change and Development in Albania*. Oxford: Westview Press.

Skeldon, R. (1997) *Migration and Development: A Global Perspective*. London: Longman.

Smith, E. (2009) 'Gap-fillers' or 'clan-destroyers'? Transnational female solidarity towards kin in the region of Fier, *Southeast European and Black Sea Studies*, 9(4): 555–73.

Smith, J. and Wallerstein, I. (eds) (1992) *Creating and Transforming Households: The Constraints of the World-Economy*. Cambridge: Cambridge University Press.

Smith, L. and Mazzucato, V. (2009) Constructing homes, building relationships: migrant investments in houses, *Tijdschrift voor Economische en Sociale Geografie*, 100(5): 662–73.

Smith, S. (2001) Doing qualitative research: from interpretation to action, in Limb, M. and Dwyer, C. (eds) *Qualitative Methodologies for Geographers*. London: Arnold, 23–40.

Sokoli, L. (2006) Familja tradicionale shqiptare dhe alternativat 'jo-tradicionale' të saj [The traditional Albanian family and its 'non-traditional' alternatives], in Sokoli, L. (ed.) *Analiza Sociologjike*. Tirana: Instituti i Sociologjisë and Rinia, 6–24.

Spatafora, N. and Freund, C. (2004) *Remittances: Transaction Costs, Determinants, and Informal Flows*. Washington DC: World Bank Policy Research Working Paper 3704.

Stampini, M., Carletto, G. and Davis, B. (2008) International migration from Albania: the role of family networks and previous experience, *East European Economics*, 46(2): 50–87.

Stark, O. (2009) Reasons for remitting, *World Economics*, 10(3): 147–57.

Stark, O. and Bloom, D.E. (1985) The new economics of labor migration, *American Economic Review*, 75(2): 173–8.

Tacoli, C. (1999) International migration and the restructuring of gender asymmetries: continuity and change among Filipino labor migrants in Rome, *International Migration Review*, 33(3): 658–82.

Tahiraj, E. (2007) *Poverty and Anti-Poverty Programmes in Albania. The Role of Social Policy in Transition and Consolidation*. York: University of York, DPhil thesis in Social Policy and Social Work.

Tarifa, F. (2008) Of time, honor, and memory: oral law in Albania, *Oral Tradition*, 23(1): 3–14.

Tarifa, F. (2007) Of mice, men and mountains: justice Albanian style, *Sociological Analysis*, 1(1): 89–125.

Taylor, J.E. (1999) The new economics of labour migration and the role of remittances in the migration process, *International Migration*, 37(1): 63–88.

Taylor, J.E. (1987) Undocumented Mexico-US migration and the returns to households in rural Mexico, *American Journal of Agricultural Economics*, 69(3): 626–38.

Tirta, M. (1999) Migrime të shqiptarëve, të brendshme dhe jashtë atdheut: vitet '40 të shek.XIX-vitet '40 të shek.XX. [Internal and international migration of Albanians: 1840s–1940s], *Etnografia Shqiptare*, 18.

Trako, I. (2008) *The Impact of Remittances on Incentives: The Case of Albania*. Buenos Aires: University of San Andrés, Department of Economics Working Paper.

Triandafyllidou, A. and Veikou, M. (2002) The hierarchy of Greekness: ethnic and national identity considerations in Greek immigration policy, *Ethnicities*, 2(2): 189–208.

Uçi, A. (2003) Mbi disa aspekte të marrëdhënieve familjare e martesore [On some aspects of family and marital relations], *Politika dhe Shoqëria*, 6(1): 17–30.

UN-Albania (2004) *Common Country Assessment*. Tirana: UN Albania.

UNDP (2009) *Human Development Report 2009. Overcoming Barriers: Human Mobility and Development*. New York: United Nations Development Programme.

UNDP-Albania (2008) *Partnering for Development: UNDP in Albania 2008*. Tirana: UNDP Albania.

UNDP-Albania (2006) *At Risk: The Social Vulnerability of Roma in Albania*. Tirana: UNDP Albania.

UNDP-Albania (2005) *National Human Development Report Albania: Pro-Poor and Pro-Women Policies and Development in Albania. Approaches to Operationalising the Millennium Development Goals in Albania*. Tirana: UNDP Albania.

UNDP-Albania (1999) *National Women Report Albania 1999*. Tirana: UNDP Albania.

UNDP-Albania and SIDA (2004) *Progress Report UNDP Korça Clean and Green Project*. Korça: UNDP Albania.

UNICEF (2009) *Albanian Migration since the 1990s and its Socio-Economic Influence on the Children Left Behind*. New York: UNICEF.

Uruçi, E. (2008) The role of remittances in the Albanian economy. Paper presented to the conference on 'Migration and Development in Albania and the Western Balkans: Remittances, Return and Diaspora', Durrës, Albania, 26–27 September 2008.

Uruçi, E. and Gedeshi, I. (2003) *Remittances Management in Albania*. Rome: CeSPI Working Paper 5.

van Hear, N. (1998) *New Diasporas*. London: UCL Press.

van Hear, N. and Nyberg Sørensen, N. (2003) *The Migration–Development Nexus*. Geneva: IOM.

Van Hook, M., Haxhiymeri, E. and Gjermeni, E. (2006) Sexual trafficking of women. Tragic proportions and attempted solutions in Albania, *International Social Work*, 49(1): 29–40.

Van Hook, M., Haxhiymeri, E. and Gjermeni, E. (2000) Responding to gender violence in Albania. A partnership effort, *International Social Work*, 43(3): 351–63.

Vanwey, L. (2004) Altruistic and contractual remittances between male and female migrants and households in rural Thailand, *Demography*, 41(4): 739–56.

Vertovec, S. (2004) Cheap calls: the social glue of migrant transnationalism, *Global Networks*, 4(2): 219–24.

Vertovec, S. (1999) Conceiving and researching transnationalism, *Ethnic and Racial Studies*, 22(2): 447–62.

Vickers, M. (1995) *The Albanians: A Modern History*. London: I.B.Tauris.

Vickers, M. and Pettifer, J. (1997) *Albania: From Anarchy to a Balkan Identity*. New York: New York University Press.

Vullnetari, J. (2009) Women and migration: a view from the village, *International Migration*, early online view.

Vullnetari, J. (2008) *The Dynamics between Internal and International Migration: A Development-Oriented Ethnographic Study in Albania*. Brighton: University of Sussex, DPhil thesis in Migration Studies.

Vullnetari, J. (2007) *Albanian Migration and Development. State-of-the-Art Review*. Amsterdam: IMISCOE Working Paper 18.

Vullnetari, J. and King, R. (2008) 'Does your granny eat grass?' On mass migration, care drain and the fate of older people in rural Albania, *Global Networks*, 8(2): 139–71.

Wallerstein, I. (1979) *The Capitalist World Economy*. Cambridge: Cambridge University Press.

Wheeler, R. (1998) *Past and Present Land Tenure Systems in Albania: Patrilineal, Patriarchal, Family-Centred*. Madison: University of Wisconsin, Land Tenure Centre Working Paper 13.

Whitaker, I. (1981) 'A sack for carrying things': the traditional role of women in Northern Albanian society, *Anthropological Quarterly*, 54(2): 146–56.

Wong, M. (2006) The gendered politics of difference in Ghanaian transnational families, *Economic Geography*, 82(4): 355–81.

World Bank (2011) *Migration and Remittances Factbook 2011*. Washington DC: World Bank (2nd edition).

World Bank (2007) *Albania: Urban Growth, Migration and Poverty Reduction. A Poverty Assessment*. Washington DC: World Bank Report 40071-AL.

World Bank (2006a) *Global Economic Prospects. Economic Implications of Remittances and Migration*. Washington DC: World Bank.

World Bank (2006b) *Albania: Labour Market Assessment*. Washington DC: World Bank Report 34597-AL.

Young, A. (2000) *Women Who Become Men: Albanian Sworn Virgins*. Oxford: Berg.

Zezza, A., Carletto, G. and Davis, B. (2005) Moving away from poverty: a spatial analysis of poverty and migration in Albania, *Journal of Southern Europe and the Balkans*, 7(2): 175–94.

Zinn, D.L. (1996) Adriatic brethren or black sheep? Migration in Italy and the Albanian crisis, 1991, *European Urban and Regional Studies*, 3(3): 241–49.

Zolberg, A. (2003) The archaeology of remote control, in Fahrmeir, A., Faron, O. and Weil, P. (eds) *Migration Control in the North Atlantic World*. London and New York: Berghahn, 195–222.

INDEX

R

S